Essential Humanities

Third Edition

Lois Parrott

Richland College

Kendall Hunt
publishing company

www.kendallhunt.com
Send all inquiries to:
4050 Westmark Drive
Dubuque, IA 52004-1840

Copyright © 2009, 2013, 2017 by Kendall Hunt Publishing Company

Text + website ISBN: 978-1-5249-6857-1
Text Alone ISBN 978-1-5249-6858-8

All rights reserved. No part of this publication may be reproduced, stored in a retrieval system, or transmitted, in any form or by any means, electronic, mechanical, photocopying, recording, or otherwise, without the prior written permission of the copyright owner.

Published in the United States of America

CONTENTS

Prologue v

Unit 1 What Are the Humanities? 1
    Chapter 1   What Are the Humanities? 3
    Chapter 2   Humanities: Time and Place 5
    Chapter 3   Why Study Humanities? 11
    Chapter 4   Disciplines 15
    Chapter 5   What Is an Idea? 17
    Chapter 6   How to Evaluate the Arts in the Humanities 19
    Chapter 7   Elements of Disciplines in the Humanities 23

Unit 2 Artists and Styles of Art 35
    Chapter 1   Styles of Art 37
    Chapter 2   Printmaking Methods 39
    Chapter 3   What Factors Influence Artists? 43
    Chapter 4   Important Artists and Individuals 47

Unit 3 Timelines and Chronology 77
    Chapter 1   What Is a Timeline? 79
    Chapter 2   What Is Culture? 81
    Chapter 3   Chronology 83
    Chapter 4   Ancient Mesopotamians 87
    Chapter 5   Ancient Egyptian Civilization 91
    Chapter 6   Greek Civilization 95
    Chapter 7   Ancient Roman Period 129
    Chapter 8   Middle Ages (The Medieval Period) 137
    Chapter 9   Renaissance 141
    Chapter 10   Baroque 151
    Chapter 11   Classical Period 159
    Chapter 12   Romantic Period 165
    Chapter 13   Nineteenth Century 169
    Chapter 14   Twentieth Century 173

Unit 4 Music and Listening 177
    Chapter 1   Music: Compositions and Composers 179

Unit 5 Acting, Theater, Film, and Dance 217
    Chapter 1   Film 219

Appendix 255
References 273

PROLOGUE

To my Readers and Students:

My intention is for you to read this book with the understanding that the purpose of this text is to give you a beginning and an introduction to the Humanities. It is my way of giving you a spark that will ignite a fire within you that will stay lit for many years. This way you will never be bored. This text will give you the essentials to understand the basics to be able to enjoy art galleries, recitals, and films in a new and exciting fashion. Wherever you travel, you will enjoy the Fine Arts because you will have the basics to know what to look for, what to read, what to hear, and what to see.

It is virtually impossible to learn all the disciplines and material in-depth in one fast-track session or in just one semester course of Humanities. However, it is possible to understand the basics in a short amount of time. This text is an introduction and brief overview of major artistic and groundbreaking trends essential to the understanding of why certain works are significant and why some creative individuals left their mark.

My hope is that you will be inspired to read more, attend additional recitals, tour art galleries and museums, listen to new music, look at artists' work, watch dance recitals, attend musical concerts, watch interviews of performers, watch great films, and travel to historic sites.

When you read the artist and musician biographies in this text, you will notice how their families and their economic, social, political, and religious factors influenced their production. You will also notice how each artist pursued their goals, handled obstacles, but continued to pursue their art form. Reading about their lives helps us understand what is meant by "artistic drive." Artists need to create. The "artistic spirit" is born into some individuals; and our world is better for it.

UNIT 1

What Are the Humanities?

WHAT ARE THE HUMANITIES?

Disciplines (subjects) of the Humanities:

- Visual Arts
- Sculpture
- Printmaking
- Photography and Film
- Architecture
- Theater
- Dance
- Music

What Are the Humanities?

The Humanities is considered to be interdisciplinary because it possesses more than one subject at a time. The subjects found in the Humanities are Painting, Drawing, Architecture, Sculpture, Ceramics, Music, Theater, Dance, Film, and Photography. The focus of Humanities is on how and why human beings achieve creatively and use their imagination. For generations, people have been using their minds creatively and finding ways to live in environments where they can be safe and secure, with enough food and water. For this reason, it is noticeable in studying the origin of the earliest known ancient civilizations that they began near rivers. Being able to stay in one location long enough to plant and harvest became the assurance of a group of people who developed a way of life, which would become the definition of community living. Since the beginning of recorded human history, it seems that humankind had the desire to create expressions, which are now considered art. These art works that remain for us to view today are sculptures such as the fertility goddess "The Venus of Willendorf" named after its place of origin, Willendorf, Austria. This sculpture is the most famous early image of a woman, Venus, found in 1908 by the archaeologist Josef Szombzthy in Willendorf (source: http://72.52.202.216/~fenderse/Venus.htm).

Cave paintings remain on the interior cave walls of Altamira, Spain and Lascaux, France. These paintings were produced by prehistoric artists who painted with a combination of materials gathered from organic material such as berries, blood, and soot. These earth tones reflect their environment and capture what was important to them at their time and place. They painted using the same elements of art as artists utilize today when they paint. For example, they used line, textures, and shapes as do many twenty-first-century artists. The prehistoric artist painted the subjects of bison, deer, and other animals on cave walls thousands of years ago. We are fortunate to have traces of these prehistoric treasures today to examine, because they give us an idea as to how they really lived. They were inventive humans who were creative and communicated by painting. This creative achievement made by prehistoric people helps us understand why communication and expressing ideas is so important everywhere around the globe. The arts can help us understand our past and help us learn to better communicate and express ourselves to others. If we learn more about our own cultural heritage, we find that we are able to listen to others better and share ideas with them. This is why it is so important to study Humanities. Studying the Humanities is vital in today's way of life. Living with the understanding of the Humanities helps us to better respond to our feelings. Humanities help us find more to live for and add more meaning to life. We learn to respond better to others' concerns and learn to respect other cultures than the one we know. Through the humanities, we learn to live a life of caring. We try to learn to walk in another person's shoes. If we do not know where we came from we will not know where we are going.

HUMANITIES: TIME AND PLACE 2

The Humanities include disciplines such as sculpture, painting, drawing, printmaking, photography, film, music, and theater. The study of humanities enables students to look deeply into themselves to make more sense of their own existence. The humanities help them to discover a better sense of who they are and give more meaning to their lives.

The humanities offer individuals a method of categorizing and placing artistic creations in a systematic approach to the study of past cultural achievements. They express ideas in tangible ways through artistic and musical expressions that were created in particular time periods. This approach gives a sense of time and place to the works that were created and an appreciation of the effort that was put into the works by their creators. Furthermore, in-depth study of the works may then lead to a desire to find out how the work was made, who did it, and why it was made. This sense of wonder and a desire to know more about the creative process is what sparks students' interest in the endeavors of artistic creators across generations. That spark will lead to a sense of self-discovery. As students study how and why the works were created, they will gain a heightened respect for the work. As they ponder and notice how the art was accomplished, they will develop a greater sense of respect toward the works of the past and be able to understand their aesthetic and artistic value.

This sense of history is unique within the study of the humanities. Artistic works take on a new meaning in their reflection of time and place. The humanities are also considered interdisciplinary: when a student studies a creative achievement, he realizes that the work reflects what was going on when it was created. If it was a musical composition, for example, the composer may have reflected a very strong feeling about a tense political struggle. The music may include tense chords, and there may be both slow and fast parts and loud and soft as well as dissonant and clashing chords to represent unrest and chaos. The stressful and tension-filled times will be heard within the composition itself. Those sounds will have been expressed through the notes written by the composer. Those sounds represent the mood and the tone of that day, and the music's timbre or quality of sound reflects the turmoil of that event. Then whenever someone listens to that composition today, he can still hear the sounds that make him feel a sense of unrest when the piece is performed or played. That is remarkable. Some of the greatest pieces of music do not go out of date but continue to speak to people. They continue to be performed and remain meaningful.

It is the same way with great paintings. A great portrait captures a sense of time and place. Some of the great artists were able to paint portraits that capture the viewers' imagination and sense of wonder. Their paintings stir a desire in the viewer to add his own ideas and points of view to the painting. If the painting is too finished or complete, it may leave nothing more to be desired. There may be nothing left to the imagination.

> **QUESTIONS**
>
> **Questions to Contemplate**
>
> Can you think of any paintings that have captured your imagination? Were those paintings ones that you wanted to see again and again?
>
> Sometimes someone goes to a film and the next day a friend asks if he wants to see it again. He may have still been thinking about the film, so he agrees to go with his friend. The second time he may actually see more in it and enjoy it even more. What type of film would someone be able to sit through more than once, noticing more of the script, visuals, camera angles, camera movement, lighting, and other creative shots with each subsequent viewing? Would a film of that quality possess characteristics that would be considered art? Most people would say that art possesses characteristics that surpass time and place and are universal in their appeal. They are also characteristically unique, creative, innovative, meaningful, and sometimes not readily understood.

Why Archaeology Is Essential When Studying the Disciplines in the Humanities

According to some historians, studying Western Art is a reflection of how people lived and what they believed in at a particular period. For people living in the West, it was important to examine the innovations of those artists who dared to resist the establishment and authorities. They were resilient when they received a "no" and continued to create their fine art forms even under duress. Some fine artists dared to create innovations that were contrary to the system. These new methods became boundless without the constraints of tradition. In several areas of the Western Hemisphere, in periods after the Renaissance, some bold artists dared to resist the authorities and spread their wings. Some of the innovations became styles that will be discussed later in the text. In Unit II, when reading biographies of individuals, notice how the fine artists' own discipline and courage influenced his or her mission.

Sometimes Great Works of Art Are Initially Rejected

Some great artworks were not accepted at first. One example is Igor Stravinsky's *Rite of Spring*. The first performance was unsuccessful. A year after the first performance, the work was performed again, and it was a success.

> History resounds with examples of new artistic attempts that met with terrible receptions from so-called experts, whose idea of what an artwork ought to be could not allow for experimentation or departures from accepted practice. In 1912, when Vasslav Nijinsky choreographed the ballet *Rite of Spring* to music by Igor Stravinsky, the unconventional music and choreography actually caused a riot: audiences and critics could not tolerate that it did not conform to accepted musical and balletic standards. Today, both the music and choreography are considered masterpieces (Sporre 23).

> Another example given by Dennis Sporre of a work that was at first unacceptable but then came to be considered great was the play *Waiting for Godot* by Samuel Beckett (1953). In the play, Beckett "does not have a plot, characters, or ideas expressed in a conventional manner. In this play, two tramps wait beside the road by a withered tree for the arrival of someone named Godot. The tramps tell stories to each other, argue, eat some food, and are interrupted by a character named Pozzo leading a slave, Lucky, by a rope. After a brief conversation, Lucky and Pozzo leave. At the end of the first act, a boy enters to announce that Godot will not come today. In Act 2, much the same sequence of events occurs. Then Lucky leads in a blind Pozzo. The tree has sprouted a few leaves. The play ends as the young boy returns to indicate Godot will not arrive that day either. If your standards require a successful play to have a carefully fashioned plot wrapped around fully developed characters and a clear message, then *Waiting for Godot* cannot possibly be a good play. Some people agree with such an assertion; others disagree vehemently. What, then do we conclude? What if my criteria do not match yours? What if two experts disagree on the quality of a movie? Does that ultimately make a difference to our experience of it?" (Sporre 23–24).

Igor Stravinsky

Stravinsky's "Rite of Spring"
Russian composer 1882-1971

Igor Stravinsky is considered to be one of the greatest composers of the twentieth century. He took lessons from Rimsky-Korsakov who taught him how to write parts for all the instruments in the orchestra. Stravinsky was a quick learner and was very interested in studying the past history of the Russian heritage and the music of the people who lived in the countryside and so he visited Ustilug, Russia. This is where he played folk instruments and came up with the idea of using orchestral instruments in the "Rite of Spring," playing solo parts in higher ranges than the players were normally used to doing. This was a challenge. Stravinsky also thought that the sounds of the unsophisticated village folk music would be exiting for the orchestra to play and this was an influence upon him as he composed the "Rite of Spring." When the bassoon played a solo part in the "Rite of Spring" someone in the audience was confused as to which instrument was being played because it was difficult to recognize the timbre (quality of sound) of the bassoon since it was higher than it normally played.

The composition of the "Rite of Spring" was a combination of unusual meters which changed frequently from one meter to another. If we look at the music, we can see that there are different time signatures every few measures right at the beginning of the composition. This was a new method as well for the listening audience so the composition was a challenge for the audience. When it is performed by symphony orchestras today, audiences may be more used to this type of music. Today there is more exposure to music from around the world. However, when the performance of the "Rite of Spring" was first heard, it was so new and unusual for those people that they were struck with terror. Many of us have become accustomed to dissonance (clashing sounds) and unusual noise types of sounds created by orchestras. We hear sound tracks for films which have many weird sounds. However, in 1913, that was a different scenario.

Some historians say that Stravinsky's religious works were notable and reflected a period of time in his life. The work he did at this time was the cantata "Symphony of Psalms" (1930) and operatic oratorio "Oedipus Rex."

In 1934 Stravinsky took up French citizenship. He had lost his property during the Russian revolution and made a living composing and performing. He was a concert pianist and an orchestra conductor at that time. Stravinsky lived in Russia, France, and Switzerland and then during World War II came to the United States in 1945, and he and his wife became U.S. citizens that same year.

Source: http://www.pbs.org/keepingscore/stravinsky-rite-of-spring.html; https://www.britannica.com/biography/Igor-Stravinsky/images-videos/Igor-Stravinsky-1920/55847

Keep This in Mind

In order to understand the play, one has to watch it and examine it in depth.

Waiting for Godot
By Samuel Beckett
1906–1989
Born in Dublin, Ireland

In this play, the author uses repetition, making one day seem the same as the next. The two main characters participate in nonsensical undertakings. The two of them look into a boot and a hat and find nothing, for example.

The two main characters Vladimir and Estragon have problems remembering one day to the next. To the viewers, it may seem as if the flow of time is somewhat meaningless for those two characters playing on the stage. The idea that time is something that all creatures deal with becomes real for viewers while watching the production. Is this the universal idea in the theatrical performance?

Whether people are able to utilize their own time wisely and make something out of their life by using their own time in ways that make things happen is also something to consider. Do viewers want to consider this idea after they watch the play? The play can have several ideas for different individuals, so is this why the purpose of the play is somewhat difficult to define? Think about the two characters and what they are doing on stage with their time as they just wait mindlessly for something that never comes.

At one point in the play the characters actually contemplated suicide, because they became so disenchanted with their wait. After they were told that Godot would not arrive they were very disappointed. However, they kept waiting in hope that Godot would still arrive.

If people are always waiting for something to come along or to happen, they do not prepare, they just wait. They wait and wait and after a while their wait just becomes an action of waiting and it is the same over and over. This may happen over and over again and then it becomes a behavior which may become a habit that makes them pessimistic. It can seem to make such individuals look forward to their own death. This is what happens in *Waiting for Godot*. In life, if we end up waiting and waiting but do not know what we are actually waiting for, then we are not really waiting for anything and our waiting seems hopeless.

How does this make a normal person feel?

Do you think that waiting and waiting makes a person really feel fulfilled or happy?

Could this play ask questions about an individual who may be waiting for something to happen but just keeps waiting and waiting so the actions of waiting become meaningless?

Why would a play like this be considered a masterpiece?

Source: http://www.jeffreybigham.com/papers/godot.html; http://www.samuel-beckett.net/godot_jeff.html

Biography of Samuel Beckett

Samuel Beckett was born in Dublin, Ireland. His father William Frank Beckett worked in the construction business. His mother worked in the medical field as a nurse and his parents wanted their son to have a good education. They made sure that he was able to attend the Portora Royal School and later he obtained his bachelor's degree from Trinity College, Dublin (1927). He was a very serious student and later it was said that he probably suffered depression while in school, and perhaps it may have actually helped him in his writing to be more creative.

He traveled to Paris, France as a young man. While there, he was attacked. That experience greatly affected him. He later said that while recovering from the wounds as he was lying in the hospital, he decided not to press charges upon his attacker. He later decided to write about his experiences in novels and plays using other names instead.

He also tried new ideas and his plays began to reflect his experiences although they were not written with conventional plots and traditional locations or time frames. He focused on themes that dealt with pessimism and depression and loneliness.

During the Second World War, Beckett was allowed by the French government to remain in Paris.

He was a citizen of Ireland; however, he was fighting in the resistance movement until 1942 when members of his group were arrested by the Gestapo.

When Beckett was awarded the Nobel Prize for literature in 1969, he did not want to make a speech at the ceremonies. Therefore, he declined to accept the award. Scholars say that he was not a recluse; since he often met with artists and admirers to talk about his work. He died in a hospital in 1989 a few months after his wife passed away.

Source: http://www.biography.com/people/samuel-beckett-9204239#synopsis

WHY STUDY HUMANITIES? 3

Students can learn to understand themselves better by studying the nature of humankind in disciplines within the humanities such as music, poetry, and art. If they take the time to look at great art and listen to enlightening music, they can learn to appreciate things around them that they might ordinarily miss. In the fast-paced life of today, events go by so rapidly that people often miss out on wonderful glimpses that artists see. If only they took the time to notice, then they too could grasp the deeper meanings of the many works that are out there just waiting for them to celebrate.

The humanities invite all people, no matter who they are, to become part of a world of seeing and feeling that brings them closer to living a life that helps them to find themselves. The humanities facilitate our ability to feel and to realize that to be human is to be a person filled with emotions.

People will go through times when they feel happy and when they feel sad. It is alright to be expressive. It is a plus to be able to express feelings and emotions. The humanities offer hope to those who are emotional and to those who are different. They are subjects that embrace peoples' differences and accept people for who they are.

Studying humanities helps students find greater depth of meaning when they look at great art, read fine literature and poetry, listen to great music, and watch great films, dance, and theater. Learning to appreciate masterpieces of art, enjoying symphony music, and understanding classic films become enjoyable.

Of course, this appreciation of the humanities depends upon where people live or have lived, because all of their opinions and ideas make up who they are, what they are interested in, and how they view the world. The way they are now is a reflection of what they have been interested in before taking a humanities course. Some students have already been involved in the theater, played in a symphony or band, or taken piano lessons, while other students were not exposed to these activities during their childhood. For this reason, it is assumed that most students are reading about information that they have not studied before, and it may take some historical and symbolic background research to fully benefit from the entire experience. However, with a little time and study, the experience can become extremely valuable and, eventually, enjoyable.

According to Doris Van de Bogart, professor and author of *Introduction to the Humanities*, if a student goes to college and studies humanities he or she will have the understanding and background to live a life wherein they will never be bored. Why is that the case? According to Dr. Van de Bogart, there are so many areas to discover and there are so many new findings every year in the humanities field that students who are interested in the humanities will always find new areas of study.

In a region south of Cairo and north of Aswan, Egypt, there are many sites where the ancient Egyptians buried their pharaohs. This area is referred to as the "Valley of the Kings." The tombs of many pharaohs are here, including that of Tutankhamun, who was only a boy when he became king. His tomb was found in 1922 by archeologist Howard Carter, and it is considered significant because the mummy was intact. South of the Valley of the Kings is a temple built by a famous pharaoh named Ramses II to represent his power and might. The temple's exterior has four large sculptures bearing the pharaoh's likeness. The temple and the sculptures had to be moved when the Aswan Dam was built. Construction of the dam caused that area of Egypt to flood. The temple, called "Abu Simbel," and the sculptures were relocated to higher ground. Next to Abu Simbel is a temple erected to Nefertari, a favorite wife of Ramses II.

Ancient Egypt

There are new finds in Humanities in many areas of the world. In the areas of ancient Egypt, there have been new tombs that have been found in the last twenty years which have not been completely opened or excavated. Over the past few years, there have been more theories about the building of the pyramids discussed by professional archeologists. Students who like to travel and who like to study about the past and how the past influences the way people live today find that studying people from other areas of the world becomes very fascinating. Students find that using the computer to look up sites and find maps and geographical and archeological sites will learn a lot about interesting artifacts and important people. I challenge you to do more than just read the book.

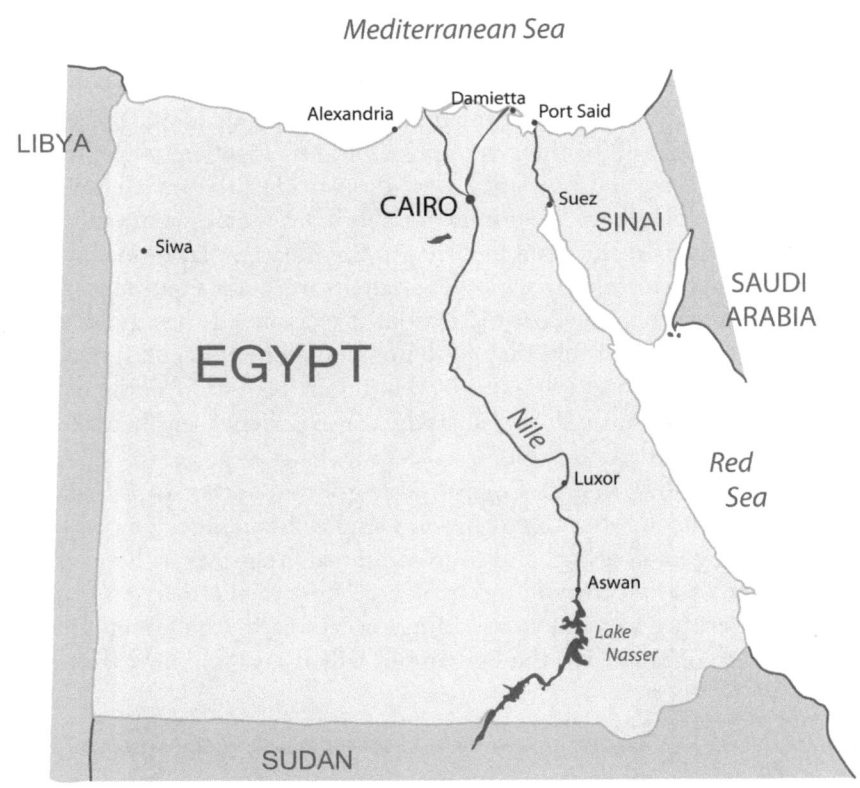

In ancient Mesopotamia, there are new discoveries about the ziggurats and other developments that are being uncovered which have come to light by archeologists in the past fifteen years. There is much exciting research to be done, which will be discussed later in the course. New research is being discovered and in Humanities, new developments constantly occur, making the study of Humanities a vibrant experience for any student.

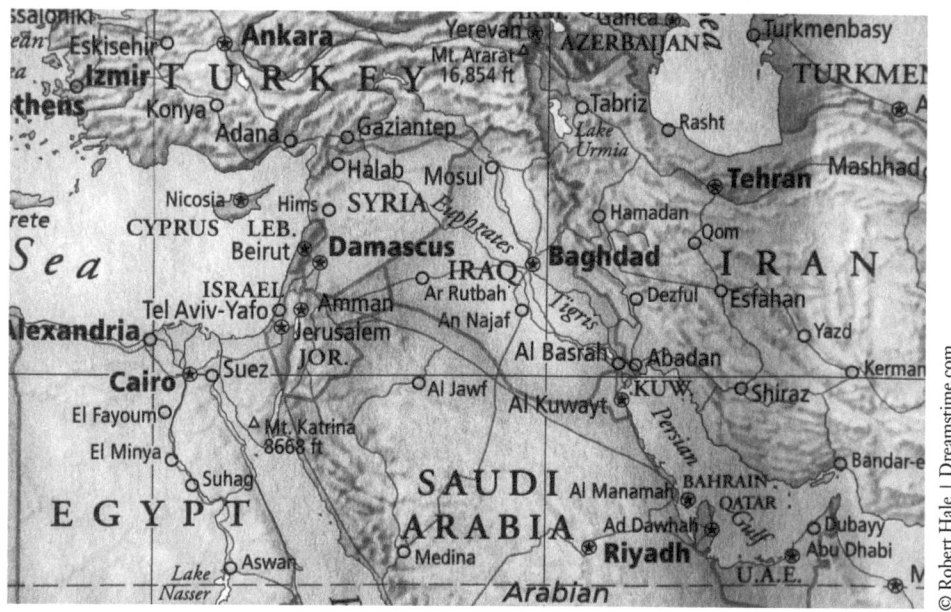

King Tutankhamun

The Boy King—a Pharaoh from ANCIENT EGYPT
Found by Howard Carter, benefactor name Lord Carnarvon from Great Britain

At age nine, the boy king became King Tut when he was made the pharaoh (king). It is said by most historians that he was only nineteen when he died accidently. The cause of his death is not known. There was an autopsy done a few years ago on his mummy and it was perceived that he died from a blow to his skull. This is not proven. He may have been on a chariot. The treasures in his tomb were made of wood and painted gold. His helmet was on his body. His body as a mummy was preserved.

The reason his tomb was so significant was that his body was still intact and had not been stolen by grave robbers. Often in ancient times other graves had been inside tombs and thieves stole the bodies with their gold helmets and rings and precious gold jewelry. That is why when the archeologist Howard Carter in 1922 found the tomb of King Tut, it was fantastic. To be able to locate the tomb and have the many treasures still in the tomb plus the body in the tomb intact was amazing. To think that the body was still mummified and the sarcophagus (containers: which there were three all together) was there with the gold around the body was truly an amazing find. Also, Carter decided to leave the treasures found in the tomb in the country of Egypt so today the pieces are housed in the Cairo Museum.

ABU SIMBEL The temple which had to be moved to higher ground when the Aswan Dam was built in the late 1960s once sat on what is now Lake Nasir. To think that a temple could actually be moved block by block was unbelievable but true. Several countries were able to send funds and workers to the area south of the Aswan Dam to the place where Ramses II's temple Abu Simbel was built. I am sure that if you look at the film about this operation you will be absolutely amazed. Flying over it, you can see the imitation mountain that was built to raise the place that the workers had to lift and move piece by piece. Each of the blocks they cut, marked, numbered, and then put back to make the temple look just like it did at the time of Ramses II.

This temple is phenomenal. It sits next to the water just down from the other temple to his favorite wife Nefertari. (Do not mix this name with the person named Nefertiti, a famous and beautiful queen. There is a sculpture in the Neues Museum in Berlin of her that is exquisite.)

The temple to his wife was also moved block by block and pieced back together. Visitors can go inside to see the columns that are in the likeness of Ramses II.

There are marvelous wall paintings of frescos on the wall outlining the accomplishments of Ramses II which reflect his travels and his power. On the walls of the temple of Abu Simbel it shows in hieroglyphics that he won a war of Kadesh with the Hittites.

DISCIPLINES

The humanities are composed of separate areas that are referred to as disciplines. These include visual arts such as painting, drawing, and printmaking as well as other areas such as photography, film, theater, dance, poetry, and architecture. These disciplines are creative expressions and achievements of the human imagination that delve deeply into the soul and spirit of the human race. Past artistic expressions offer unique insights into culture that help people to understand their world. Through art, they learn how people lived in the past, which helps them to live better among themselves.

Each one of the individual areas or disciplines has elements unique to its own structure. The way in which those elements are organized makes up its style. By looking at the elements unique to each discipline, students become more aware of the style and learn to distinguish one style from another. It becomes an enjoyable exercise to see whether students can figure out how and why an artist organized his or her work. As they study the artistic elements, an awareness and sensitivity toward style and chronological time periods develop. For some students, this will come very quickly, and for others it may take longer. It may involve taking time out to actually study the historical background along with the elements of art because an awareness of time and place are factors that often influence an artist's work.

The humanities are disciplines that differ from the sciences. They may change with time, but they also embody an element of the past that is different from changes in the sciences. Take for example a piece of equipment in a technology class that needs to be constantly updated for it to be useful. Think about how a computer that sat on a professor's desk in 1998 would look and work in a classroom today. Compare a decade-old basic computer with a CRT monitor and a phone modem to today's basic computer with a high-resolution flat screen and DSL and imagine how obsolete the old one seems to be. That old computer would probably be sitting on a curb awaiting its fate on trash pick-up day. Now think about a great painting. It could be ten years old or a hundred years old or a thousand years old, and it would still be hanging on a wall and students would still be looking at it and admiring it. It will remain meaningful. It is not necessarily being replaced with a more contemporary painting like the computer in the previous example. This is not to say that there are not other types and styles of paintings being painted in other ways and with new types of materials, but art serves a different purpose than technology.

QUESTIONS

Questions to Contemplate

What similarities and differences can you find between the sciences and the humanities, and what are the characteristics that make each of them unique?

Do you utilize both of these in your daily life? Do you need both?

Which do you find that you utilize more? Explain your answer and discuss your responses with a friend.

Discuss some of your own opinions and ideas about how the sciences and technology serve us in our society.

How are the humanities very different from disciplines such as accounting or an area of study that is highly technical? What makes those disciplines so different from the humanities?

WHAT IS AN IDEA?

The humanities are disciplines that honor and respect differences of opinion and ideas. Artists and performing artists create their art and ideas from their own vantage points and their own personal experiences. They are usually very creative individuals and often considered creative thinkers as well. Paul Baker defines an idea as "a space wherein lies the awakening of your own creative self."

When people go to a museum, art gallery, recital, musical event, poetry reading, dance recital, theatrical event, or lecture, they should try to keep in mind Paul Baker's definition of an idea. This will open their eyes and allow them to experience the event with a new mindset. Being able to open ones' mind to view an event from another vantage point creates a more enjoyable experience.

But some individuals find it difficult or challenging to view art from a different point of view because they have preconceived ideas of what art or performances should be like or look like. For those individuals, some works fall short of their expectations, and they become disappointed. They are often heard saying "That is not art" or "What a bad performance." Their experience depends on their ability to "walk in the other person's shoes," so to speak. Their appreciation and enjoyment will depend on whether the individual has the ability to be open minded and not make rash judgments. Being able to keep calm and just look and listen before forming an opinion makes an individual a better judge.

It is important to try to understand the intentions of the artist or performer if the viewer wants to fully comprehend the scope of an artwork or performing art.

QUESTIONS

Questions to Contemplate

How does the artist project his or her ideas to the world in order to be understood?

Do you feel it is necessary for art critics to understand a painter's artwork for it to be considered art?

Are some types of art appreciated in some areas of the world and not appreciated in other areas of the world today? Why or why not?

Do you believe that an artist needs to be able to reflect and project the surrounding world to be remembered from his or her own time and to be considered a great creative and innovative artist? Why or why not?

HOW TO EVALUATE THE ARTS IN THE HUMANITIES

Evaluating the arts within the humanities can be challenging. It takes time and effort. Criticizing art requires time to analyze when someone wants to respond with an educated viewpoint. To be able to critique a work with an educated response is more challenging than just deciding whether someone thinks it is art or not. A first response to an evaluation of an artwork may be whether someone likes or dislikes the work of art. There is nothing wrong about feeling that way. But if that is all that is accomplished by an experience, it is only a superficial involvement.

If it is a performance piece, this would also pertain to the situation, and it would depend upon whether the viewer was entertained by the performance. To say "I like it" or "I do not like it" is a response, but it does not really answer the question whether it is actually art. It does not answer the question, "Why is it art?" or "Why is it not art?" To answer the question about whether the work or performance is art takes more than a superficial, spur of the moment, or reactive comment to make a meaningful evaluation. A little in-depth study and research may include some background information about when the work was written, created, or first performed. Other valuable information that may be interesting and helpful would be knowing who created it. There may be other information pertinent to that particular discipline within the humanities, depending upon whether it is a painting, sculpture, print, photograph, play, musical performance, dance performance, or film. Delving into a work's historical context, the background of the artist, and the particulars of the discipline provides a comprehensive view into the work.

An interdisciplinary humanities textbook titled *The Introduction to the Humanities*, by Doris Van de Bogart, offers a basic and fundamental approach to the process of evaluating the arts in the humanities. Her categories of evaluation have been found to be useful to students and have worked in most situations and disciplines within the humanities over the years. These categories are

- Sincerity
- Craftsmanship
- Magnitude
- Universality

Van De Bogart considered these four components to be valuable tools in evaluating the performing, visual, and musical arts. They work surprisingly well for many types of events and can be a barometer for measuring the quality of a performance or activity.

HOW TO EVALUATE THE ARTS IN THE HUMANITIES 6

> **Sincerity** The artist is genuine and honest in his approach, ideas and endeavor and does his work with care. He is not just trying to make money quickly. He is patient. He does not copy work of others or from other time periods other than when he first starts studying and he learns all the techniques first. He has great technical ability and understand art historical periods. He reflects his own time.
>
> **Craftsmanship** The artist understands the necessary technique and has all the perfection and skill to be able to create the work to its utmost capacity in sound or in the visual appearance in the end result
>
> **Magnitude** The artist is able to leave behind some expressive responses for others thathave left or leave an impact which is meaningful which leave an impact
>
> **Universality** The artist is able to express feelings to others that are universal feelings which mean that they are feelings which go beyond just one group of people or just on type of people or just on type of place

> **Interdisciplinary** More than one discipline or subject together: for example, a film has graphic design, music, acting, editing, sound, and lighting. All of these elements must work well together for the film to work well.

An artist needs to be in touch with herself and her world to be able to create an expression of what she feels about the world in which she lives. If she copies or does work that is overexaggerated just to draw attention, she may be insincere in her endeavor. A viewer should ask himself the question, "Is the artist sincere?" He may think it is not possible to judge sincerity unless he is able to meet the performers or the artist. Because this is not always possible, he needs to look for the qualities of sincerity that are found in the final product. Is the work overdone or melodramatic? He will know that a fad is short lived; therefore, he knows that for an object to be art it must outlive a fad. Is there an element of trickery? A work of art must be genuine and must have been done by an artist to fulfill her own reasons. Is she portraying something that is just a fad or does it look too commercial? Is it a product that will sell? Is that its only purpose? Or is it art?

The second component is the craftsmanship of the work. This is also called technique. Evaluate whether the artist knew how to work in her media and whether she worked well with the process and the methods in reaching her goal. Did the musician understand her instrument and have the proper skills to develop the type of sound that she wanted to produce? In other words, did the musician understand how to play the instrument well? Did the artist go beyond technique? Music is not created just by playing notes. How did the composer or performer express herself? Was the performer just presenting the work because she was obligated to, or could the audience tell whether the performer was really sincere in her feelings about the work?

The third component is the magnitude or the level at which something is created. Is it for the moment? Does it represent a trite theme that is not timeless? In other words, will it be short lived? What level of meaning does it represent? Is it something the audience will want to see or listen to again? Did it leave them with a sense of awe? What impact did it have on them? Is it something that they will remember for a long time, or will they forget about the experience soon after they saw or heard it?

The fourth component is universality. Does it possess the type of ideas that all people in all times and from all places have in common? Life and death, search for meaning in life, and the emotions that all people experience from all parts of the world are what make something universal. Those are the universal feelings that artists write and paint about. They express the unchanging fundamental human conditions of all people. How people deal with emotions changes, but emotions are part of what makes people human.

Of course, the test of time is the best way to judge master works. But when someone looks at contemporary works, he can use these four components to evaluate them because it is not possible to project the art's acceptance in the future. Understanding the arts is a lifelong learning experience that gives a sense of fulfillment and satisfaction. A meaningful education is one way to enhance daily life. A humanities course should be one that offers interesting experiences that can be remembered and valued in years to come.

ELEMENTS OF DISCIPLINES IN THE HUMANITIES 7

Elements of the Visual Arts

Line	A moving dot; a line shows direction
Perspective	The illusion of depth
Shape	An enclosed line; shapes can be rounded (biomorphic attached to life forms or geometric)
Form	Shapes that seem to have volume or three dimension and can be geometric or flat and not with height or with width
Color	The absence or the presence of light; in paintings, color can give the viewer a sense of a sad or happy feeling
Subject	What it is about? It is like a topic?
Texture	The feeling of the surface
Value	The effect of lightness or darkness

Line

The first mark a child makes when she learns to draw or write is a line. It is the earliest type of expression. A line is a moving dot, and the basic tool used by visual artists. A line can be straight, curved, thick, or thin. It can be jagged or flowing, smooth or bumpy. The visual artist utilizes line in her artwork to express certain feelings. For instance, if she wants to present chaos and disorder, she may use diagonal lines to create a feeling of tension. Line was used thousands of years ago by artists who painted on cave walls in Altamira, Spain, and Lascaux, France and is still the most basic tool used by artists today.

Shape

A line that is enclosed becomes a shape. A shape can be a geometric shape like a rectangle, or it can be a rounded or oblong shape. When it is rounded and attaches itself to natural shapes, it is considered to be a biomorphic shape. A biomorphic shape is part of the biological world. If you take a look at biological organisms such as cells, you will recognize images and shapes that are biomorphic, or organic.

Many artists who like to use abstract organic shapes use biomorphic forms or shapes inspired from nature. Piet Mondrian's late works did not look organic, but some of his early abstract forms were inspired from the branches of trees. Henry Moore, a sculptor from England, was inspired by pieces of bone and created sculptures from shapes that were similar to vertebrae. In Dallas, Texas, one of his large sculptures, *Dallas Piece*, was inspired from some pieces of bones that he had in his studio. The architect of the Dallas City Hall, I. M. Pei, selected Henry Moore's work to be placed in front of it because it was completely opposite to the stark geometric shape of the city building.

Color

Color is the absorption or reflection of light. Color is used by the visual artist to create a mood.

The use of warm colors is useful to an artist for creating a happy scene. Artists and painters often use colors such as yellow or orange to create a bright or happy atmosphere. Various color combinations used by artists tend to create certain emotional responses. Many famous paintings are known because of how the colors and shapes were put together and organized. Those paintings are identified and recognized as major works of art and are studied by students today.

Reds, yellows, and some oranges are considered to be warm colors. Blues and greens tend to create more subdued reactions and emotions; therefore, they are referred to as the cool colors.

In a well-known 1937 painting by Pablo Picasso about a bomb that fell upon civilians, Picasso purposely painted using gray scale (from black to white with gray in between). This is referred to as using value, or light and dark. Picasso may have used value instead of color as the predominant element to draw attention to the shapes rather than colors. By leaving out the warm colors of tints and shades of red, which could have been used to symbolize blood, the viewer is forced to notice the fragmented shapes instead. This was a very innovative and powerful move on the part of an artist in 1937.

Guernica Painting by Pablo Picasso

Guernica, by Pablo Picasso, has a subject of war. When General Franco allowed Hitler's military to bomb the town of Guernica, Picasso was working on a mural for the Paris Exhibition (1937) but was in a dry spell. When he heard about the bombing, he knew what he would paint.

Guernica is considered to be one of the best examples of a great work of art representing the inhumanity to man.

Francisco de Goya also represented in his subject matter the innocent victim before a firing squad, an inhumane behavior of mankind. This also is an example of a major work of art that is about the subject of war.

Although these paintings are not pleasant as far as their subject matter, they are still considered to be great works of art.

Symbolism seen in *Guernica* is disturbing, as it generates many feelings in the individuals who view it. When Picasso was asked to explain the symbolism behind *Guernica*, he remarked, "It isn't up to the painter to define the symbols. Otherwise it would be better if he wrote them out in so many words!"

Colors have their own value. The value of a color is its lightness or darkness, but the hue or name of the color is still the same. For example, yellow is a color or hue that is naturally light. If you take a black-and-white photograph of a painting that has the color yellow in it, the color yellow will appear in the black-and-white photograph as a very light gray.

In *Guernica*, a painting by Pablo Picasso, he purposely used gradations of gray tints and shades in the various shapes and patterns all over the huge canvas to create a repetitive and organized yet chaotic arrangement of horror. In this work, Picasso brings viewers to a point where they cannot help but feel the pain even though there is a lack of color used by the painter.

Picasso's *Guernica* is in the museum in Madrid, Spain. It is 11 feet tall and 25.6 feet wide. Picasso painted in grey scale because he, too, first heard of this horrific event by reading about it in a newspaper. Since the newspaper was not in color during the 1930s it may be the reason for his painting in black and white values. Others have said that it may be that since Francisco de Goya's painting of the "Execution of the Citizens of Madrid" (also referred to as the "Execution of the Third of May") was in color, he decided to do his with more powerful emphasis on shapes and leave out color. Artists that are innovative and want to reflect their own time will use other forms and elements of art to draw attention with another treatment. Great artists are able to express events in other ways and not copy other artists and other time periods.

This painting is considered a masterpiece. When some young students first look at the painting they may not understand why it is considered great. It may take some understanding on their part. It may take a few minutes of understanding how to judge and evaluate art. It may be that the individual looking at the work would want to stand in front of the actual work in Madrid, Spain. Of course, this is not always possible. The next best thing would be to go to a site and watch a film and see Picasso (he died in 1973 but there are actual films with footage of him) working in his studio. (Unlike Michelangelo, who died before the age of film, we actually have Picasso on film in his studio.)

It's a wonderful experience to travel to the museum or location where an artwork is on display. If you can go see the site of the building, sculpture, or painting, it is fantastic. It takes some planning but it is worth it. It is fun and life changing. Because of the information age, another neat way to see artwork is online, where we can see its location in the museum. Viewers can experience the size and shape, as if being there. It is easy to go to the computer and look up a painting or a great building or a sculpture and find out who did it and where it was located or where it is today. I suggest anyone who does not understand a work of art to go online and become acquainted with such great works of art. Then, someday, if you can visit the museum where some artwork is on display and see the size of the work and do a little research and actually see it you will get it. You will be amazed at how it looks in the context of the space. You will then become an "art lover."

It takes a little time, a little research, a little patience, and open-mindedness.

The interpretations of *Guernica* are varied because Picasso did not explain his work. Most great artists don't. Some art professors have told me that interpretations of *Guernica* are varied and that the bull and the horse are important images in Picasso's work because he was Spanish. He used the bull to represent strength and sometimes to represent himself in his work. The horse also represented some people and the innocence of the civilians who were victimized. Accounts vary depending upon your source. Picasso was against Fascism and wanted to represent his feelings about how he felt about the brutality of the bombing of the innocent people of the town of Guernica by the dropping of the bomb. Picasso was a deeply emotional person and he did make a statement publicly once about the painting and said that he wanted to show his feelings about how he felt about the people of the town of Guernica.

Source: http://www.pablopicasso.org/guernica.jsp

Warm Colors: Red, yellow, orange

Cool Colors: Blues and some greens

Value: Gray tones, from white to black

Notice that white and black are not on the color wheel and are not considered to be colors.

Tints, Shades, and Tone

A tint is when a color has white added to it. A shade is when a color has black added to it. A tone is when brown is added to the color.

Texture

The feeling of the surface is the definition of texture. It means whether the surface *appears* to be rough or smooth, but it is also the feel of the surface.

Vincent Van Gogh, a late-nineteenth-century Dutch artist, used thick paint in many of his paintings, especially when he was emotionally troubled. He is remembered as one of the leading post-impressionist painters who utilized texture and color in an unusual manner.

He had an artistic style all his own and left many paintings behind because he only sold one during his lifetime, which was actually only exchanged in trade. Today Van Gogh is considered to be one of the most significant painters who ever lived.

Students sometimes ask why some artists were able to sell their work during their time while other artists had trouble making a living from their artworks. That may be a question to ponder. Artists who remain meaningful and unique seem to be those who have a style that stands out. It is not easy for a student in art school to find his or her artistic style. The assignments are often filled with having to do work similar to the masters, and many times the work needs to look like the instructor's. This process reflects whether students understand their assignments, and it also represents their ability to understand a master's work.

But upper-level art students must also perfect a style of their own if they want to become an artist in their own right. In painting classes, some students are able to learn to copy the works of the masters and then go beyond the copy phase to develop their own style and truly become artists.

Artists reflect their own time and place. They have the talent, skill, and know-how to project the world around them in their art. An artist is able to see and perceive in ways that many people do not notice.

Perspective

Perspective is the illusion of depth. This element does not have to be used if a work is not intended to be an illusion or appear to look three-dimensional. Some art uses overlapping to create a sense of depth or to portray the illusion of time. This technique was perfected during the Italian Renaissance.

When perspective is used, the objects in the background are smaller and appear to be farther away in the distance. These objects also get this appearance from the use of thinner and lighter paint to give an appearance of dimness. An object in the distance or in the background near the horizon line is made to look very faint and light in color. The artist may use a tint of a color by adding white to it.

Form

The form of a composition is the overall design and how the artist utilized the elements.

How did the artist use the elements together?

The following is a quote about how form and content are related when looking at a work of art.

"Form is the total effect of the combined visual qualities within a work, including such components as materials, color, shape, line, and design. Content refers to the message or meaning of the work of art – what the artist expresses or communicates to the viewer. Content determines form, but form expresses content; thus the two are inseparable. As form changes, content changes, and vice versa."

Source: Patrick Frank, *Art Forms*, 9th ed.

Subject

What was the work about?

Did the composition have a subject? Did you recognize an image? Was it a building? Was it a person (or portrait)?

Did it have a plant or a table with flowers or a vase on it? (It would be considered a still life.)

Did it not have a subject, and was it simply colors or lines or shapes? Then the work would be considered nonobjective art.

Nonobjective art has no subject; it uses elements for the sake of form itself in an arrangement.

Value

Value is the use of white, grey, and black and the absence of the pigments you see on the color wheel such as the primary colors (red, yellow, and blue).

What gradations from white to black do you notice in the artwork when you examined it?

An example:

In some artworks, artists may leave color out in order to better emphasize the use of shapes. Some scholars say that Pablo Picasso did this with *Guernica* to reflect the fragmentary pieces left after the bomb and the devastation of the act of terror.

Elements of Music

Melody
Single succession of tones

Harmony
Two or more tones sounding together

Rhythm
The beat or the pulsation

Tempo
Rate of speed

Dynamics
Loud or soft, or the degrees of loudness or softness

Timbre
The quality of sound or how one distinguishes between one instrument and another.

The elements of music need to be heard individually to recognize them and for the listener to learn to distinguish the styles of music that composers use in their work. If someone is singing all by oneself, that melody is considered to be a texture. A single sound is a thin texture that is referred to as monophonic texture. This is easy to remember because the word *mono* means "one" and *phonic* means "sound." One instrument played by itself is also considered a monophonic texture.

When two instruments are played together and each one plays a separate melody, the two melodies together are a polyphonic texture. Two people singing two melodies together is also considered polyphonic texture. *Poly* means "many."

When someone plays or sings a melody that is accompanied by blocks of sound (chords), this is homophonic texture. A hymn or a piece such as "America the Beautiful" is homophonic texture. Homophonic texture is the sound that is heard when a folk singer sings while strumming the strings of a guitar. Many symphony orchestra compositions are also written in homophonic texture.

Three Textures

Monophonic: One line of melody

Polyphonic: Two or more melodies together

Homophonic: One main melody with blocks of sound accompanying it

http://www.dallassymphony.com

Elements of Theater

Knowing the elements of theater is helpful to students when they view a theatrical performance or read a play.

Script
The language used by the actors playing the roles in a play. The parts in the written document written by the playwright. The written document, or script, is the first element of theater.

Plot

The structure of the play which consists of the exposition, the complication, and the denouement.

Exposition

This portion of the play introduces the characters and their backgrounds and personalities.

Complication

This element gives the audience a reason to be interested in the story and characters and keeps their attention. A conflict may be created to frustrate the audience and gain their interest in the plot.

Denouement

This device is a period of adjustment at the end of the play that resolves the complication.

Elements of Architecture

The visual elements of art are used by architects to plan and draw. Architecture is a three-dimensional art, which means that it consists of height, width, and depth.

Line

The use of a moving dot to show direction. A line is a tool used by the architect to render the schematics.

Shape

Lines are enclosed to create shapes that are used in architectural drawings.

Scale

The relationship of the size of the building to the size of the human form.

Function

The basic purpose of a building.

Context

The environment surrounding a work of architecture.

Color

The color can be from the natural color of organic materials or manmade such as synthetic or chemically mixed colors. The use of color in architectural structures depends on the location and weather conditions as well as the function and purpose of the structure.

Elements of Dance

Movement
A dancer moves the body in curved or straight angles. The movements create horizontal, vertical, or diagonal lines.

Sound
Dancers move to sound. The sound is usually a rhythm or beat. The sound can also be organized as music. Many types of traditional dance forms are performed to music.

Theme
A theme, or dancing to a subject, is somewhat like a story in Western dance. In some parts of the world, people do not dance to themes. Some modern dancers avoid a theme (just like some modern painters avoid a subject in a style called nonobjectivism). Ballet is a form of dance that has a theme or subject that is used to tell a story. Ballets that were written in the eighteenth century became very long. Two well-known ballets are *Swan Lake* and *Romeo and Juliet*.

Choreography and Staging
Where to go on the stage and placement of where to dance.

Set Design
What is built on the stage that sets the mood and that the dancer has to dance on and around.

Lighting
The way the lights shine on the dancers and how they are lit.

Elements of Film

Script
Organization of the shots as well as the words and phrases spoken by the actors.

Sound and Audio
Actual sounds captured by filming, as well as special sounds added in the editing phase.

Camera Angles and Camera Movements
The way in which the camera moves in order to capture images to portray mood, expressions, and feelings.

(Bishop, Philip E., *A Beginner's Guide to the Humanities*, Prentice Hall, 2003)

Acting
The actresses and actors portraying characters, making situations believable.

Lighting
Use of light to capture mood, draw attention, and create suspense if needed.

Costumes and Makeup
These add information and detail helpful to create believable situations. They also draw attention to the characters and provide hints to help tell the story or create suspense.

Editing
Placing the pieces of film together in a fashion to create the story. This may also be the arrangement of scenes to create mood, explain characters, present points of view, and tell a story.

Music Used to Enhance Film and the Acting in Film
An example of music used in a film that many students are familiar with is "Star Wars." "Star Wars" was composed by the renowned John Williams. The instrumentation selected by the composer helped the scene become more believable and drew an emotional response from the audience. The strings were used to help the audience respond in conjunction with the actors to feel more sentimental and the brass instruments were used to create a presence of triumph and victory. The music helped convey romanticism and exhilaration. Williams won an Academy Award for his work as a composer and as a conductor. His work writing scores for films has certainly given other composers someone "to look up to" and transformed the film music industry. Even though "Star Wars" is not as old as films like *Citizen Kane* or *North by Northwest*, this film's soundtrack has earned the title of being legendary.

Source: http://www.billboard.com/articles/news/6812919/star-wars-main-title-theme-deconstructed

John Williams was born in New York and moved to Los Angeles. He studied at the Juliard School of Music, attended UCLA, served in the Air Force, and worked in his early career in the film industry with Bernard Herrmann who was the composer of "North by Northwest." Williams was the conductor of the Boston Pops and composed many soundtracks for famous films such as *Saving Private Ryan, Amistad, Seven Years in Tibet, The Lost World, Rosewood, Sleepers, Nixon, Sabrina, Schindler's List, Jurassic Park, Home Alone, Far and Away, JFK, Hook, Presumed Innocent, Always, Born on the Fourth of July,* the Indiana Jones trilogy, *The Accidental Tourist, Empire of the Sun, The Witches of Eastwick,* the Star Wars trilogy, *E.T.: The Extra-Terrestrial, The Empire Strikes Back, Superman, Close Encounters of the Third Kind, Jaws,* and *Goodbye Mr. Chips.*

Source: http://www.johnwilliams.org/reference/biography.html

Music Is Used in Film Scenes to Help Create Mood

Scene from film: *The King's Speech*, Director Tom Hooper
Musical Score Alexandre Desplat
Use of the musical composition, "The Symphony No. 7 in A Major" by Beethoven.

Director Hooper's achievement was his use of film elements enabling viewers to feel as if they were there alongside the stuttering King George VI. The camera zoomed in on the king's twitching mouth awaiting his words while in the background, an anxious speech coach played Beethoven's *7th Symphony*.

The music used in the film *The King's Speech* during the first wartime speech given by the king was Ludwig van Beethoven's "Symphony No. 7 in A Major: Allegretto." As King George VI concluded his first wartime speech, the film audience heard the "Piano Concerto No. 5 Op. 73 (Emperor) in E-Flat Major: II. Adagio un poco mosso" by Beethoven. During the first therapy session when the king's voice is being recorded, the music heard in the background is "The Overture to La Nozze di Figaro" by Wolfgang Amadeus Mozart.

One reason the audience was so interested in the film was that viewers could relate to the main characters: King George VI and his speech therapist. Subjective shots were successfully used in order to draw the audience into the emotions of the characters.

The success of the film comes from the achievement of the director and the director of photography to ensure that the audience felt that they were right there alongside the king. Emotionally, the audience invests an enormous amount in the character, and they empathize with his problem of stuttering. (The seriousness of the time and the importance of his role as the king and the role of his country in the war is also brought out in the film and his ability to speak clearly is important.) The use of cutaway shots and camera movements add to the tension inside the sound room as the king speaks in front of the microphone which shows his mouth forming the words and almost making incorrect sounds, but the camera cuts back and forth between the close-up of the king's mouth and the reassuring speech therapist, who moves his hand assuredly and the king's voice sounds loud and clear over the loudspeaker. The camera pans the room where his wife and family are seated and then to the technical assistant who looks very restless and uptight. The music of Beethoven's *7th Symphony* plays in the background and the volume of the music goes up and down in dynamic levels. When the king's words are dramatic and he asks his countrymen and women to support him and his country, the music swells to a loud sound and large chords are heard with the entire symphony playing. The use of close-up and wide-angle lenses were intentional to create suspense for the audience, and the top of the king's face was cut off to create an even greater close-up image. Closing in on the actors' faces helps viewers to really get under the actors' skin, and use of good camera movement and lighting makes it compelling and keeps viewers engaged with the anxious monarch.

In the last speech in the film *The King's Speech*, the actor who plays King George VI, Colin Firth, gives his speech in the sound room with his speech therapist who says to him, "Just say it to me as a friend." The speech therapist looks directly at King George VI through a close-up camera shot of the large round microphone, looking reassuringly into the eyes of the king. The camera then cuts to an extreme close-up of the king who blinks his eyes and makes nervous twitches in this quick cutaway to the king. The king looks uneasy, agitated, and nervous. The extreme lighting contrast goes from dark bluish grey to black to light white to grey tints. The size of the sound room is accentuated by the lighting and the placement of the microphone directly in the center of the room. The closeness and tightness of the room and the low, slow, dark sounds of the music all add to the intensity of the mood. The camera closes in on the king's face for a partial view, and most of his face is shot in a shadow with his profile in the lit area with a light glow on his face. Then the camera shows the microphone in the middle of the shot again and moves around in motion. The speech therapist (Lionel Logue, an Australian speech therapist in real life, played in the film by Geoffrey Rush, actor) continues to conduct the king who stands nearby. The speech therapist stands in front of the king, acting as if he were a symphony conductor. As Lionel Logue stands in front of the king, giving him hand signals and position facial expressions, the sound of Beethoven's *Symphony No. 7* continues to build and swell during the scene. The king's dynamic level of voice also follows the swell, up and down in volume when his message gets louder, and more compelling and more serious. The king asks his British people to stand beside him and to help him with his cause and to be faithful and that then with the help of God they will prevail. The scene begins with a close-up of the king's mouth and a nervous facial expression with his eyes blinking, and ends with his eyes open and his full face and form looking confident.

Viewers first feel the king's nervousness and tension from the way the camera draws them into the sound room, looking into the dark room, hearing the somber sound of Beethoven's *No. 7 Symphony*, and seeing the lighting used by the director of photography and the film director. The use of these elements helps enhance the scene and influence the audience to better understand the meaning of the film.

It makes a difference to look at how the elements of film help tell the story—for example, how low light was used on the king, with a touch of highlights, to create suspense. The director of photography chose to show only portions of the king's face and only partial lighting to give the viewer a sense of tension and a feeling of anticipation and uneasiness. This subjective shot by the camera helps viewers feel the tension that the king was feeling. The shot of the speech therapist when his expression was calm and he smiled directly at the king and nodded at him to give him positive strokes and assurance was important to the story and helped the king speak much more clearly into the microphone. King VI continued to speak as a cutaway shot drew the audience to a room of individuals, including his wife and daughter who were sitting in the front row listening intently to his speech. His wife's expression helped the audience feel the same extreme nervousness as she felt when she closed her eyes as if meditating or praying. The camera zoomed in on the main technician in the sound room who also looked tense and had a very serious facial expression, then the camera panned around the entire room to show how the room was filled with technical tools and serious-minded employees working at the equipment. The music continued to play in the background as the king's speech improved and the audience began to think he would make it through; and his speech pattern began to sound confident as he spoke, asking his British citizens to please stay calm and remain united even if the days ahead were going to be dark and challenging.

MUSIC HAS AN INFLUENCE ON OUR MOOD WHEN WE WATCH FILMS

When we watch a film we are influenced by sounds and that is why the first film makers that only had the option of adding sound such as a piano realized that the audience became more exited if they heard something.

Very quickly, the film makers realized that sound was also important for audiences to understand the breadth of the story if they could see as well as hear at the same time. After a while some of the theaters had live performance with small orchestras; however, that became quite expensive. Eventually, technology improved and sound became a possibility and everything changed for the film industry.

Music in film establishes the setting and draws attention to the characters. Music can help create the atmosphere and mood.

Music in film can help the audience understand what is about to happen.

Source: http://www.veryshortintroductions.com/view/10.1093/actrade/9780195370874.001.0001/actrade-9780195370874-chapter-1

Music can invoke feelings of inspiration or despair, happiness or sadness. It can help the audience understand what is approaching, and about impending doom.

Music can create fear, without the listeners' knowledge. Music touches listeners quicker than visual. It causes a very quick response rate and seems to have a universal sound that translates to people from around the globe, which is quite extraordinary and remarkable. Music has been called a universal language for several reasons and some say it is because it crosses boundaries of age, ethnicities, and localities. Would you agree or not? If one asks good directors and film editors, they know that music will make or break their film. If you study the greatest films ever made it is interesting to note that great music was created for the film. Great music was used in great films.

Great films will have utilized music that allowed the audience to have connected with the music to help enhance the main actor's character or to help understand the message of the film or to help understand the main story line.

Great films will not use music that is tiring or overdone. Music that is used over and over or that is heard and then becomes so obvious that one hears it over the dialogue is not considered wise. Music in film is used to enhance, not to drown out the conversation.

In *Jaws*, the theme music by the great movie composer, John Williams, was very suspenseful and the sound track (music) was rather simple in its melody; but it was very effective. Director Steven Spielberg knew how to utilize music in an effective manner and he created a powerful film. *Jaws* is still considered a film that is a good example of music used effectively.

Source: http://www.centerdigitaled.com/artsandhumanities/Music-Makes-Movies.html

UNIT 2

Artists and Styles of Art

In this unit, you will study the lives of artists and how they were influenced by the time and place they lived and the people they knew. Be sure to study the photos in the accompanying "website."

Many of the artists had barriers to overcome and some had family situations that were either helpful or detrimental. You may find that reading about an artist's life will be very helpful in understanding the type of art that an artist paints, sculpts, or draws. If you look at a series of an artist's work and not just one or two pieces, you are much better off. Be sure you do that.

I personally feel that it is a disservice to an artist if you form an opinion on the basis of one piece of artwork. Great artists spend their life and their genuine effort and strength in their art and they do more than one or two works of art. However, many times, posters or books may print only one or two of their most popular work.

STYLES OF ART

Impressionism: The artist renders a fleeting impression of an object, person, or scene based on observation in open air.

Pointillism: The artist juxtaposes small dots of color, which blend to produce tone and shape.

Expressionism: The artist expresses feelings in terms of distorted lines and strong colors rather than trying to accurately represent the subject.

Cubism: The artist renders objects or persons in geometric forms.

Surrealism: The artist produces paintings of the unreal which appear photographically real or fantastically abstract.

Op Art: The artist organizes lines and colors so that the eyes cannot find a stable pattern in which to focus.

Pop Art: The artist creates or renders objects that reflect the age of consumerism, drawing attention to how much the mass media influences people's interests, using popular culture as a subject.

Conceptual Art: The artist produces art pieces or large-scale works or collaborative projects in which the idea is more important than the object. These works do not necessarily have a long material life.

Abstract Expressionism: The artist finds that his or her art can be created by using ideas from the subconscious mind and so explores their use. The lines and colors are to represent only very abstract lines and should not create forms that look like recognizable shapes.

Psyexpressionism: The artist finds that his or her art can be created by battling out a progression from the non conscience. By being in an isolated environment and in tune with the art form, the artist layers paint over and over again in thick lines and shapes until they seem to proliferate and form mutual realism.

PRINTMAKING METHODS

PROCESS OR METHOD

Intaglio	Relief	Planographic	Stencil
WORK OF ART:			
Etching	Woodcut	Lithograph	Silkscreen
Engraving	Wood engraving		
WHAT PRINTS:			
Ink comes from below the surface (the ink is wiped off with a cloth, but the ink that is down below the surface in the grooves is forced out onto the paper)	Ink above surface	Ink on smooth surface	Ink goes through holes in silk

Printmaking

Printmaking has been around for many centuries. Albrecht Dürer (1471–1528), a German printmaker who lived during the Renaissance, was mainly a wood engraver. He is still considered to be one of the best engravers or wood etchers to have ever lived. He did very detailed work at a time when the printing press had just been invented and illustrations for books were being printed. Many of his prints were of religious subjects, such as Jesus' life and Crucifixion. He also depicted other major topics from the New Testament.

An Edition

An edition is considered to be the entire collection of a print or the entire amount of similar prints that the artist makes from one plate, screen, or lithographic stone. It can be a collection of any number, but usually a round number such as 20, 50, or 100. The group or edition is then penciled in as the numerator with the total number as the denominator. For example, the first print of a twenty-print edition is signed and numbered as 1/20, the next one as 2/20, and so forth.

Such prints should all be of equal quality, and the works should be signed by the artist in pencil and numbered. Always be sure that the dealer will allow a piece of art to be removed from a frame. Be sure to wear white cloth gloves, and be careful with the artwork so as not to damage it. If you look at the art and can see its back side, look for an indentation in the back to see if it is genuine. If a work is a reproduction, such an indentation may be missing—dealers sometimes try to sell reproductions as if they were originals. Be careful, and seek out good art galleries when buying artwork.

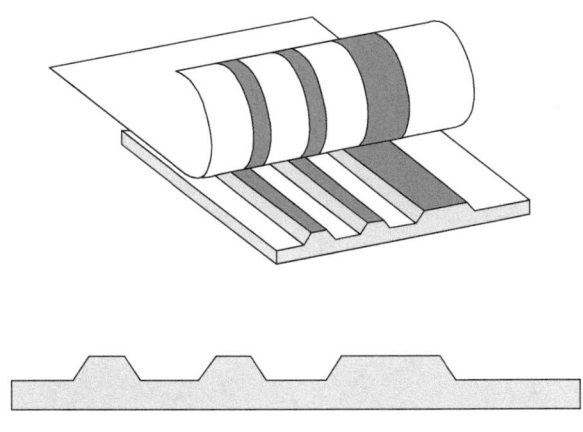

Relief printing.

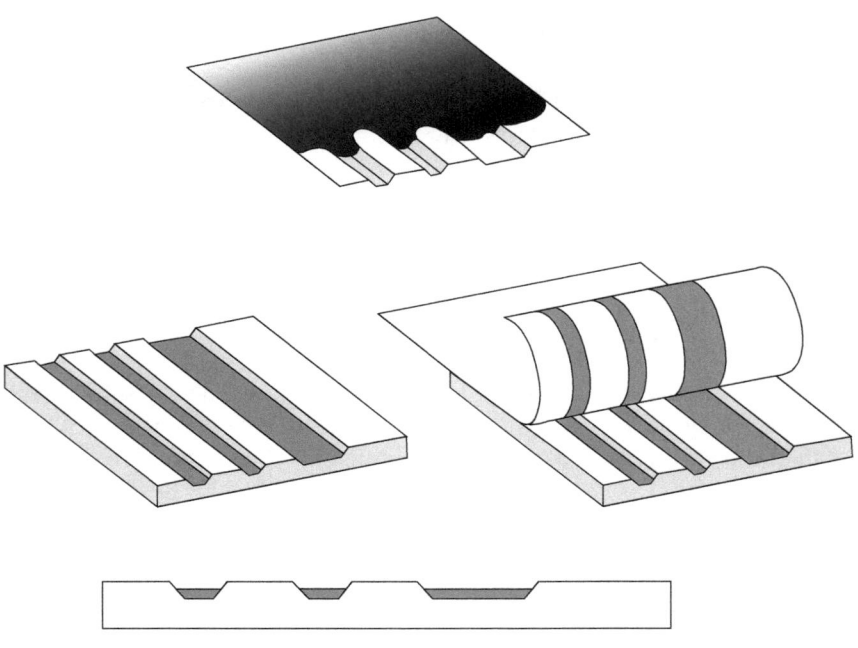

Intaglio process.

© Kendall Hunt Publishing Company. Reprinted by permission.

Printmaking is a very detailed type of art that has been around for centuries. Art schools continue to teach printmaking just as traditional artists such as Rembrandt and Francisco de Goya did it in their day. The differences between etching and engraving are observed in the studio when a student studies art and looks at the difficult and painstaking processes up close. The greatest prints created are studied by artists and students today. These can be seen in museums around the world.

When we look at these paintings on our monitors and in textbooks, we do not see the texture of the ink on paper. It is only second best. If you have had the opportunity to visit the Kimbell Museum in Ft. Worth, Texas or the Meadows Museum in Dallas, Texas or the Metropolitan Museum in New York City, the Prado in Madrid, Spain, Louvre Museum in Paris, France, the National Gallery in London, England, or the Rijksmuseum in Amsterdam or many other museums around the world, then you have seen for yourself close up what I mean. If you have the opportunity to go to an artist's studio, or talk with artists about their work, I hope you will. This gives a closer look at what an artist goes through in order to create and come up with ideas. You will also be able to find out if they are genuine about what they do. For so many of us, we have to just read about artists from the past that lived before video and television and media. However, today it is possible to find interviews with artists on film and in media. This should help us evaluate their work more closely and we should be able to understand their work better.

You may have lived in areas of the world where there are museums with art from the Western and the Eastern Hemispheres. I hope that you will take the opportunity to visit museums and art galleries every time you have the opportunity. The only way to fully see real art and appreciate it is to see it firsthand. This text is helpful in categorizing artists' work and setting their work into a time and place. Categorizing and recognizing the style that the artist's work represents is fun.

An etching is the product or the art work. The process or method that the artist uses to create an etching is called an intaglio process or method. A student should watch a printer do this work in an artist's studio or watch the process on a film in order to understand how it works. When visiting a gallery or going to a museum the final product is shown. Therefore the metal plate that the artist works on is not seen by the viewer. The metal plate used by the artist is scratched on after the plate is prepared and then placed in a pan of acid in order to eat away at the lines so that the ink can stay below the surface in the grooves. The plate is wiped with a rag so again the ink stays below the surface in the grooves. The plate is run through a press with the paper on top of it with a piece of felt material on top of it so that the edges are not torn. The eye can see the edges on the back of an original print since it will have the depression (indentation) on it. This way if you want to purchase a print you should know that it is a genuine print and not a photographic replica. Always be sure your work is signed. It has been a tradition for a printer to sign a print in pencil.

Please take advantage of the "Timeline" in the accompanying website and look at as many works of art as possible to become acquainted with each artist's style. There have throughout history been differences in the way artists have perceived their world; therefore the artists' ideas and value give us a glimpse into their domain and thinking. This is why a master artist will have a unique style.

In this unit, you will notice that the master works of Albrecht Dürer, Rembrandt Van Rijn, Francisco de Goya, Katsushika Hokusai, Vincent Van Gogh, Edgar Degas, Mary Cassatt, and Pablo Picasso (to list a few) were painters as well as excellent printers. In your study of artists and their work you will want to pay close attention to what types of subjects they used.

Practical Information to Know about Printmaking

The reason it is interesting to know about printmaking is many established artists such as painters also create and sell their prints. If it is out of the question financially to purchase a painting by an important artist, it may be possible to purchase a print instead. This of course depends upon the artist and the type of print produced. Prints are less expensive than a painting because there are more of them. The entire edition may consist of often 20, 50, or 100 identical prints.

The prints that investors usually purchase from an edition are numbered as the first or the last print of the edition. For example, the number for the first of an edition of 50 would be 1/50 and the last one of that edition would be 50/50. Other numbers would be 1/100 and 100/100.

If you purchase a print from a reputable dealer or at an art gallery, be sure to ask for a lower price if the print is not the first or the last. Also, be sure that the dealer allows you to see the back side of the print to check for indentation such as an etching on the back side. The back side will have left an indentation from the etching metal plate which was used in the process. Be sure as well that the artist has signed his or her name. Traditionally, original prints are signed in pencil.

When you have time to visit museums and art galleries you will find that it is fun to see the original art works. Prints and paintings do not reproduce well in photographs or in copies seen on your monitor or in your textbook or from a website. I suggest that you study them from a text before you go since then you will have such a better time when you actually get to see the size and the colors, texture, value, and shapes of the original.

WHAT FACTORS INFLUENCE ARTISTS? 3

The factors that influence an artist can be social, economic, political, religious, and geographical. In the humanities, an artist is anyone who creates, such as a musician, writer, dancer, painter, printer, photographer, screenwriter, actor or actress, director, or architect.

Family life influences artists, because the people with whom they spend the most time have the greatest impact upon them. A death in the family can shake up an artist, profoundly impacting his or her work. Being married (or unmarried) or part of another relationship can also play an important role in an artist's life, influencing his or her work. For example, the death of Pablo Picasso's sister deeply affected his work—some of the images in his work symbolized the sadness that he felt and the ways that he struggled with her death. Other artists had illnesses which influenced their work and which can be heard in some of their sounds, such as in the melancholy chords of Frederick Chopin. Writers often use happy incidents when telling funny stories or writing comedies. Situations that happen in artists' lives directly influence their work.

Monetary status influences artists, because life requires money if only as a means for paying bills. In many cases, art takes a long time to become valuable. Artists often receive very little monetary compensation for their art when it is first produced. They may not be understood at first, and may be unappreciated. It may take many years for their work to be recognized, no matter how good it is. Rembrandt Van Rijn, for example, painted what today is considered a great painting, named *The Night Watch*. But when he painted it, he was unable to obtain the funding for his commission, and he eventually went bankrupt. When he died, he remained extremely poor. Vincent Van Gogh did not sell his paintings, so famous today, such as *The Starry Night* or *The Sunflowers*. His brother sold art, but even he could never sell one of Van Gogh's paintings.

The time period influences an artist and what he or she paints, composes, performs, or describes, for each artist represents a particular time, reflecting the events of his or her day. For example, Auguste Renoir was a successful painter who was from a family of means, able to enjoy painting the outdoors and beautiful, sunny afternoons at the terrace café. He enjoyed life, and many of his paintings reflect blissful scenes and a carefree life. Francesco de Goya, on the other hand, was a court painter who lived during a major political upheaval during which his country came under foreign occupation. He painted *The Execution of the Citizens of Madrid* and created prints of the *Disasters of War* which express the horror and terror of the situation. Artists often reflect their own times and the events of their lives, whether good or bad.

Religious beliefs often influence artists. Some artists select topics that are unrelated to religion, but other artists are influenced a great deal by their religious beliefs. Because art is very personal, an artist may intentionally reveal his or her reality by using religion or religious symbolism in his or her art. For example, Salvador Dali's paintings are considered to be surrealistic in style, but he used many images of Christianity, including Mary (the mother of Christ) and Jesus Christ, in some of his paintings. Rembrandt Van Rijn was a painter and a printmaker known for his portraits, but later in life he created many religious prints on the topic of the life of Christ. Many of those religious prints were never commissioned and were never sold. They may have been created for the artist's sake alone. Did Rembrandt need to create? Do you think creating these prints of the life of Christ and his trials and tribulations could have actually helped Rembrandt through the difficulties in his own sad life?

Education influences an artist's work. Where an artist is trained and with whom he or she is able to study may make a big difference. Artists who have parents who are able to teach them the trade at an early age have a head start. Beethoven was able to be taught by Franz Joseph Haydn, whose lessons were a great influence upon his career. Pablo Picasso's father was an art instructor and taught Picasso to paint. Michelangelo's father sent him to a very good sculpture school when he was a young boy, giving him the opportunity to learn a number of important techniques. Howard Carter, a great archeologist who was able to decipher hieroglyphics and who is credited with finding King Tutankhamen's tomb in the Valley of the Kings in Egypt, was able to learn much of what he knew because he accompanied his mother, who worked at the British Museum, when boxes of Egyptian artifacts arriving at the museum were uncrated. Because of his mother's influence, he was being educated at the museum, something that greatly affected his career.

The country and culture in which someone lives can be a major influence upon his or her art. For example, someone living in certain areas of the world or as a part of certain religions might not wish to represent the human form on a sacred building. Those living in other areas of the world would find a holy image or figure in a stained glass window natural. In some areas of the world, people build with domes and arches, and in others they build very flat, low buildings. Buildings and architectural structures reflect both the function and availability of their materials.

Many times artists' and individuals' works and research are not known until after their deaths: Vermeer was one such example.

For more than 200 years after his death, Vermeer was overlooked by all but the most discriminating collectors and art historians. His few pictures were attributed to other artists. Only after 1866, when the French critic W. Thore-Burger "rediscovered" him, did Vermeer's works become widely known and heralded as genuine. http://www.ibiblio.org/wm/paint/auth/vermeer/

The thirty-five (or thirty-six) paintings generally accepted as by Vermeer are divided between Europe (22) and America (14). The *Saint Praxedis*, which would be the thirty-seventh painting by Vermeer, is only weakly supported by authorities, and it is only rarely on public view. Vermeer's *Concert*, once housed in the Isabella Stewart Gardner Museum in Boston, was stolen on March 18, 1990, and has not been recovered. If you have any information regarding this theft, please report it to the FBI Art Theft Program. http://www.essentialvermeer.com/maps/mapeurope.html

Women in History

Since antiquity, women have created art and not received recognition for doing so. It is difficult to obtain a proper history of women in art because many records have been manipulated, and a great number of works by women have been credited to their male teachers or relatives, as it was believed that no truly great art could be created by a woman (Heller, 1987). A large number of artists from antiquity remain unknown, and many are of the opinion that perhaps "anonymous was a woman" (NMWA, 1998, p. 1). We know that women were creating art during this period through discoveries of unaltered records and images of women artists working, yet there are relatively few known female artists of this time. Hypothetically, if not in truth, we may conclude that works were better received with artist unknown, rather than to be attached to the name of a woman. Clearly it was an unacceptable notion that a woman was capable of creating great art. (*Source:* Jeannie Shubitz, *Women, Art and Gender: A History.*)

If someone does not make an impact or influence on a group of people, then that someone does not go down in history as having an impact.

If your work is found after you are gone, it is possible that the work can be influential in future generations. If someone else finds your work or your writings later, then the work may be used to influence others. An example of this is the way in which Pablo Picasso "resurrected" the art of and the interest in El Greco (Doménikos Theotokópoulos). This artist was from the period of time between the Renaissance and the Baroque Period, often referred to as "Mannerism." El Greco elongated his spiritual figures, such as saints found in the Catholic Church, to show the difference between regular individuals and spiritual figures.

The reason many artists were not able to impact the "art world" when they were alive was their art was not seen by the influential people from places where there would have been a significant amount of information spread about their work. If a creator has his or her work shown or distributed only in a small area, say, where they were living, then it is likely that they will not become famous. It may be that their work is discovered, however, after they are gone. An example of this is when Pablo Picasso became interested in El Greco's art. Upon rediscovering it, Picasso prepared El Greco's work for a revival. Picasso was influenced enough by El Greco's work that one can notice similarities in a few of his compositions.

During the late nineteenth century, if naturalist Charles Robertson had not traveled to the Illinois countryside recording the movements of bees and categorizing them, we would not know their role on our current environment. However, Robertson was not famous during his own lifetime but recently scientists have found his work to be valuable. "Bees provide a unique insight," Lane said. "They are a window into our impact on the environment because they are directly impacted."

In the end, all bee researchers have Robertson to thank, for the study could not have been carried out without his in-depth research, according to Marlin.

"I would say that he was probably obsessive—you almost have to be obsessive to do this kind of work," he said. "The man's amazing." (*Source:* H. Zolkower-Kutz, "Researchers Buzzing About New Bee Study.")

A Few Examples of Women Artists Who Did Paint during the Renaissance and Baroque Periods

Catherine de Vigri
A religious painter during the Renaissance Period
1413–1463 born in Bologna, Italy

This artist was born into an aristocratic family and was later known as Saint Catherine de Bologna.

She became a nun and established a monastery for the poor in the area where she grew up. She learned to paint from her father and paint altar pieces of religious subjects for the Catholic Church.

Source: http://hubpages.com/education/History-of-Female-Renaissance-Artists.

Sofonisba Anguissola
1531–1625 born in Cremona, Italy

This artist was born into a noble family with five girls. Their father taught the girls to paint. Sofonisba was allowed to travel to Rome and was intrigued with the work of Michelangelo. She painted for twenty years and it has been documented that her work was mainly commissioned by King Philip the First of Spain.

Source: http://hubpages.com/education/History-of-Female-Renaissance-Artists.

Baroque Period Artist
Artemisia Gentileschi
1593–1656 born in Rome, Italy

Gentileschi was an Italian Baroque painter and is considered today to have been unique because of her use of high contrast between light and dark. She did portraits which were extremely realistic and detailed. She was able to get some work but was not accepted by many of the powerful people high in the Catholic Church so she was not able to get commissions for altar pieces. She moved to Venice and to Naples in search of work.

Many of the subjects that she did paint were topics representing strong women. She especially painted those women who had gone through extremely hard times. Gentileschi painted suffering women from myths and biblical stories. Her subject matter usually depicted victims, suicides, or warriors.

Source: https://en.wikipedia.org/wiki/Artemisia_Gentileschi

IMPORTANT ARTISTS AND INDIVIDUALS

Giotto 1276–1337

Italy (Italian)

Giotto was an artist who lived in Florence, Italy, during the late thirteenth and the early fourteenth centuries. His full name was Giotto di Bondone, and his work was distinct, for it bridged the gap between the Middle Ages and the beginnings of the Renaissance. He used strict symbolism, painting a gold glow around the gold halos circling the faces of saints and Jesus and his mother. But the wall paintings that he did in Padua were unique because of his ability to show how human beings felt towards one another, something very new to the world of painting. Little is known about his personal life. He has been called a transitional artist, for his paintings embodied both the elements of the past Gothic look and the beginnings of the new Renaissance style. Giotto painted altar pieces for cathedrals on wood panels with tempera paints. His subject matter was the Madonna and Child. His paintings were unique, with flat areas lacking shadow and using little perspective. Some of the areas in his frescos incorporated a few areas that depicted some use of volume and a little contrast between light and dark. He began to introduce the use of perspective and humanism into his work. Being able to render individuals' emotions and feelings was a new and innovative technique that would soon catch on. Giotto paved the way for other artists in the Renaissance, and that is what made him important (Fischner-Rathus 358).

In Doris Van de Bogart's *Introduction to the Humanities*, she states that John Canady, a modern art critic and historian, thought that Giotto's thirty-eight fresco paintings in the Arena Chapel in Padua were extremely influential on the future of emotion and passion in religious art from that time on (Van de Bogart 98). Giotto gave the Italian Renaissance a jump start.

Albrecht Dürer 1471–1528

Nuremburg, Germany (German)

Albrecht Dürer was sent to study in the workshop of Michael Wolgemut for four years. After he studied, he wandered through northern Europe for an additional four years, until his father, a goldsmith, asked him to return to Nuremburg.

He left home again for a short time, traveling to Italy, where he studied the great artists of the Renaissance. He was intrigued with the use of perspective and was a master at creating illusions by using very thin black lines. He perfected the art and craft of using solid, porous pieces of wood that he first carved and then inked. He perfected the art of wood engraving and is still known today as one of the best wood engravers. Dürer was also a painter. He painted a picture of himself (a self-portrait) where one can see how he signed his name on his work with a large A and a large D inside it. Dürer looks very serious in his self-portrait which gives the viewer a sense that he took the role of artist very seriously.

Pieter Brueghel 1525-1569

Flanders/Belgium (Flemish/Belgian)

In the Netherlands at this time, the accessibility and the purchasing of art became available to dealers and the rising upper-middle-class buyers. Previously artworks had been commissioned by aristocrats such as the royalty and religious centers (churches). This offered artists such as Pieter Brueghel the Elder the opportunity to sell his work. Brueghel's travels to Italy influenced his interest in humanism, which helped him understand the importance of how man and nature are interrelated. One notices this aspect in his well-known painting *Hunters in the Snow* (oil on wood). The painting reflects how he represented nature and man side by side as he depicted a cold clear day with men, along with their dog, among a cluster of trees and birds on the left, as they look on to a town with a pond of frozen ice with townspeople ice skating. In the far distance one can view the mountains. (*Source:* Adapted from Lawrence S. Cunningham, John J. Reich, and Lois Fichner-Rathus, *Culture and Values, A Survey of the Humanities* [8th ed., vol 2, pp. 480-481].)

Pieter Bruegel was also referred to as Pieter the Elder, for he had a son, Pieter the Younger, who also became a painter. His son made copies of his father's work.

Because of this situation, you may see some reproductions of works having the same name and looking similar but with different dates on them.

The country where Pieter Bruegel the Elder was born was called Flanders, which makes him Flemish. Flanders is modern-day Belgium; today he would be considered Belgian.

There is little known today about his personal life, but it is known that he was highly educated, a painter who was interested in the humanistic ideas that were relatively new in his country at that time. He had been commissioned to paint for the Hapsburg Court (Schloat 12).

Brueghel painted humble people who worked hard. He wanted to show how difficult their work was while showing respect for their labor. In a series of paintings of an entire wedding, he painted several scenes of events that occurred at the wedding, from the guests eating to the guests dancing. The dancing of the guests is very lively, and viewers can almost imagine that they hear the music being played as they look at the painting in the museum.

The painting of the dancers reflects a happy scene, and the people in attendance are eating and enjoying themselves. The mood is light. It is a time of joy and happiness.

The title of the painting is *The Wedding Dance*. Brueghel portrayed the dancers as in movement by his mastery of line and shape and by the reddish-orange color he used throughout his work. This painting is a masterpiece that reflects how he was able to capture a scene with its mood using space, form, line, and shape. As a great artist, he understood how to use the elements of art to create a composition that reflected the mood he wished to portray.

Leonardo da Vinci 1452-1519

Vinci, Italy (Italian)

Leonardo da Vinci was born in Vinci, a small village in Italy. His father sent Leonardo to a school of a goldsmith named Andrea Verrochio, who was very impressed with his student's ability as a painter. In the Florence of that day, the Medici family had a lot of influence in the world of art. Because it did not notice Leonardo's talent, he left Florence to pursue other opportunities.

Some stories say that da Vinci was invited to go to Rome before he made a decision to go to Milan, Italy. He had been invited to paint some of the walls at the Vatican but decided to go to Milan, where he painted the mural *The Last Supper*, from 1495 to 1498, which would become one of his most famous works (Hobbs and Duncan 125–127). He began working for Lodovico Sforza then, who was Regent of Milan at that time.

While working in Milan, da Vinci designed war machinery and sketched many studies having to do with science, anatomy, and engineering. He designed the altar piece for a church, and painted the *Virgin of the Rocks* in 1483. Leonardo also experimented with materials and produced countless sketches and drawings for an equestrian monument that was never built.

The *Mona Lisa*, painted from 1503 to 1505, may very well have never been finished. The actual name of the painting may have been that of the wife of Francesco del Giocondo—perhaps "del Giocondo," or, as most books would have it, "Gioconda." Francesco del Giocondo may have been a Florentine citizen of the merchant class. The *Mona Lisa*, as the painting is most often called, has an unusual background that gives the figure of the woman a realistic, three-dimensional appearance, particularly in her hands and in the appearance that she has just turned to look at the viewer. Her eyes appear to gaze at each viewer in the room, no matter the location. Most paintings of the day were related to religion, not women from the merchant class (some sources say that her husband was a Florentine banker), which in itself makes the painting unusual (Hobbs and Duncan 128).

The *Mona Lisa* also has a landscape in its background that gives it depth and makes it possible to imagine that the subject is a real person living in the real world. She appears to be someone not of the aristocracy, nor the mother of Jesus Christ or a religious person to be worshipped, even though such things might have been much more common themes and subjects. Why, then, do you think this painting is so famous and thought to be so innovative for its time? What types of other portraits were being painted at that time in history, and why did this painting end up in France, in the Louvre?

Leonardo da Vinci brought the *Mona Lisa* with him when he left Italy on his way to France where he was invited by King Frances I. Da Vinci kept the painting with him until his death. Because this painting was in the possession of the King of France, it became the possession of France and is now in the French museum. It has had an impact upon painters for many generations and represents the naturalness and grace of the Renaissance even today.

The painting is oil on panel, 30¼ by 21 inches. It is in the Louvre, Paris, France (Gilbert and McCarter 388, 477–478).

Raphael Sanzio 1483-1520

Italy (Italian)

Raphael only lived for thirty-seven years. He was one of the most well-known portrait painters of the Italian Renaissance. He was born in Urbino and studied with the important artist Pietro Perugino during his youth. At twenty-six, he was commissioned to paint many rooms at the Vatican, where he painted the famous *School of Athens* (Schloat 12). The

School of Athens was painted during the same period in which Michelangelo was painting the ceiling of the Sistine Chapel. Pope Julius II had both artists working on many projects at the Vatican during that period, a time when they were in competition with one another. For the large wall painting in the room where documents were signed by the pope, Raphael chose the subject of Athens, reflecting his interest in the ancient history of the Greeks, which was being studied at that time. Raphael selected that theme and chose to portray the two central figures as the two Greek philosophers Aristotle and Plato. Some say that those two philosophers appear to resemble the faces of his two competitors of his day and time—Michelangelo and Leonardo da Vinci. Plato's white hair and long beard, for example, seem to depict da Vinci. The background of the painting has arches and, above them, clouds and a beautifully painted sky. The arches give the painting a great sense of depth and a feeling of enormous space such as is felt when walking inside St. Peter's, which was being designed at that time (Schloat 12).

Michelangelo Buonarrotti 1475–1564
Italy (Italian)

Michelangelo was born in Tuscany, Italy, in 1475. His teacher, Domenico Ghirlandaio, taught him how to paint when he was in his early teens. His father never married his mother (Gilbert, McCarter 390). Michelangelo is probably mostly known for painting the ceiling of the Sistine Chapel after he managed to build scaffolding seventy feet above the floor. He painted 5,760 square feet of ceiling at the Sistine Chapel, in the Vatican. Michelangelo was not interested in painting when Pope Julius II asked him to paint the ceiling of the Sistine Chapel (Fiero 202). He was expecting to sculpt a project for the pope instead but was unable to do so, because the artists of that period were not their own masters. The pope had other plans for Michelangelo. As a child, Michelangelo had attended a sculpting studio, where he had studied with the future Julius II, and now Michelangelo was unable to go against the pope's wishes. Michelangelo is said to have started out with a design of drawings of disciples; when asked why he wanted to do disciples as the paintings on the ceiling, he answered that they were all living as people with little means whom he felt were somewhat poor. But Michelangelo abandoned that idea after he came down from the scaffolding after a few days and didn't like what he saw. He realized that the figures were not large enough. Because the ceiling was so high, he had to make his paintings much larger. He then started completely over, using a different portion of the Bible as inspiration—the moment of God's creation. He chose the separation of light from darkness, the creation of the heavenly bodies and Earth from water, the creation of man, and the expulsion of man from the garden, as well as many other scenes.

Although Michelangelo, who preferred to sculpt, wanted to execute forty sculptures as an enormous monument to the pope, that work was never completed. Between 1498 and 1500 Michelangelo created a work of art that has epitomized his ability to handle marble in the method of the Classical Greek style while drawing from the Renaissance's religiosity to gain work. He was expected to be able to sculpt work that would fit within the popes' and the Church's belief system. The work that brought him fame, showing just how much talent he had even as a young sculptor, was the *Pieta*, a magnificent work that is still in the Vatican, in the chapel area to the right after entering St. Peter's Basilica. The sculpture was actually flown to the World's Fair in 1964 to Flushing, New York, where people could actually touch it, it was so close to them. It was seen by several million people. But times have changed. The sculpture was struck with a hammer a number of years ago but was not badly damaged. It was repaired and is now behind a panel of bulletproof plexiglass, no less marvelous to lay eyes upon and considered one of the most fragile pieces of marble still to be in excellent condition.

Michelangelo gained fame and another great work, the *Pieta*, that of Jesus with his mother Mary after he was taken from the cross. Those two early works are his most well known.

Before Michelangelo went to live in Rome, he was in competition with another well-known artist, Leonardo da Vinci. Da Vinci had been given a large piece of marble by the city fathers to create a sculpture but never managed to get it completed and gave it to Michelangelo. Michelangelo was in his twenties when he took the marble block and made his famous sculpture of David, the young boy who fought the giant Goliath. *David* was executed between 1501 and 1504 and is now displayed in the Gallery of the Academy of Florence. (It was originally outside the Palazzo Vecchio.) The sculpture is nearly eighteen feet high. *David* was one of the first sculptures by which Michelangelo was able to gain notoriety.

Peter Paul Rubens 1577–1640

Flanders (Flemish)

Peter Paul Rubens grew up in Germany while his father, a peasant, worked in exile because he was a Protestant. After his father died in 1589, Rubens was brought up as a Catholic. His studies included working for the Duke of Mantua while he was traveling in Italy for eight years. Many of the years of his life that followed were spent in Flanders, until his wife died. He then served as a diplomat in Spain and England. He opened a studio and hired many qualified artists to complete the volumes of portraits that he and his staff were commissioned. He also received commissions to paint religious works for cathedrals. A very important set of paintings for the Luxembourg Palace were of the arrival of the future queen of France, who was coming from Italy to reign in France. In these Baroque paintings, Maria de Medici is depicted as protected by mythological figures such as Neptune. Rubens and his first wife had three children. Four years after his first wife died, he remarried and had four more children. Peter Paul Rubens died at the age of sixty-three.

William Shakespeare 1564–1616

Stratford-upon-Avon, England (English)

William Shakespeare has been called the greatest writer of plays. He wrote thirty-seven plays, which vary from comedies to tragedies. He also wrote short poems and 154 sonnets. Some say he was also an actor who played several leading roles on stage.

At age eighteen, in 1582, William married Anne Hathaway, a local farmer's daughter who was eight years older than he was. They named their first daughter, born six months after they were married in 1583, Susanna. They later had twins named Judith and Hamnet, born in 1585.

Shakespeare was the greatest English writer, and possibly the greatest writer in any language since the Golden Age of Greece, according to many English scholars. Shakespeare studied Aeschylus and Euripedis and their work in the Greek plays they wrote during the great Greek Era of tragedy and comedy. The elements of theater had been studied by Shakespeare, who used those elements and structure in his work. Shakespeare's plays can be divided into three major categories: comedies, tragedies, and histories.

Shakespeare was born in the town of Stratford-upon-Avon, England. His father, William, attended the local grammar school in Stratford, where he studied Latin rhetoric, history, and literature. He was not only a writer but also an actor and a stock holder.

Shakespeare left Stratford-upon-Avon and joined a repertory theater company, which performed for an admission fee.

In 1594, Shakespeare began working with a theatrical group who performed for the royalty, including Queen Elizabeth. Shakespeare's plays began to be more recognized, and a time came in his career when a couple plays a year had to be written and performed on stage in London. Shakespeare wrote both tragedies and comedies. Shakespeare's most famous plays, including *Hamlet, Romeo and Juliet,* and *King Lear* are tragedies.

Many of William Shakespeare's plays were set at a time in history from the Roman Period to the Renaissance. These Shakespearian theatrical productions are still performed today because they have a universal appeal. They are comprised of interesting stories, useful narratives, meaningful dialogues, and are bursting with word meanings deep with symbolism. The main characters are studies of individual personalities and the audience responds to them with an emotional and responsive appeal.

Shakespeare—Hamlet

Hamlet, Shakespeare's most famous play, was first performed in 1601 and published in 1603. The Hamlet story was a widespread legend in northern Europe, and Shakespeare's source for the play may have been Belleforest's *Histoires Tragiques* (1559). Shakespeare's play may also have used as a source a lost play supposedly by Thomas Kyd, usually referred to as the *Ur-Hamlet*. Shakespeare's *Hamlet*, however, has its own unique central element in Hamlet's tragic flaw, his hesitation to avenge his father's murder.

At the beginning of the play, Hamlet mourns the death of his father, who has been murdered, and also laments his mother's marriage to his uncle Claudius within a month of his father's death. Hamlet's father's ghost appears to Hamlet, telling him that he was poisoned by Claudius and asking him to avenge his death. Hamlet hesitates, requiring further evidence of foul play. His uncertainty and hesitancy make him increasingly moody, and everyone believes that Hamlet is going mad. The pompous old courtier Polonius believes Hamlet is lovesick over his daughter Ophelia.

Despite Claudius' apparent guilt, Hamlet still cannot act. Nevertheless, he terrorizes his mother and kills the eavesdropping Polonius. Fearing for his life, Claudius sends Hamlet to England with his friends Rosencrantz and Guildenstern, who have orders to have Hamlet killed. Discovering the orders, Hamlet arranges to have his friends killed instead. Returning to Denmark, Hamlet learns that Ophelia has killed herself, and her brother Laertes has vowed vengeance on Hamlet for Polonius' death. Claudius happily arranges the duel. Both Hamlet and Laertes are struck by the sword that Claudius has had dipped in poison. Gertrude mistakenly drinks from the cup of poison intended for Hamlet. Before Hamlet dies, he fatally stabs Claudius.

In the play, Shakespeare appears to suggest that traditional beliefs about revenge are oversimplified, arguing that revenge does not solve evil if evil lies in a complex situation: "The time is out of joint; O cursed spite/That ever I was born to set it right." He also seems to maintain that revenge itself is morally wrong. In *Hamlet*, as well as the other tragedies (*Othello, King Lear,* and *Macbeth*), Shakespeare explores with great psychological subtlety how the personality flaws in the protagonist lead almost inevitably to his own destruction and the destruction of those around him.

Hamlet
William Shakespeare
Act 3, Sc. 1
Hamlet:

> To be, or not to be: that is the question:
> Whether 'tis nobler in the mind to suffer
> The slings and arrows of outrageous fortune,
> Or to take arms against a sea of troubles,

And by opposing end them? To die: to sleep:
No more; and by a sleep to say we end
The heartache and the thousand natural shocks
That flesh is heir to,—'tis a consummation
Devoutly to be wish'd. To die, to sleep;
To sleep: perchance to dream: ay, there's the rub:
For in that sleep of death what dreams may come,
When we have shuffled off this mortal coil,
Must give us pause: there's the respect
That makes calamity of so long life;
For who would bear the whips and scorns of time,
The oppressor's wrong, the proud man's contumely,
The pangs of despised love, the law's delay,
The insolence of office and the spurns
That patient merit of the unworthy takes,
When he himself might his quietus make
With a bare bodkin? Who would fardels bear,
To grunt and sweat under a weary life,
But that the dread of something after death,
The undiscover'd country from whose bourn
No traveller returns, puzzles the will
And makes us rather bear those ills we have
Than fly to others that we know not of?
Thus conscience does make cowards of us all;
And thus the native hue of resolution
Is sicklied o'er with the pale case of thought,
And enterprises of great pith and moment
With this regard their currents turn awry,
And lose the name of action.

Rembrandt van Rijn 1606–1669

Leyden, Holland (Dutch)

Rembrandt learned to paint as a teen in a studio of Peter Lastman, who had been taught by a famous Italian artist named Caravaggio, famous for using a painting technique that drew sharp contrast between light and dark, called chiaroscuro. This dramatic use of light and shadow was a technique that Rembrandt used during his career as well. Rembrandt's work has a certain quality about it that is timeless and captivating. Rembrandt was not just a realistic painter. Although he painted realistic work, trying to make someone represent what he or she looked like, his images were indeed deep. He was concerned with the personality of the sitter and the deep meaning within the individual, which was psychological rather than superficial.

Rembrandt moved to Amsterdam when he was twenty-five years old and remained there until he died, at the age of sixty-three. His early work was mainly portraits, and he was so busy that he hired assistants for a short time. His style throughout his entire life can be seen by looking at his etching of himself and his self-portraits, done in oil, pen, and ink. Rembrandt also did landscape painting throughout his career in Amsterdam, during which he married twice. His first wife was from a family that had a favorable enough economic level in Amsterdam that Rembrandt was fortunate enough to be able to start a business painting portraits. He found that to be profitable for a while, but he gradually lost sales and commissions. Several factors accounted for his professional demise. After he lost his first wife in childbirth, several other of his children died at very young ages, after having his female housekeeper move in with him, he was shunned. He then went bankrupt and moved to what was referred to as "Amsterdam's worst ghetto." He became dependent upon his son for a while, but his son died right before Rembrandt died in 1669. Rembrandt outlived his entire family.

Rembrandt is considered to be one of the greatest portrait painters. His work is great because it is genuine and honest. His portraits were likenesses of individuals but went beyond that to express personality, the subjects' innermost parts without saying a word. That this depth is evident upon each viewing of one of his paintings is the timelessness of Rembrandt. His self-portraits take you through the life of a young man who has it all—happiness, fun, glitter—and then at the end has nothing but himself. He is still the same, but he is stripped down to who he is alone, a lonely but satisfied and resolute gentleman. He is somber but not bitter. He may be somewhat sad but he is accepting. It is sad that Rembrandt was somewhat of a stubborn man. Seeing that he lost commissions and never even got paid for painting the famous group painting *The Night Watch*, perhaps Rembrandt did want to produce a painting that was more interesting in its composition, choosing to have the figures in the arrangement where some are hard to see and identify. It seems that he may have lost work by caring more about maintaining his artistic integrity than about receiving payment for his paintings. He certainly underwent major hardships, including having his work seized by the government.

Amsterdam is where many of Rembrandt's works can be seen. The apartment where he lived in an upper level while working on his religious prints of the life of Christ using copperplates for his etchings is now the Rembrandt House Museum. The State Museum or Rijksmuseum is where one can visit to see more of his famous works, including the painting with Captain Cocq and the lieutenant in the center with those around them in shadow or hidden from full view. The arrangement is creative, and the viewer's attention is drawn to two full figures who are in the middle of a conversation. The two seem almost oblivious to all the crowded folks behind them. No one has ever been able to explain why Rembrandt placed the older-looking "short woman" to the central figure on the left side. Whether it was added to communicate a certain meaning or to add a light area is unknown. His commissions dried up somewhat after this work was painted, and from then on Rembrandt was not in demand as a portrait painter. After this, he began to work more on etchings and paintings of religious subject matter.

In *The Night Watch* the use of line and the angular shapes created by the flags and the weaponry create a strong background for the two central human figures, making them more noticeable. The use of strong contrast between light and dark create the mood, and the intensity of the light and shadow give the painting an almost ominous feel. That may be why for so many years the painting was incorrectly labeled *The Night Watch*. Whoever first called it that may have thought that someone was lost, with a group of people being sent out to go find him or her. The painting evokes a feeling of worry, but the two central figures seem almost apart from the rest of the crowd. The painting did not seem to make sense at the time that it was painted, and supposedly Rembrandt was unable to receive payment for the painting, for some of the individuals in the painting did not like the composition and refused to pay their fee. The painting was supposed to hang in the company of the Banning Cocq Company but never did. Another version of the story is very different, describing how the painting was rolled away then placed on a wall, then trimmed to fit a wall on a pub, and then misnamed. But no matter the story, the painting is a masterpiece. It is a moment in time, capturing the feel of a certain place. It gives us such a great sense of the humanness of the men and the use of three dimensions to create depth and spaciousness. Rembrandt was able to create on a flat piece of canvas an amazing composition that has stood the test of time to become a universal work of art. Those two men in the center toward the front of the canvas, once two average Dutch men going about their business making a living in Amsterdam in 1642, are now remembered not by their names but in a different way. Take a closer look; imagine what they may be saying to each other as they walk and talk. Taking time just to wonder is why some people take time to look at art. Think for a moment; go back in time and consider the connections that we all have with people from times past.

Also, think about how many years this was before the invention of the camera. Rembrandt did not have a photograph, a camera, or a television. He created this painting in his studio, yet the men are casual and appear to be talking and walking, as if to depart from their place of business. It is a moment in time composed in an arrangement that offers viewers an opportunity to spend time gazing at many areas of the canvas and the wealth of captivating figures. The arrangement has been considered to be one of the best compositions ever produced from that period.

Historians have labeled this painting a Baroque style of art from that period. It reflects the style of the Baroque period: contrasting areas of light and dark, diagonal lines used to break up space, ornate decoration, precision, and accurate detail. Some areas of the work are decorated with ornate and highly detailed work, such as on the clothing of the gentleman and the figure of the short older female figure. The arrangement was actually of a military organization, such as a guard, preparing for an exercise. The work measures 12 feet 2 inches by 14 feet 7 inches, and is located in the Rijksmuseum, Amsterdam, Holland (Gilbert and McCarter). In 1975 a patient from a Dutch mental institution visited the Rijksmuseum in Amsterdam and managed to gouge twelve deep slashes into the painting. It was repaired at the museum and still hangs in the Rijksmuseum in Amsterdam (Gilbert and McCarter 474).

Johannes Vermeer 1632–1675

Delft, Holland (Dutch)

Johannes Vermeer produced less than thirty-five paintings in his life. Those that exist today are exquisite. They reflect everyday activities in the lives of those in the middle of a task. Although Vermeer's work was not noticed by a large audience during his lifetime, a Parisian art critic took note and published a monograph on Vermeer's art. Vermeer's work is considered to be about everyday life and is thus referred to as *genre painting*.

His work is so detailed, and its texture so smooth, that seeing it in the museum it seems almost unbelievable that it could be possible to do such detailed, believable work. But because Vermeer was so accurate and detailed in his work, he probably did not have time to do any more than he did, for he ran a tavern to support his family of eight children. Johannes Vermeer died at the age of forty-three.

Honoré Daumier 1808–1879

France (French)

Daumier's father hoped to keep him from being an artist by apprenticing him to an usher in the Paris law courts but was unsuccessful. Daumier learned about law and injustice, but his understanding of politics and his interest in art led him in a direction contrary to his father's wishes. In the long run, Daumier became one of the leading printmakers in history, creating his biting satires that are still displayed in courts today.

In 1832, he was employed by the weekly paper *La Caricature* to create illustrations and was imprisoned for six months after depicting a politician as a Gargantua devouring the heavy taxes of the people. One of Daumier's most famous paintings was *The Third Class Carriage*. But Daumier began having trouble with his eyesight, and by 1875 he was completely blind. (Daumier is a realistic painter also grouped into the Romantic Period but he is difficult to label. Daumier may also have been influenced by Impressionism.)

Honoré Daumier created artwork that drew attention to the social injustices and ill treatment of people living in difficult economic and cultural environments in his day. His painting *Third Class Carriage* has left us as viewers today more likely to understand his political views as we are able to see a glimpse into how he illustrated the social ills of his day and time.

His work has been divided into two parts: from 1830 to 1847, when he was a lithographer, cartoonist, and sculptor; and from 1848 to 1871, when he was a painter whose art was representational and somewhat reflective of some Impressionistic tendencies as far as his style. He worked constantly throughout his life and produced approximately 4,000 illustrative drawings and 4,000 lithographs.

Théodore Géricault 1791–1824

France (French)

Théodore Géricault is known as one of the best Romantic painters. He was born in Rouen, France. Known for his love of horses, Gericault died at the age of thirty-three in an accident while he was horse racing. One of the most famous and dramatic works which art historians view as a masterpiece is his *Raft of the Medusa*, a painting that he did after hearing about a shipwreck. (Source: Doris Van De Bogart (author) Introduction to the Humanities, Barnes and Noble, Inc. 1977. ISBN: 0-06-463277-6)

The *Medusa* was a ship owned by the French, filled with immigrants from Algeria. The crew on the ship experienced a wreck and since there were not enough lifeboats, a raft with a chord pulled the immigrants along. It managed for some distance until the chord broke. Originally, the raft was carrying 149 people; however, by the time help was sought, only some of those were still alive on the raft. For days the raft floated defenselessly upon the water. No help came. By the time there was a ship to help, of those on the raft, only 15 survived.

The painting represents the moment in time when the survivors on the raft desperately strain to draw attention to a ship that they finally see. They desperately tried for days to draw attention to their plight with no success and finally saw a ship that finally rescued them.

This painting is sixteen feet by twenty-three feet and located in the Louvre Museum in Paris, France. Romantic paintings by artists seem to evoke deep emotional response.

Source: Edmund Burke Feldman, *Thinking About Art* (Englewood Cliffs, NJ: Prentice-Hall, 1985)

Jacques Louis David 1748–1825

France (French)

Jacques Louis David was a student of Joseph Vien who won the Prix de Rome in 1775. He studied in Paris at the Royal Academy after returning from his studies in Italy.

Under Napoleon's regime, David was a major painter who executed works that had symbolic meaning and that possessed connections with political situations. Because he was especially knowledgeable about the history of Rome and wanted to reflect the ideals of fighting for one's country, he used themes from ancient Roman legends. The Roman ideas of duty toward country and of fighting for a cause, even to death, were used in a famous work of a father with his sons saying an oath before departing for battle. That famous painting, along with other of his political paintings, are still thought of today as masterpieces. These formal compositions are filled with representational work, a close look reveals that the works are filled with political meanings. For example, in the painting about a Roman father entitled *The Oath to the Horatii*, the sons take an oath before their father to fight even if it means that they have to die for their cause. The work is Classical—reserved and orderly. It has emotion, but even the emotion is restrained, and the painting does not feature flamboyance or extreme, intense emotion.

In another painting, which shows a writer in a bathtub, the artist David left some of his canvas almost blank, giving the painting a somewhat empty feel. The writer, Marat, suffered from a rare skin disorder and sat in the bathtub in order to feel well enough to write. But he was unexpectedly attacked by an intruder, a political opponent who walked into his apartment and stabbed him to death. The painting is stark and barren, and the person in the bathtub is actually a corpse. The painting might seem to be Romantic in style for dealing with such an intensely emotional situation, but its style is actually Classical. Some areas are without action, and the letters inscribed in the painting are Roman, a device used at that time by Classical painters.

Neoclassical in style, however, David is difficult to label and his *Death of Marat*, 1793, is almost more realistic than neoclassical.

The painting was a result of a commission which David had received after marrying the spirited Marguerite Pécoul, whose father was a wealthy building contractor and the superintendent of construction at the Louvre in 1782. In the *Oath to the Horatii*, David uses clear lighting and very somber expressions. He represents the courage of the three Horatii brothers as they face their father and vow to offer their lives to assure victory for Rome in the war with Alba.

Source: http://www.britannica.com/EBchecked/topic/152567/Jacques-Louis-David

Francisco de Goya 1746–1828

Spain (Spanish)

Francisco de Goya lived in Spain and may have supported himself as a bullfighter as a young man. By the age of twenty he had moved to Madrid, Spain. As a teenager, Goya was adventurous and had several close calls while in dueling matches. He was very serious about wanting to be an artist but was unable to win a scholarship to study at the Academy of San Fernando, the foremost art school at that time near where he lived. He was upset, but a court painter named Francisco Bayeu apprenticed him and helped Goya learn the art of decorating ceilings and painting portraits. Goya assisted his teacher and then left to study for a while in Italy (McCandless).

Goya returned to Spain and became one of the leading court painters (Gilbert and McCarter 158). His paintings of the royal family appeared to flatter the family of the king but actually reflected the greed and arrogance of the individuals he painted. Goya painted a portrait of the entire family of Charles IV, king of Spain during the late nineteenth century, in which one of the women has her face turned and an elderly woman looks somewhat unattractive. It seems odd to many today that Goya was able to get away with what he did, especially for that day and time and in such political situations as those in which he lived. In the same painting, in the back and to the left, Goya himself is depicted behind an easel, painting. The painting was "nicknamed," supposedly by the king himself, *We Are All Here*, because the entire royal family is pictured. Goya was a remarkable painter who was also personally concerned about the social and political issue of his day. He was extremely troubled by individuals who were placed in asylums, who he thought to be treated worse than unwanted animals.

One can view his paintings of *The Madhouse at Saragosa* and imagine what it may have been like at the asylum he visited. Goya was representing the struggles of humanity in his work. He personally suffered from a difficult marriage because he and his wife experienced the deaths of all but one of their many children. Goya also suffered severe bouts with diseases that represented many setbacks for him throughout his career. He became totally deaf after one grave illness, first having ringing in his ears for some time and eventually losing his hearing entirely. At one point in his life, he became totally isolated and a recluse. During this period, he painted large, dark, somber canvases about Saturn, myths, skeletons, and an old lady. He was undergoing a terrible time mentally and was very depressed. But when he was able to come out of that state of mind, he created a beautiful painting, one of his last, called *The Milkmaid of Bourdaux*.

Goya has been known as one of the best printmakers. His *Los Caprichos* prints were satirical studies of how human beings are somewhat unaware, uncaring, corrupt, and devious. His etchings about the atrocities of war were titled *The Disasters of War* and were of superb craftsmanship. The pictures of fighting in the streets show dead bodies being taken away in a cart and a woman with a baby on her back loading a cannon, among other scenes. But although his paintings and etchings were emotionally charged, they were not sentimental. They are difficult to label, even though historians may call them Romantic because of the Romantics' propensity for social and political rebellion and support of freedom of expression. Goya's paintings and his prints express universal truths and are executed with great skill and technical ability. They show the horrors of war and "man's inhumanity to man" but do not stop at that. Rather, they take a stand and *denounce* man's inhumanity to man (Gilbert and McCarter 158, Van de Bogart 242).

Katsushika Hokusai 1760–1849

Japan (Japanese)

The name Hokusai means "star of the northern constellation." Hokusai was born in 1760 in Edo, now called Tokyo, Japan. He supposedly had fifty names and lived in ninety houses over the course of his life. He never opened the packet of money he received after his first book of sketches were published, and he was considered an "odd sort of fellow," for he seemed not to care about money. He is remembered today in Japan as one of the greatest artists ever to have made prints. Hokusai was a versatile artist, spontaneous and creative, and was both a painter and a printmaker. He was a master craftsman at his art and knew how to use the tools that were essential for the difficult techniques he used to make his woodcuts. It is said whenever his rent came due, he refused to open the money packet he had earned and was then thrown out. After finding another place to live, he would work a while and then be forced to move again—and again. Hokusai did not believe in material things and seemed to care little about money, content to be a great, if eccentric, artist (Gilbert and McCarter 216).

Assessment of Hokusai

Hokusai embodied in his long lifetime the essence of the *Ukiyo-e* school of art during its final century of development. His stubborn genius also represents, in its seventy years of continuous artistic creation, the prototype of the single-minded artist, striving only to complete a given task. Moreover, Hokusai constitutes a figure who has, since the later nineteenth century, impressed Western artists, critics, and art lovers alike, more, possibly, than any other single Asian artist.

Source: https://www.britannica.com/biography/Hokusai

Hokusai had a long career and after he turned sixty years old, he produced most of what critiques say were his most important works. After his death, many of his prints were displayed in an exhibit in Europe and artists such as Henri Toulouse-Lautrec, Paul Gauguin, and Vincent Van Gogh were influenced by his work.

Source: *World Book Encyclopedia*, vol H (Chicago: World Book Scott Fetzer Company, 1992), 289-290. ISBN 0-7166-0092-7

Auguste Rodin 1840–1917

France (French)

One of the world's most well-known sculptures was created by Auguste Rodin, who sculpted an enormous number of renderings of the human figure. His depiction of a man sitting with his chin resting upon his hand is his most famous. The man is in a trancelike state, thinking. Rodin preferred to work first in clay or wax and then cast his work in bronze. Rodin wanted to have the surface of the texture help create the mood. The rough texture can create a suitable conductor of light, with a different feel from that of marble. But his works were not understood when they were first created. For example, his sculpture of a man walking was missing some portions of the human form, reminiscent of ancient artistic relics. His doors to the gates of hell were also difficult for viewers to comprehend. Thus, because his work was difficult to sell, he made a living from his ornamental sculptures for commercial firms (*World Book Encyclopedia*).

Claude Monet 1840–1926

France (French)

Claude Monet lived as a young boy in Le Havre, France, but was born in Paris. He is sometimes given credit for starting the movement of Impressionism, because his painting of a sunrise, *Impression Sunrise*, gave the movement its name.

Claude Monet painted outdoors and used colors, avoiding black and white. His shadows were made of colors, not merely black or brown. Painting outdoors and using colors to depict everything created a new way of painting.

Monet was influenced by two English painters when he visited England in 1872. The style of Constable's landscapes, which were of English countrysides and the cathedrals and buildings in the area, gave Monet some ideas about mixing color. The paintings of Turner, with his use of texture and creative way of expressing the atmosphere with its steam or smoke, was very interesting to Claude Monet. Both of those painters' styles helped Monet create a new way of painting that incorporated their techniques and ideas into his developing method. Monet then became aware of the way that light reflected off of surfaces such as water.

Claude Monet was an artist who made some of his income in his early career from painting portraits. He had been already known at age fifteen as an artist with talent, and when he lived in Le Havre he was known as a caricaturist.

Eventually Monet would sell his work, but he had difficulty at first making a living from his art. He was able to move when he was in his forties to a small town north of Paris, called Giverny, where he painted outdoor scenes. He became fascinated with the atmosphere and with the effects of the sunlight and other light on surfaces. Even though his work was not accepted during certain parts of his career, he continued to paint atmospheric conditions to show the way that weather conditions can change the way a viewer sees buildings and places.

He painted a cathedral façade in the town of Rouen to show how the sun shone on the cathedral at different times of day, making the cathedral look different during the morning, at noon, and in the evening. Monet was able to set up his easel in the apartment that he rented across from the Rouen Cathedral, from which he watched the effect of the sun on the surface of the façade as the sun rose and moved across the sky.

In 1890, Monet purchased a home at Giverny, and ten years before he died, he was able to build a large studio in which to paint. He had difficulty with his eyesight during the last years of his life; even surgery was unsuccessful. He died of lung cancer in 1926.

His studio, grounds (with their lily pond and bridge), and home have been made into a museum to let visitors see where he lived and painted. The location is very beautiful and worth visiting.

Auguste Renoir 1841–1919

France (French)

Auguste Renoir has been known for the bright red-orange color that he used in many of his outdoor scenes picturing groups of people having pleasant outings talking together in the afternoon by the water.

Renoir was famous for lively group scenes of his friends, who congregated at one of his favorite restaurants where his fiancé would meet him with her little dog and eat lunch. His friends would casually talk and visit outside in an informal setting by the water, and Renoir would enjoy watching the sun cast shadows at different times during the afternoon. He was a master of light and color.

Renoir studied precision and drawing at an early age. He was an artist who knew the techniques of portraiture and how to draw depth and perspective. He had taken lessons from artists who taught him how to draw accurate renditions of reality. Renoir traveled to Italy in 1880. He studied in Italy where he was an apprentice to a porcelain painter. He learned how to paint windowshades and was able to master that art in the studio of artist Charles Gleyre. Renoir knew that Impressionism was useful to him, for he had tried working with its methods of color theory. He enjoyed working with the ideas of color in which he had been influenced by studying the works of the Impressionists with whom he had come into contact while in Paris. Renoir was interested in meeting the leading Impressionists, and the artists who influenced him most were Claude Monet and Edouard Manet, whom he supposedly met.

As he aged, Renoir continued to produce major work, but he suffered from extreme pain as he worked, from arthritis. He had to have a family member bandage his paintbrushes around his hands in order to be able to paint toward the end of his life because of his condition (*World Book Encyclopedia*).

Edgar Degas 1834–1917

France (French)

Edgar Degas has been known as an artist who captured a moment in time. His subject matter included dancers about to go on stage or reaching for their slippers or getting ready to practice. He drew with pastels and painted with oils. He was known for his spontaneous work and for being able to design compositions on paper and canvas that viewed ballet dancers from a variety of viewpoints. Degas watched for hours as they practiced and as they prepared to go on stage at performances in Paris. He also watched the ballerinas in rehearsals, which helped him know how to paint and draw such impromptu positions of dancers. His works took a new approach to the way that artists painted, portraying the day-to-day activities of working women who danced as they tried to perfect their art. It was not something that artists had been painting frequently in Paris at that day and time. Degas was especially interested in the casual poses of the dancers as they prepared for their performances.

Degas has not become known as a sculptor, even though his bronze sculptures are museum quality. The bronze sculptures that he created were only made for the use of the study of the human form, not for exhibition. However, even today they are considered to be of superb quality and of artistic merit. Degas has been considered an artist from the Impressionist period who used exceptional craftsmanship to pursue his unique style (*World Book Encyclopedia*).

Mary Cassatt 1844–1926

Allegheny City, Pennsylvania (American)
Mary Cassatt's father, Robert Simpson Cassat (later Cassatt), was a successful stockbroker and came from a family of banking. The ancestral name in his family was actually Cossart. Mary's family moved from Lancaster, Pennsylvania, and then to Philadelphia, where she began school at the age of six.

When she was very young, her family traveled, and she was able to attend the Paris World's Fair of 1855. She saw the work of the French artists Jean-Auguste-Dominique Ingres, Camille Corot, and Eugene Delacroix at an early age.

At the age of twenty-one she left Philadelphia, much to her family's chagrin, to travel to Paris to study art. It was not a vocation that was acceptable at that time, and for her to be traveling alone on a ship all the way to Europe was quite troubling to her family. But Mary was adventurous; she knew that if she was going to become an artist she had to go to Europe to study. When she was young, she had seen enough to know what she wanted. When Mary arrived in Europe, she was not readily accepted and had to prove herself worthy of her craft. But she was of an independent nature and did not give up easily. She recognized the strength in tie between women and their children, and that is what she began to draw. Her pastel work began to be shown. She saw the work of the Impressionist painters who lived in Paris. She met Claude Monet and Camille Pissarro and began to show her work in some of the exhibitions. One of the artists who was interested in her use of spontaneity was Edgar Degas, who was painting dancers in rehearsal. She and he met and struck up a somewhat difficult but professional friendship. It has been reported that Degas commented that her work was not so bad, for a woman's. Cassatt was not entirely accepted by her male peers, but history places her with some of the Impressionists in some books, although she was an American artist. (An artist is considered to be from the place of his or her birth.)

Cassatt's best work is probably her paintings of children with mothers. She worked with pastels and also did woodblock prints, perfecting the process of lithography in her art. Many of her paintings were done in oil, but she also used other media in her outpouring of artistic work. Her innovative printmaking style was also influenced by the prints that were then being imported from Japan.

Paul Gauguin 1848–1903

Paris, France
Paul Gauguin was born in France. His work became known as part of the movement of Impressionism; however, much of his work does not appear like other Impressionist artists. His work is much more flat and decorative in appearance. He used rhythmic lines and opposite colors in his work. His subjects were the women from the island of Tahiti when he traveled to that island. His work, as well as his friend van Gogh's, are not always easy to place into a category.

Gauguin has been known for his paintings of decorative flat areas of color of patterns and shapes of beautiful women from the South Pacific. He traveled to that area from France and was able to sell his Tahitian canvases at that time in Paris. His dealer was Vincent van Gogh's brother. During this later portion of Gauguin's career, his art became well known.

As a stockbroker, he became interested in art and admired pointillism. In his midthirties, he left his wife and family and traveled after taking lessons from Camille Pissarro. His early works were influenced by the Impressionist style of painting, and he became acquainted with many of the Impressionist painters while living in Paris. He met van Gogh, and before he left France to travel to Tahiti, he lived for a short time in a town where the two painted in the town and fields outside Arles, France (Janson, H. W. and A. F. Janson 776).

Vincent van Gogh 1853–1890

Holland/Netherlands (Dutch)

Vincent van Gogh has been known as the artist who cut off his own ear, but he did not. He did, however, cut part of a lobe off when he argued over a girl with his friend Paul Gauguin. Van Gogh was a great painter and printer who left behind unusual and outstanding works of art. But van Gogh was a troubled person. He signed his name *Vincent* because he wanted people to know him; he wanted attention and tried getting it from his teachers, but he never made it through art school. He was told that he could not draw using perspective correctly and that he was drawing with his paint instead of painting with it.

Vincent had a brother named Theo who was very close to him. Theo was an art dealer who had left home to be trained and had moved to Paris to work in a firm that dealt with successful artists. But Vincent never sold a painting in his life, although he was able to barter one painting, *Red Vineyards*. Theo tried to sell Vincent's work and felt very troubled about not being able to help his brother sell his work. Theo was so distraught over Vincent's death that he died six months later, leaving behind a wife and a very young son who they had named Vincent, Jr. Vincent lived in Holland as a young boy and was a son of a Dutch Reformed Church minister. He wanted to become a missionary and did attempt that, but he was too emotional and gave away all of his own material possessions, feeling so sorry for other people that he could not help anyone else.

When Vincent was twenty-seven years old, he went to stay with his brother in Paris. He painted for nine more years, producing his art. After living in Paris for two years, he moved to Arles, in the southern part of France. He painted with Paul Gauguin at that time, creating many of his landscapes. Vincent realized that he needed help and committed himself to an asylum in Saint-Remy for treatment, where he created many paintings using intense color. In 1890, he left there and went to Auvers-sur-Oise, where his brother Theo had hired a doctor named Dr. Gachet to help make sure that his brother would be able to care for himself. Vincent was living in a small, upstairs apartment above a business establishment at that time. One day, Vincent took his easel and paints and left for a walk outside town, as he had made a habit of doing. He walked down a road and began to set up his easel to paint. Before he went, he had asked the shopkeeper to borrow his gun to shoot at crows. Instead, Vincent shot himself in the stomach, and three days later, he bled to death with his brother at his side (Gilbert and McCarter 24).

Vincent Van Gogh's sister-in-law became interested in her brother-in-law's art after her husband, Theo, died, and she decided to do some research. She traveled to where Vincent had worked and gathered up some of the canvases that had been stored in a neighbor's barn, and Vincent her son and she decided to go to the Dutch government to try to convince them to create a museum for his art. They succeeded, and the Vincent Van Gogh Museum is where many pieces of his work are now located, from his early dark brown and earth-toned works to his late works, which are very bright and colorful.

Henri de Toulouse-Lautrec 1864–1901

France (French)

Henri de Toulouse-Lautrec was from the family of the counts of Toulouse. He suffered throughout his life from a rare bone disease that stunted his capacity to grow at a normal rate. When he was a child, he broke one of his bones in his upper thigh, and he later broke his other upper thigh. This gave him an appearance of being shorter than normal and a subsequent inferiority complex. As an adult, because his legs never grew to be the length of other adults', he had difficulty walking normally, especially for long distances. Toulouse-Lautrec once painted a self-portrait that showed how the appearance of his physical form seemed to be dominated by the unusual proportion between his torso and his legs.

Toulouse-Lautrec's mother always took a great interest in her son, and when he wished to move to Paris and work as an artist, she became extremely worried about his potential new companions. Some stories say that she sent a bodyguard to live with him for protection. Toulouse-Lautrec, who had to walk with a cane, lived in a Parisian area of nightclubs and bars. He felt more accepted in that environment, and his surroundings are evident in his paintings and lithographs. One can only imagine how a mother descended from nobility felt about her son living in such wretched conditions. Toulouse-Lautrec had constant difficulty with his health throughout his life, but his crippling illness did not keep him from his art. He sat for hours in cabarets, theaters, and circuses, composing his drawings in preparation for the prints he created in his studio. Some history books claim that van Gogh met Toulouse-Lautrec in Paris briefly.

When Henri was in his late thirties, he became even more physically inhibited as his medical condition worsened, but he continued to paint and draw. Even though it became even more difficult for him to walk, he was determined to go to the cabarets and draw. Although he himself was unable to dance, he created posters for the Moulin Rouge nightclub. He became known for his ability to produce mass-produced lithographs which were hung publicly to advertise upcoming events. At that time, Japanese wood block prints were a popular import. Their simplicity and beautiful design and execution influenced artists such as Toulouse-Lautrec and the Impressionists.

A look at Toulouse-Lautrec's posters makes his style evident, with their strong silhouettes accompanied by printed words incorporated into his designs. Each work was easy to read from a distance. The positive shapes of dancers combined with a background of lettering created posters that were striking. Toulouse-Lautrec made use of color and line effectively, and his patterns provided exceptional models for other artists involved in advertising design many years down the road. He introduced the concept of poster-making into the realm of the fine arts when the idea of associating advertising and art was unheard of.

During spring 1901, Henri became paralyzed and was taken home to live in one of his family's estates. He died a few weeks later, with his family at his side. Today Toulouse-Lautrec is considered to have been not only one of the best lithographers of the Impressionists but of the past hundred years.

Henri Matisse 1869–1954

France (French)

Henri Matisse's art has sometimes been compared to children's paper cutouts. Matisse meant his work to look as if he were trying to simplify his subject matter, whether human figures or plants. During the 1930s, he actually did cut up paper to plan his canvases. Matisse would paint paper and then rearrange it to create mural-sized compositions. When he was ill, toward the end of his life, he sat in a wheelchair and continued to work using cutouts (Gilbert and McCarter 148).

Matisse was born in Le Cateau, France. Although Henri's father wanted him to study law, Henri did not want to become an attorney, and at age twenty-one he had an appendicitis attack that helped him make his decision. While he was recovering, his mother gave him some paints; later in his life, Matisse said that his life's direction had been altered by his bout of appendicitis. When he recovered, he enrolled in the famous Paris art school Ecole des Beaux-Arts. His teacher was Gustave Moreau (Phipps and Wink 336.)

Matisse married a woman named Amelie Parayre, and together they had three children, all three of whom chose to be professionally trained in art; one became an art dealer in New York City. Pablo Picasso and Matisse were friends for several years and painted some of the same subjects. Some of the same art dealers who sold Picasso's art works encouraged art collectors to consider purchasing Matisse's work as well.

Edouard Manet 1832–1883

France (French)

Edouard Manet was influenced by the art of Velasquez and Goya when he traveled to Spain. Manet was a son of a wealthy bourgeois family. He registered as a merchant marine as a teenager and entered art school, where he studied for seven years while spending much of his time practicing in the Louvre, where he studied and copied paintings to learn his craft.

Manet helped organize artists who had been rejected by official exhibitions in Paris and gave them support. He encouraged them to paint outdoors and to continue to show their work. He also shocked the public when he painted a nude meant to be a parody of a Francesco de Goya painting, except that Manet painted the woman looking directly out at the viewers, something that was completely shocking to critics. Some stories say that the woman may have resembled someone whom the critics recognized, which may have escalated criticism of the work. Nevertheless, Manet's work received acclaim, although he also received some negative reviews about his painting (*Encyclopedia Americana* 214).

Kathe Kollwitz 1867–1945

Prussia

It is no wonder that Kathe Kollwitz's art was about children and young men who were in despair. She saw both world wars firsthand, and her grandson and son, both named Peter, were killed in each one of the wars. Kollwitz painted, drew, and made prints of the situation of the helpless mothers who came to her husband's clinic where she had an artist's studio.

Kollwitz is now considered an Expressionist for her noteworthy ability to convey feeling and expression through her artistic media. Most of her work was done in black and white, and her major works focused on social and political themes.

Kollwitz was an active and educated woman who was ahead of her time. She has recently been recognized as a brave woman who even in those times made a way for herself to express deep and intense emotions in her remarkable prints.

Kollwitz was born in Konigsberg called Prussia at that time. Her parents allowed her to take art lessons, and she learned to draw at an early age. Kathe considered herself to be more of a printer than a painter, but not until she set up her studio after getting married. She had to set up a studio to run the press she needed to produce her prints, and to contain the many materials needed in such a studio, such as a press, ink, tools, plates, and still other equipment. Kollwitz became an excellent printmaker able to produce etchings, lithographs, and woodcuts. Because she saw her husband at work, helping him on occasion and always closely connected to his work, she made her work reflect the suffering of the families who came to receive medical help. One of her well-known prints shows death seizing a child. Others show the suffering of mothers' faces over their ill children. Kollwitz felt it her duty to portray the emotions of families when they lost a loved one in the war, which in turn helped her cope with her own grief. She was never able to really get over the feeling of duty she felt about drawing attention to the futility of war. Although she opposed war, she understood it, having lived in and through it. She identified with mothers who brought in their sick children or families who brought in injured soldiers, and she always felt their pain. She was filled with so much emotion that she had to let it out by drawing; she once said that while she drew hurting children she wept. Kollwitz never felt that she could do enough to help at the clinic, so she went to her studio and drew. She was involved in her own way, politically, trying to change the ways people thought by drawing attention to what suffering did to mothers and their families. She once called it her task "to voice the never-ending sufferings heaped mountain-high. This is my task, but it is not an easy one to fulfill. Work is supposed to relieve you. Did I feel relieved when I made the prints on war and knew that the war would go on raging? Certainly not." (Gilbert and McCarter 182)

Kollwitz is considered now to be German; however in some books she is still considered from Prussia, which is now part of Germany.

Source: This is from information gathered from the Museum tour in Berlin, Germany Käthe Kollwitz And Berlin's Neue Wache
Source: http://theculturetrip.com/europe/germany/articles/k-the-kollwitz-and-berlin-s-neue-wache/

The Diary of Kathe Kollwitz

On a personal level too, Kollwitz's life—like so many Germans of her generation—was scarred by war. With the outbreak of the First World War, her sons Hans and Peter volunteered for service. Not yet of age, Peter required his parents' consent to fight, which Kollwitz and her husband duly provided. Peter was killed on October 22, 1914, just months into the conflict, a loss which Kollwitz admitted she never recovered from. She later wrote:

> 'I sometimes think, it was then that I gave up my strength. At that moment I became old. Began the walk to the grave. That was the break. The stoop to such a level, that I could never again stand straight'...

Kollwitz's first major recognition was obtained from her prints of the subject matter pertaining to events that actually happened and she experienced. They were about the Peasant War of 1902–1908. The prints (from woodcuts in black-and-white shapes) reflected images about how the poor were being oppressed.

Source: *World Book Encyclopedia*, vol. 11 (New York: Scott Foster, 1992), 364

Diego Rivera 1886–1957

Mexico (Mexican)

Rivera was born in Guanajuato City, Gto. Mexico. He lived and worked in the twentieth century and was considered controversial for disagreeing with the Mexican clergy. He portrayed Mexican life and was considered radical because of his political persuasion.

Rivera was a muralist who painted about the lives of the many underprivileged and hardworking people of the lower classes. He was considered a social and political painter and at times had difficulty obtaining support to have his work shown because of his controversial subject matter.

The working man in the assembly line in the Ford plant in Detroit, Michigan, can be seen in the fresco wall painting that was painted at the Detroit Institute of Arts. In that fresco, an entire day in the life of assembly plant workers at the Ford plant was painted in the fresco, demonstrating how the workers made cars using steel, processing and drilling the metal. Even the punching of the time clock and lunch break were included in the large wall scene.

Rivera's famous murals in San Francisco and Mexico City include *Escuela de la ciudad*, *La Historia de la Cardiología*, *Hombre en una Encrucijada*, *Desembarco de Españoles en Veracruz*, and *El Buen Gobierno* which, though enormous, were still of high-quality craftsmanship. Rivera married the famous Mexican painter Frida Kahlo (Gilbert and McCarter 149, 196).

Vasily Kandinsky 1866–1944

Russia (Russian)

Vasily Kandinsky was a law professor at a Russian university before he became an artist. He was part of a group of artists known as the Blue Riders, who used color in a nonrepresentational manner. Kandinsky's paintings were meant to represent ideas not from the material world. His paintings were created from the use of the elements of art: colors, lines, and shapes. His paintings have been considered some of the first abstract artwork to have been created to influence the art world during the early twentieth century. His artistic creations directly affected the art world and helped instigate the theories that formed around the ideas about how sounds could be seen through colors and lines and how abstract shapes could be considered art. Kandinsky felt that painting colors and abstract shapes could be a form of universal communication, but that was not an accepted concept at the time. Scientific findings such as the splitting of the atom made a big enough impression upon Kandinsky to give him the courage to overcome feelings of obligation to represent the visible and obvious material world (Phipps and Wink 335). Kandinsky, who has been credited as one of the first abstract artists, died in 1944.

Grant Wood 1891–1942

American Grant Wood was born in Anamosa, Iowa, but he lived mainly in Cedar Rapids, Iowa. After studying at the Academic Julian in Paris in 1933, he began to paint in the Regionalist style in the midwestern part of the United States, working with close attention to sharp detail. Wood taught painting at the University of Iowa. His best-known works are *American Gothic* and *Spring in Town*.

"Grant Wood was born on a farm near the small town of Anamosa, in 1891. By painting simple scenes of the land and people he knew best, he helped create an important, all-American style of art. Grant Wood's paintings show the love he had for the people and customs of the Midwestern United States. Grant Wood particularly loved the farmland of Iowa. While growing up, he enjoyed feeling the soft, warm soil between his toes as he walked barefoot through the fields. In his painting *Young Corn* it seems like the round, friendly hills are protecting the farmer and his children while they work in their fields.

"Grant Wood showed an interest in art at a very early age. He often drew pictures with burnt sticks his mother gave him from her stove. Even though Grant drew pictures every chance he got, everyone thought he'd grow up to be a farmer like his father. Grant seemed to enjoy his farm chores, and had his own goats, chickens, ducks and turkeys. When Grant was ten years old, a very sad thing happened to him. His father died, and his mother found that it was too difficult to keep the farm running. She decided to move her family to the nearby city of Cedar Rapids. It was a hard move for Grant. He missed his farm pets, and felt out of place at the new city school. Some kids even made fun of him. Because of his good sense of humor and his talent for drawing, things eventually got better for Grant. In high school he made friends and was always busy working on projects, like designing scenery for school plays and drawing pictures for the school paper and yearbook. After he graduated in 1910, Grant did a lot of different things. He took art classes, taught art, made jewelry, learned carpentry, decorated people's houses and cared for his mother and his sister Nan.

"One day, while Grant was looking for something interesting to paint, he discovered a farmhouse with an unusual window. The arch-shaped window was based on a style of European architecture from the Middle Ages called Gothic architecture. Grant liked the contrast of a European window on an American farmhouse. After he made sketches of the house, Grant looked for just the right people to go with it. He thought his family dentist and his own sister, Nan, would be perfect for the farmer and his daughter. Grant entered *American Gothic* in a big show at the Art Institute of Chicago, and won the third place prize. People all over America loved the newspaper pictures they saw of it. Soon, Grant's paintings started to become very popular. One reason for this was that many people felt Grant's art was easier to understand than a lot of the new modern art being done. Another reason Grant's paintings became so popular was that they came along during a rough time in history known as the Great Depression."

Source: http://www.grantwoodartgallery.org/grantwood.htm

Andy Warhol 1928–1987

Pennsylvania (American)

Andy Warhol's real name was Andy Warhola. He graduated from a high school in Pittsburgh and went to Carnegie Institute of Technology in Pittsburgh. He earned his BFA in 1949 and became employed by *Glamour* magazine but was considered controversial. He received attention in the film industry for some of his off-the-wall ideas. His film about a person sleeping gained him artistic recognition, and he continued to make films and create art. In 1968 he was shot and severely injured, but he recovered from the incident.

When he was young, his father died and his mother and brother had to move to an upstairs apartment which he later described as very dismal and depressing. He was not a healthy child. In an interview, Andy related how his older brother would come home and open a can of tomato soup for his lunch during the winter months for him, when he had to stay home alone. With his father dead, his mother had to stay at work. He remembered how lonely he was but how important the kindness behind that can of soup was to him every day when his brother rushed home from school.

Warhol was a talented artist who drew and worked on perfecting his skill at printmaking. He began using ink and silk to produce silk screens. Warhol produced silk screens of Marilyn Monroe, a film icon who rapidly rose to fame. The images he created of Monroe are iconic, as well (Fichner-Rathus 7).

Warhol also did a series of silk screens of Campbell's soup cans. He may have been drawing attention to the way people sometimes see the package more than the content, or he may have been drawing people's attention to how so much of society is driven by the packaging of products. Could it be that sometimes the package is what sells the product more than the product itself? Was Andy Warhol drawing attention to the way that our society had become almost like one row after another of the same things?

In 1987, Andy Warhol died of a serious complication following a ruptured spleen, at age fifty-nine.

Pablo Picasso 1881–1973

Malaga, Spain (Spanish)

Born in the city of Malaga in the Andalusia region of Spain, Pablo Picasso was the first child of Don José Ruiz y Blasco and María Picasso y López. Picasso's family was part of the middle class. His father was a college professor who taught Pablo to draw and paint at an early age. When Picasso was in his teenage years, his father was a painter and an instructor who specialized in naturalistic depictions of birds and other game. After studying art in Madrid, in 1900 Picasso made his first trip to Paris, then the art capital of Europe. There, he met his first Parisian friend, the journalist and poet Max Jacob. Jacob helped Picasso learn French, opening to him the world of French (particularly Parisian) literature, which he incorporated into much of his artwork.

Picasso's work has been divided by art historians into certain stages, most commonly accepted as the Blue (1901–1904), Rose (1905–1907), African (1908–1909), Analytic Cubism (1909–1912), and Synthetic Cubism (1912–1919) periods.

Pablo Picasso was influenced by his father and his entire family. When he was in his early teens, his beloved sister died—something he later described as having an immense influence upon his life. Picasso gave few interviews, saying that attempting to explain his paintings would be like barking up the wrong tree. (He said it in Spanish, however; something is probably lost through translation.)

Picasso was so upset by his sister's death of malaria that he said later that when he painted a bull and young women together, he was depicting his memory of her terrible death and how helpless she had been to protect herself against the epidemic that spread through his town when he was a child. He once said that he had prayed that she would be spared. He could not understand how such a beautiful girl could die, so young and beautiful. To Picasso, the bull represented the power that left him no control over what happened. He never forgot how beautiful his sister was, and throughout his long life he etched the bull and innocent young women.

For Picasso, the bull also represented the horror of war, agony, and despair in other works, the symbol of the death, disease, despair, and helplessness he saw and felt. It may have been represented in other ways in his art in various forms and styles throughout his many phases. Picasso lived a very long life and has been credited with more paintings than any other painter in the twentieth century. When he died, he did not leave a will, but Jacqueline, his widow, was still alive. A museum was built to his honor in Paris, France, and much of his work was placed there, in the Picasso Museum.

Salvador Dali 1904–1989

Figueras, Gerona, Spain (Spanish)

Salvador Dali was born in Figueres in Catalonia, Spain. He was eighty-four years old when he died in 1989. He was considered to be a painter and printer who did mainly etchings, lithographs, and some engravings. He also did many murals on walls. He was also known as an extremely innovative and creative filmmaker from Spain.

Dali grew up in a small town in the northern area of Spain and lived there throughout his youth. In 1927, at the age of twenty-three, he went to Paris, where he met artists such as Joan Miro and Pablo Picasso, whose influence on his artistic career would help him become even more committed to being an artist who painted and drew from his imagination but yet who used recognizable imagery. His images were based on realistic objects to begin with, but by the end of his composition his work had evolved into many shapes and morphed to realms enough to make the head spin. As the years went on, Dali would become known as one of the leading Surrealists for his use of ideas drawn up from deep within his subconscious.

According to Milo Wold and Edmund Cykler in *Music and Art in the Western World*, Dali's style was inspired by the developments of Freudian psychology and linked closely with post–World War I developments and research associated with new methods of dream interpretation. The style of Surrealism that Dali created had a unique appearance and was difficult to explain, and Dali was not known to verbally explain his work. He once remarked to a reporter he didn't want to say much about his art, because if he had intended to explain his work, he would have become a poet instead of a painter.

At the age of ten Dali was already drawing realistically. He entered the famous Royal Academy of Art in Madrid, but an instructor was not pleased with his political views and became upset with his mannerisms. Dali was accused of causing other students to question authority.

Dali was expelled for inciting students and accused of creating an atmosphere that caused other students to be disruptive. He was ticketed and thrown in jail for a short period of time (Phipps and Wink 334).

His sentence was considered to be valid because Dali's actions were prompted by beliefs different from the authorities' and because his behavior was considered overly eccentric.

Two of Dali's most memorable paintings are his renderings of limp watches and mountains entitled *The Persistence of Memory* and his interpretation of Leonardo da Vinci's *Last Supper*. Dali's different interpretations and alternate viewpoints made him a leader in the Surrealistic movement through his paintings, murals, and many exquisite prints. He was a versatile and leading twentieth-century artist (Phipps and Wink 334).

Louis Armstrong 1900–1971

United States (American)
Louis Armstrong was born in New Orleans, Louisiana. Stories say that Armstrong started learning to play the cornet when he was five or six years old, picking up leftover firewood when riding on a cart and playing an old bugle. He worked, trying to make money, and dropped out of school when he was in elementary school. He always liked listening to music and wanted to play the cornet, an instrument similar to the trumpet that plays the same notes but is slightly shorter. He was able to earn $5.00 and bought a cornet at a pawn shop. He did not take lessons but taught himself instead. According to Dennis Sporre's instructor's manual, one New Year's Eve Armstrong shot off a gun into the air to celebrate. He was picked up by authorities and sent to reform school. Later he described how at the reformatory he was able to learn to play the cornet and take lessons. He had been upset to be sent to the reform school, but in the long run, he said, he learned a lot, and had he not been picked up that night, he might never have been able to learn to play the cornet the way he did.

Armstrong had a style of his own that made him great, and popular around the world. In interviews later in his life, he talked about how a bad incident turned into something that became a turning point in his life. He learned to read in reform school, and later said how important that education was to his life.

In 1922 he left for Chicago with his cornet in one hand and a trout sandwich that his mother had made for him in the other. He was off to change the world of music, and he changed the world of jazz. He had a major influence on other players and musicians and made a lasting impact on the way musicians improvise.

He became a world traveler and an ambassador of sorts, spreading American ideas to the world. People across the globe knew who Louis Armstrong was. He had a style of his own with its variations of rhythm and pitch. He popularized scat singing, alternating between lyrics and syllables. He played the trumpet so well that he caused other trumpet players to have to compete with him. He created new trends in jazz all over the country and eventually the world (Sporre, 21; *World Book Encyclopedia*).

Georgia O'Keeffe 1887–1986

American United States (American)
Georgia O'Keeffe was born in Wisconsin. Her artwork was first shown by a friend of hers to a photographer whom O'Keeffe eventually married. According to one story, O'Keeffe sent some of her drawings to a friend, writing that they were not to be shown to anyone. But her friend showed them to Alfred Stieglitz, a successful photographer with a studio. A year later, in 1917, Stieglitz organized a one-person exhibit for O'Keeffe. The artist found that her painting style was more original when she painted in the Southwest—and she certainly had a unique style of her own. One of her trademarks was taking a flower or object and painting a section of it at an enlarged scale. In 1924, Alfred and Georgia were married. Stieglitz spent most of his time in New York City, and O'Keeffe spent most of her time in New Mexico (Gilbert and McCarter 90).

Sir Alfred Hitchcock 1934–1980

London, England (British)
Alfred Hitchcock was born on August 13, 1899, in London, England. In 1934, he moved to California, where he began making films. *North by Northwest,* made in 1959, was a successful film about a twice-divorced, sleekly handsome debonair mistaken for someone else. Cary Grant, Eva Marie Saint, and James Mason starred. The famous scenes of the crop duster airplane swooping down upon Cary Grant in a field out in a barren area with no crops to be dusted is a classic movie moment, as is the well-known chase scene involving the sculptures of the presidents of the United States at Mt. Rushmore, South Dakota. *Psycho* was made in 1960; Anthony Perkins played a demented son who operated a motel. *The Birds* was made in 1954. *The Man Who Knew Too Much* was made in 1934.

In each film Hitchcock placed himself somewhere in a scene, even if only for half a minute, as when he got on a bus at the beginning of *North by Northwest*. He was known for his ability to create suspense, making an audience enjoy even the emotions of terror. Hitchcock died of natural causes on April 29, 1980, in Los Angeles, California. Shortly before his death, he was knighted by Queen Elizabeth.

Jackson Pollock 1912–1956

Cody, Wyoming (American)
Jackson Pollock was in his prime at only forty-four years old when he died in an automobile accident. He was born in Cody, Wyoming, the youngest boy in the family of a rancher who moved around quite a bit in his life. Pollock had a somewhat troubled youth, during which the problems that would eventually cause his death from an automobile accident first started. The main problem seems to have been alcoholism and his family's movement from place to place.

At age eighteen, Pollock moved to New York and studied with Thomas Hart Benton, a regionalist painter at the Art Students League. He was hired during the Great Depression to work for a federally funded program in which artists were hired to paint murals in public buildings. He managed to produce one major work suitable for installation approximately every six weeks. He realized at that time that he had to do something about his drinking problem, and he sought help through psychotherapy.

Pollock met another artist whom he would marry, named Lee Krasner, and they exhibited their art. The years between 1948 and 1952 were when most of the paintings known as his "drip" abstract paintings were accomplished. Pollock experimented with using lines and throwing streams of paint from buckets to create lines on canvas that failed to become shapes. Those lines intersected and still remained lines. The idea was to play with his own subconscious feelings. Some of his canvases were very big, and he actually walked onto the canvas and threw paint down in streams of lines onto the surface. The finished product was a mixture of several colors of lines in layers of textures. They were vibrant and full of patterns that seemed to some people to go against every definition of art they had ever known. To Pollock this was expression, and since his death his paintings have become known as "action painting." His drip paintings are his most important works and their style has been called Abstract Expressionism. Pollock certainly shook up the world of art. His art may still be difficult for some individuals to understand today unless they realize that art can be an expression of a time and place and that in art lines and colors can be used to create art for the sake of lines and colors (Gilbert and McCarter 53).

Anna Marie Holmes

Canada (Canadian)

Anna Marie Holmes was the first Canadian-born ballerina to perform in Russia and was able to perform during an era when it was very difficult to be invited to that part of the world. She was invited to dance with the Kirov Ballet (www.balletadriatico.com). She was able to travel to Cuba and dance there as well. She was in demand as a dancer for several years until she became a choreographer and teacher in the early 1990s with the Boston Ballet.

Anna was married to David Holmes while living in Winnipeg, Canada, during the 1970s, when Norman McLaren, with the Canadian Film Board, was filming experimental films on dance and creating educational documentaries. David and Anna created the documentary *Tour en l'air* which proved to be an informative documentary about the lives of ballet dancers that showed the ups and downs of their way of life.

Their practice and devotion to their art was evident. The entire hour was extremely interesting and informative for students of humanities to watch. At the end of the documentary the filmmaker produced a short film that received international acclaim, *Springwater*. The musical score was slowed down, and David was the choreographer. The ballet dance was their original dance, and they took it to several countries on tour.

Zubin Mehta

India (Indian)

Born in Bombay, India, Zubin Mehta grew up in a musical environment. His father, Mehli Mehta, founded the Bombay Symphony. Despite this musical influence, Zubin's initial field of study was in medicine. At the age of eighteen, he abandoned his medical career to attend the Academy of Music in Vienna. Seven years later, he conducted both the Vienna and Berlin Philharmonic Orchestras. From 1961 to 1967 he was music director of both New York Philharmonic Orchestra and Montreal Symphonies. He was appointed music director for life of the Israel Philharmonic in 1981.

Counting concerts, recordings, and tours, Zubin has conducted over 1,600 performances on five continents with his extraordinary orchestra. Since 1986, he has also acted as music advisor and chief conductor of the Maggio Musicale Fiorentino, the summer festival in Florence, Italy.

In 1978, Maestro Mehta became the music director of the New York Philharmonic Orchestra. During his thirteen years in New York, he conducted over 1,000 concerts, holding the position longer than any music director in the orchestra's modern history. One of Zubin's many highlights occurred in 1988, when the orchestra embarked on a ten-day tour of the Soviet Union that culminated in an historic joint concert with the State Symphony Orchestra of the Soviet Ministry of Culture in Moscow's Gorky Park. In May 1991, the maestro concluded his tenure in New York with three performances celebrating the hundredth anniversary of Carnegie Hall, followed by a series of performances of Schoenberg's Gurrelieder. Twice in 1992 Zubin returned as guest conductor of the New York Philharmonic: first for the world premier of Olivier Messiaen's last orchestral work, *Eclairs sur l'Au Dela*, and later in the gala *A Philharmonic Celebration: 150th Anniversary Concert*.

Frank Lloyd Wright 1869–1959

United States (American)

Frank Lloyd Wright designed the Guggenheim Museum in New York City and the theater center in Dallas, Texas, and he developed the idea for a mile-high skyscraper. But the most well-known residence that he built was the one for the Kaufmann family as a weekend house named Fallingwater in Bear Run, Pennsylvania. Today, it is a museum. Fallingwater was built in 1936 and has a waterfall built into the topography of the landscape, with the structure's architectural plan based on the form of the cantilever.

From 1915–1922, Wright designed the Imperial Hotel in Tokyo which withstood the earthquakes (*World Book Encyclopedia*).

Henry Moore 1898–1986

England (British)

Henry Moore was born in Castleford, England, in 1898. As a student attending the Royal College of Art in London, he became interested in art from the Prehistoric Era and visited Stonehenge, near Salisbury, England. Stonehenge intrigued him at that time and stuck in his mind throughout his entire career, influencing him in two ways. First, he wanted his work to have an evident connection with ancient civilizations, and second, he wanted to be able to do large-scale pieces (interview, July 1979). In his art history classes, he studied African sculpture and Mayan art from the Yucatan Peninsula. Both styles of art were an influence upon his own; he was interested in their forms and shapes, and both are evident in his own sculptures. His selection of organic shapes was purposeful, designed to reflect their natural beauty as well as his interest in the art of the Mayan and African cultures. He collected wood scraps and stones for use when he made models as trials for sculptures before deciding which ones he would enlarge. His large sculptures were executed and eventually caste in bronze if he had the funds to make a finished product. Because he did not have the funds to cast in bronze until late in life (an expensive operation), he had to wait for commissions.

In 1936 a work in elm wood of a reclining figure reflected how he had become interested in using nature as his inspiration and as a way to find examples for his surfaces. Some critics said that he used caves and hillsides and cliffs as his inspiration for sculpting during that part of his career (*World Book Encyclopedia*).

Henry Moore valued the art of ancient cultures and wanted to tie the past to the present. As he progressed in his career and his work was increasingly shown in exhibits, he became more successful. He wanted to do larger works so that he could work in bronze. He was able to cast large pieces of bronze outside the Lincoln Center in New York City in 1965, which was a boost to his career. In the early 1970s he was given a commission to erect a large bronze titled the *Dallas Piece* for the Dallas City Hall in Dallas, Texas, which was an enlargement of a group called a vertebrae series. The *Dallas Piece* is one of the largest pieces he did. The *Sheep Sculpture*, which was placed behind his studio in England, was one of his later works and is known to have been one of his personal favorites.

Interview with Henry Moore

I have always been interested in reading about the lives of artists. When I was a student, some of my art history professors told stories about artists that sounded so real it was as if they had met the artist about whom they were lecturing. I was so interested in what they were saying that if I had not known better, I would have thought they had—as if they had been friends with artists who lived 400 years earlier, with Michelangelo, with Leonardo da Vinci.

From those talks, I realized that when I spoke to my students, I wanted to be able to relay important and correct information about artists' lives that was current and also exciting.

It occurred to me that there was still a very famous artist alive with whom I could possibly talk so that I could share what I learned from him with my students. For that reason, I wrote Henry Moore a letter. Surprisingly he wrote me back, and my husband and I planned a trip to his studio in July 1979. We took photographs, toured his property, saw his studio, and talked with him.

I opened up the interview by thanking him for allowing us to visit him at his home. I told him that I thought that he had a beautiful place and that the grounds with their plants and flowers were lovely. He replied, "The flowers and the plants are all done by my wife. She does all of that herself."

I told him that I taught and that my students would greatly appreciate being able to see photographs of his studio so they would be able to see how an artist works and comes up with his ideas.

He said that he taught for a number of years. I asked if he was glad to be able to finally be a full-time artist and not have to teach, but he said that he never gave up teaching and that he was still mentoring some students.

He said he was interested in meeting me since I was a teacher, he having taught so many years, and that teaching was something that would always be very important to him.

He asked me if I had been able to talk to Malcom who had been working on his enlargement piece, commissioned by Raymond Nasher of Dallas, Texas. We talked about that piece and a few other works he had been commissioned to do.

I asked him which works he felt the best about and he mentioned the *Dallas Piece* and the *Sheep Sculpture*. The model of his *Dallas Piece*, called a Marquette, was in his studio. He told me about it and how he came up with the idea (it came from a collection of bones). He also told me about the *Sheep Sculpture* and why he had placed it on his own property. He had purchased a strip of property and decided to make the sculpture out of bronze, a hard surface, while making the surface appear as soft as a sheep's wool.

He also talked about his youth, and about how he was influenced by World War II. He was caught in the Underground (subway) in London overnight when London was bombed, and he sketched scenes of the terrified people. He said that his drawings were sold by Kenneth Clark, an American art dealer, which is what helped him become recognized as an international artist. He was able to start making a small amount of income from some of his art, which allowed him to move to Perry Green. He said that he first rented part of the house where he lived. Eventually he was able to buy the house, and he retired from teaching.

At the end of the interview, he explained that he always wanted to sculpt big pieces of bronze—that for him was the measure of his success. He said that the *Dallas Piece* was one of his large pieces, and that he was going to continue to try to work until he was unable to do any more work. He explained that he had several Marquettes in his studio ready to be made into enlargements.

Mr. Moore was very thoughtful and gracious, and a humble, nice person. He showed me his drawings and said that he had collected way too many things. He said that he was a very lucky person, because he never really felt as if he ever had to work, because to him, art was just such a great life. He said that being an artist is like being on a perpetual vacation, doing something you enjoy all the time. My husband and I thanked him for the interview, and I told him how much it meant to me to actually meet him, and to have had an opportunity to now be able to tell my students I had met a great artist. He stood up and said, "I know what it is like, because when I was young, I got to meet Picasso."

Christo and Jeanne Claude

Christo born in Bulgaria
Jeanne Claude born in Morrocco

Christo Javacheff, an American artist of Bulgarian birth, studied at the Fine Arts Academy in Sofia (1953–1956), after which he spent six months in Prague. There he encountered Russian Constructivism, which impressed him with its concern for monumental visionary structures. Like his contemporaries, Christo rebelled against abstraction, seeing it as too theoretical. Christo began by wrapping everyday objects, including tin cans and bottles, stacks of magazines, furniture, automobiles, or various objects such as *Wrapped Luggage Rack* (1962; New York, Jeanne-Claude Christo). From 1961 he collaborated with his wife, Jeanne-Claude [née de Guillebon] (*b* Casablanca, 13 June 1935). Industrial materials, usually polypropylene sheeting or canvas tarpaulins held in place with irregularly tied ropes, were used for the wrappings. The use of fabric sometimes involved wrapping an object.

Jeanne Claude (1935–2009)

Jeanne Claude spent her younger years in and out of many different schools. She was a fast learner, but her behavior held her back. Her mother's fourth husband, however, helped change her life, and she adapted to a more stable lifestyle. Her mother was the first female officer to enter liberated Paris with Free French forces. Her mother and father were married illegally on an army base. After their separation, her mother gave birth to Jeanne-Claude at 17. Jeanne Claude died in 2009 from complications of a brain aneurysm.

Both Jeanne-Claude and her husband were born June 13, 1925. They worked on projects such as the *Valley Curtain* in Colorado, which was a massive piece of orange fabric that hung between two mountains. After that, they went to California to erect a fence of white nylon fabric about twenty-five miles in length over ranchers' properties and then into the Pacific Ocean. The fence was white, a conductor of light, and represented what fences do, such as building boundaries. It was up less than two weeks. A big project called the *Mastaba* has been attempted in New York City, Houston, the Netherlands, and the United Arab of Emirates. The mastaba has been an ongoing idea of Christo and Jeanne-Claude for over twenty years. The word *mastaba* means "bench" in Arabic. The shape of a mastaba is somewhat like a pyramid's trapezoidal shape, and the way it has been drawn in Christo's plan has many multicolored stainless steel oil barrels in it, making the shape of the mastaba. Christo and Jeanne-Claude spend their own foundation's finances and by the sale of his art have already raised much of the funding for the approximately $1 million project. Together they have created other projects, which wrapped some islands off the coast of Florida, a portion of a beach in Australia, and part of a city block in New York City. They also built a gate along a pathway in Central Park, New York City, using a wooden framework and orange fabric. All these projects were released at the same time; the gates were up for less than three weeks. The idea of New York City as the gateway to the world may have been part of the gates' underlying meaning. What other ideas do gates represent to you?

UNIT 3

Timelines and Chronology

WHAT IS A TIMELINE?

A timeline is a way of organizing the past, using years in a manner similar to the way a mathematical number line uses numbers. The Romans organized their calendar (continued in Europe) based on the approximate year of the birth of Christ, with years after his birth designated "anno Domini" (in the year of the Lord, abbreviated A.D.), and with years before his birth referred to as "before Christ" (abbreviated B.C.). Instead of the designations B.C. and A.D., some modern books use "before the Common Era," abbreviated "B.C.E.," and "Common Era," abbreviated "C.E." A timeline is also called a chronology.

_____ B.C. / A.D. _____

WHAT IS CULTURE?

The term *culture* can be defined as those artifacts and characteristic evidence of shared existence that are left behind after a group of people is gone.

I once went to a lecture series by a renowned lecturer and anthropologist named Dr. Parker Nunley from Richland College. Dr. Nunley defined civilization like this: "After all the people are gone, what is left behind are the artifacts and their art and music and any visual form of a written language. That is what we refer to as culture." Therefore, culture is what is left behind to ponder and to study after all of the people of a particular group are gone.

Webster's Dictionary Definition: "The beliefs, customs, arts, and institutions of a society at a given time."

What Is a Civilization?

A civilization is a group of people who have unique common characteristics, such as language and location. The people usually live in an area near water so that they can plant and harvest crops.

General Characteristics of Civilizations
- System of writing
- Government
- Type of religion or spirituality; some type of ceremony or rituals
- Urban life
- Trade and commerce
- System of transportation
- Way of communication

Webster's Dictionary Definition: "A relatively advanced stage of social, political, and cultural development."

CHRONOLOGY 3

Civilizations began when people settled in areas where land and water were available for farming. After planting crops, they remained in their settlements long enough to reap the benefits of their planting and harvest. Until human beings developed these agricultural abilities, they were unable to coexist in settlements long enough to reap the benefits of crops and communities. Remaining in a settlement long enough to develop a community became a characteristic of civilization. Living together brought about the establishment of systems of rules and regulations that enabled people to get along and to know what was expected of them in various social and political situations. Over time, these systems of laws or policies became the basis for new forms of government for groups of people in the regions where early civilizations developed. Each civilization developed systems unique to its own needs and values.

Another characteristic of early civilizations was the establishment of a belief system, or a cultural method for the celebration of traditions. People began to create pottery and weavings to be used in these events. No longer nomadic, they created objects and containers that they used to store grain and other foods. Many of these containers were decorated, and any of these utilitarian objects that remain today are considered some of the earliest existing artwork, useful in deciphering what early cultures believed and valued.

Some such objects are sculptures and paintings, said to be from prehistory (before written history). The Paleolithic Age, when people began to gather food while moving from place to place as nomads, is a prehistoric time period (Sporre).

Even the earliest artifacts reflect the culture and beliefs of human beings, giving us a glimpse into what their lives may have been like over 20,000 years ago. Imagine what it was like for Paleolithic peoples to travel from place to place gathering food. Gradually, over many years of nomadic living, people finally became permanent settlers, able to produce food, and thus civilizations were created. People were food producers, planters, and harvesters; lived in communities; and spoke a common language. They also held traditional celebrations and held to religions, and from their utilitarian art and architecture culture emerged.

Prehistoric Period

- Paintings from the prehistoric time period are considered to be great works of art. Artwork found in a cave in Lascaux is considered among the best representations of Paleolithic art. One example of early artwork is the *Venus of Willendorf*, considered to represent a fertility goddess. The sculpture was found in a location called Willendorf, in lower Austria.

- It is not certain exactly when the *Venus of Willendorf* was sculpted, but it is believed to have been between 30,000 and 25,000 B.C. The name "Venus" is from the Roman time period, and is given by art scholars to any depiction of a woman who represents feminine beauty and fertility. The Greek name for a sculpture of a woman was *Aphrodite*; the name *Venus* is a simply a more modern name given to this work of art. (Works of art, such as sculptures, are often named after locations.)
- Lascaux is on the Vezere River in France.
- According to several scholars, including author Dennis Sporre in *Reality through the Arts*, a group of children discovered the cave where the paintings were found while investigating a tree uprooted by a storm.

PREHISTORY

Terms to Consider (see website for definitions of terms and more detailed information):

Aphrodite: goddess of love (the word used by the Greeks); Venus was the word used for this god by the Romans

Civilization: a group of people living together with common interests such as a system of laws, language, religion and ceremonies, architecture, and art forms

Culture: the artifacts and the structures left behind after people are no longer living

Gilgamesh: a mesopotamian king in the oldest known epic which covers topics about death and a friendship between Enkidu who dies

Hammurabi: ruler in ancient Mesopotamia who developed the first written code of law known as the Hammurabi Code

Neolithic: New Stone Age

Paleolithic: Old Stone Age

Pyramid: large architectural structure from the ancient Egyptian Period

Society: group of people who live together agreeing upon similar ideas

Venus: the Roman goddess of love; copied from the Greeks (see website for more information)

Ziggurat: large architectural structure built by the ancient Mesopotamians which had a temple on top

Old Stone Age (Paleolithic)

1. Food gatherers
2. Nomadic tribes (moved from place to place)
3. Art styles: magic religion, spiritualism, fertility sculptures, cave paintings

New Stone Age (Neolithic)

1. Food producers
2. Community living
3. Art styles: celebrations, ceremonies rituals burials of the dead, artwork on pottery, ceramics, weaving, jewelry, gold and silver pieces

Prehistoric Period Accomplishments

During the Prehistoric Period, there were the earliest people from the Paleolithic Period who roamed from place to place gathering food. Over a long period of time, people began to stay in one place and the time period referred to as the New Stone Age (called the Neolithic Period) was when people started to settle. This period, the Neolithic Period, was the period when people started to live permanently near rivers so they would have water nearby and they gradually developed methods of planting and harvesting crops. This way they were able to use their agricultural skills to produce food and develop a lifestyle of community living. With community living, after some time, people were able to advance and live together. They developed ways of living together by developing laws, ceremonial practices, architecture, language, and art forms such as making containers and creating designs on containers to store grain and other items.

Research

Define each term in depth, and research the dates when the earliest known civilizations began. Also research inventions such as the wheel, the first written code of law, and the first monument built in stone for an Egyptian pharaoh.

- Locate interesting objects with which you are unfamiliar and find out how many centuries they have been in existence.

During the Neolithic period, communities grew and people developed lifestyles that fit their religious, social, and political needs. Communities began to specialize in the production of certain goods and products, which could then be traded with neighboring communities in exchange for their goods and products. Thus trade and commerce came into existence. For example, if one group of people had an excess of barley, and another group had an excess of wheat, the two could trade with one another. Both transportation as well as communication were necessary, however, in order for groups to be able to carry out transactions. In the process of barter and trade, large pots and containers with unique designs and shapes were made by each group, and eventually those containers became identifying objects unique to specific communities. Thus, each of the communities developed its own unique types of utilitarian objects. This exchange among groups of people also resulted in other art forms, such as weaving. Although the craftsmen who used lines, colors, and shapes to create identifying designs may not all have been artists in their own times, their work is considered invaluable today. As we study these early artifacts, we learn how ancient people lived many hundreds of years ago in the earliest known civilizations.

Characteristics of Early Civilizations

- language and writing
- religion
- architecture
- decoration
- weaving
- government
- trade and commerce

Can you think of any additions to this list?

ANCIENT MESOPOTAMIANS

One of the earliest societies to develop a civilization, which has left behind many major contributions and influenced people around the world, is that of the ancient Mesopotamians. In order to understand the history of the earliest peoples of the area, it is important to note that their name derives from the region. The name used in humanities is a geographical name, which may be confusing to students who are not aware that the names in art history and humanities are usually derived from the names of their geographical origin. The area once known as Mesopotamia is now home to modern-day Iraq, parts of Iran, parts of modern-day Turkey, and Syria. When studying some regions of the world, note that not all names have changed. Egypt, for example, is still located where ancient Egypt was.

Many groups of people settled in Mesopotamia, the Sumerians earliest of all. Then came the Babylonians, Assyrians, Hittites, Chaldeans, and Persians. The Sumerians developed in the region referred to as the "land between the rivers," around the area of the Tigris and Euphrates rivers. Sumer was made up of city-states governed by priest-kings. The Sumerians are credited with the invention of cuneiform, an early type of writing consisting of carving made on tablets. Another contribution of the Sumerians was the invention of the wheel. Although we do not have exact dates for when the Sumerian civilization developed, some early objects and markings are dated as early as the years 3500 to 3300 B.C. Marble statuettes from the Abu Temple, Tell Asmar, Iraq, circa. 2900–2600 B.C., represent the concept of a higher power and are a reflection of early peoples' polytheism, in which their many gods were closely linked with the forces of nature (Fiero 9). The images of the gods worshiped in this region are fierce, and it was in this region that the first written code of law was found: the Code of Hammurabi. Hammurabi is recorded as having attempted to systematize legal practices, and his code was the first example of recorded law among the Babylonian rulers (Fiero 10).

One of the epics attributed to the Mesopotamians is the *Epic of Gilgamesh*, the first literary epic in recorded history. An epic is a story in which the main character is a hero who encounters a major challenge, and whose response to that challenge confirms one of the chief values of his community. The characters in the epic are Gilgamesh, his friend Enkidu, and a character named Utnapishtim who saves humankind from a great and devastating flood. In the story, Enkidu travels on a great trip; his entire journey is a search for eternal life. Gilgamesh also wants to have everlasting life, but he discovers that he, too, is a mere mortal. The story is much more complicated than this and is worth reading in its entirety. It is an important and significant literary piece, because it is the first recorded written work that reflects both the human need to accept death as well as the desire to live forever (Fiero 10–11).

The Epic of Gilgamesh

The *Epic of Gilgamesh* raises questions that are universal. This epic is a search for the meaning in life. Gilgamesh asks questions that we still ask ourselves today, such as: What is the meaning of life? Why do we exist? and Why do we have to die?

The story of Gilgamesh was written down in approximately 2000 B.C.E. according to the authors Lawrence Cunningham and John Reich. The story is about Gilgamesh, a very brave Sumerian ruler, who according to many accounts ruled around 2700 B.C.E. and lived in the ancient city of Uruk. In the story, Gilgamesh is a powerful ruler and king who oppresses his people. His countrymen pray for help and Enkidu is sent to fight Gilgamesh according to this myth. Instead, these two individuals become friends. Gilgamesh and Enkidu then travel together.

Gilgamesh is approached by the Queen of Heaven, Ishtar, a goddess, whom he rejects after she makes advances toward him. This turns out to be a disastrous situation for Gilgamesh because he will be punished by having a bull sent to kill him. Gilgamesh kills the bull instead. As a punishment for this, however, Enkidu is killed, which is a tremendous blow to Gilgamesh. The experience is so troubling that it changes Gilgamesh's outlook forever as he becomes aware of his own impending doom. (He had not been aware of his own death until that point.) As his journey continues, Gilgamesh's travels bring him upon Utnapishtim, who has been given eternal life. The epic ends with Utnapishtim telling Gilgamesh a story about the flood which has similarities to the biblical story of Noah and the flood. At the end of the epic poem, Gilgamesh returns home and has to accept the fact that he too will die.

Source: Lawrence S. Cunningham and John J. Reich, *Culture and Values: A Survey of the Western Humanities, Volume I.*

ZIGGURAT

The ziggurat was a place where the citizens gathered and according to some historians, citizens may have brought agricultural goods to the ziggurat and there may have been a market around the site. The ziggurat was a useful gathering place for the community where people gathered for both spiritual and physical nourishment. The ziggurat was created for the patron saint of the city of Ur. The ziggurat was built while King Ur-Nammu of the Third Dynasty of Ur ruled. This ziggurat was constructed for the moon god Nanna, the patron saint of the city of Ur.

In the 1920s Sir Leonard Woolley, in a joint project with the University of Pennsylvania Museum in Philadelphia and the British Museum in London, partially excavated the site of the present ziggurat which is located at the Ali Air Base in Iraq.

Source: https://www.khanacademy.org/humanities/ancient-art-civilizations/ancient-near-east1/sumerian/a/ziggurat-of-ur

Tell Asmar Statues

The Tell Asmar statues are some of the best-preserved ancient Mesopotamian sculptures still surviving and date to about 2750 B.C. They established social hierarchy and communicated larger truths about the world (Sporre).

Early Sumerians played stringed musical instruments such as lyres, harps, flutes, and drums. These instruments have been found in tombs in good condition as recently as the twentieth century. Tablets written in cuneiform writing were found together with a harp during an archeological dig in the ancient area of Mesopotamia. After this find, three professors from the University of California spent several decades deciphering the tablets and making a replica of the instruments in order to recreate ancient musical sounds. Scholars have long pondered the uses of ancient musical instruments such as these, including things hinted at by looking at the carvings in relief on their surfaces. Music could have been used in religious events, such as dedications, coronations, and weddings, as well as in other ceremonies and rituals.

One harp (lyre) was found in excellent condition in the tomb of Queen Puabi. When it was recreated, scientists discovered that it used the traditional Western intervals used by pianos and symphony orchestras. Many older textbooks have credited ancient Greeks such as Pythagoras with the invention of the fourth and fifth intervals, and this concept was taught for many years. Pythagoras was a wise man and was certainly aware of harmony, the octave, and many other musical concepts, but these concepts may have been understood before his time.

When harps and lyres were found that used fourth and fifth intervals as well as the octave, the harp became included in music appreciation classes. It was exciting to have new information about an instrument from approximately 2600 B.C. and intriguing to imagine what music may have sounded like in ancient Mesopotamia thousands of years ago. The lyre, or harp, found in the tomb of Queen Puabi was an extraordinary find, but more research is needed about the tablets in the tomb, as well as of how the harp might have been tuned, and other museums in the United States and Great Britain have harps and lyres that could be researched as well.

Ancient Mesopotamian Accomplishments

Ancient Mesopotamians accomplished major architectural feats.

Here are a number of them:

Arch: a curved shape that helped create structures

Astronomy: a study of formations of the stars; used to help understand when to plant and harvest crops

Irrigation: a system used to water crops; it involves moving water to plants to help them grow

Wheel: an invention used for transporting things and people

Ziggurat: a large architectural structure with a temple on top

Astronomy: the study of the stars and constellations

Cuneiform writing: the type of writing used for record keeping and communication

Mathematics: used by high priests (scientists) in architecture and to study the stars in order to understand the best times to plant seeds

ANCIENT EGYPTIAN CIVILIZATION

Accomplishments of the Ancient Egyptians

- science of embalming
- irrigation
- ship building
- plowing, agricultural improvements in planting and harvesting food
- sculpture
- mathematics
- life after death belief
- relief carving and fresco paintings in tombs
- hieroglyphic writing

The ancient Egyptian civilization developed along the Nile River between 5000 and 3000 B.C. The flooding of the Nile River left a rich silt that increased the fertility of the land, so the ancient people were able to plant and harvest there; ultimately, they developed a civilization along the vast Nile River valley. Egyptology is the study of Egyptian history and culture, including the science of mummification, a method used to preserve the bodies of the dead.

Egyptian history is usually broken down by scholars into three periods: the Pyramid Age, Middle Kingdom, and New Kingdom. The pyramids were built in the earliest era, and the temples at Luxor and Karnak were built over many years, but the bulk of the work on them was done during the New Kingdom. The pharaoh at that time, Ramses II, became very powerful. Because of his military prowess as well as his many years of service (he would die at about ninety-two), he had his sculpture and name carved on the temples, publicly expressing his power and might. Four sculptures of Ramses II were carved on the exterior of the temple Abu Simbel, as well as in numerous rows of columns on the interior.

For nearly 3,000 years, pharaohs and queens ruled in dynasties until Egypt was finally conquered. Their land was isolated and protected by the natural boundaries of the desert and mountains. The yearly rainfall alone would not have allowed for the growth of grain and crops had it not been for the yearly flooding of the Nile River. The Nile was the lifeblood of the Egyptians, and the ability to understand the flooding patterns became a way of life for the ancient Egyptian farmers. They perfected the use of the plow, used a mechanism now called a nilometer to measure flooding, and forecast the weather. Use of the nilometer to know where to plant and understanding the distance of the flow of the Nile's waters were two of the main elements of the pharaohs' reign over their people. Pharaohs were expected to guide and direct their people by providing for a productive harvest, and it was crucial that each pharaoh understand how far the water would recede in order to determine where to plant the grain. This, like other such issues, was calculated by the leadership of the pharaoh and his staff, who were excellent mathematicians and scientists.

The Egyptians believed that the body had to be preserved, or embalmed, through a process called mummification. In this process, the body was dried and then placed in a coffin. After the Pyramid Age, bodies were placed in a resting area referred to as the "Valley of the Kings," deep in a rocky tomb. The location of the Valley of the Kings was along the Nile River, in the middle of Egypt. Inside the tombs were burial chambers where the mummies of the pharaohs were placed. Each mummy was decorated inside the coffin using hieroglyphics, a system of picture-writing. The walls and even ceilings of the tombs were decorated with relief carvings and paintings that depicted the life of the pharaoh, usually showing him in battles or other situations illustrating valor or great bravery.

Some temples represent how some of the Egyptian pharaohs and queens wanted to be remembered for their escapades, experiences, and activities. Two extraordinary examples are those of Ramses II and Queen Hatshepsut.

The sculptures outside Ramses II's temple of Abu Simbel were sixty feet high (Gardner). However, Ramses II's temple had been built near the future site of the Aswan Dam, so in the 1960s Abu Simbel had to be moved to higher ground. The temple was literally cut apart and then pieced back together and was placed on an imitation mountain near the water. UNESCO and several countries helped provide technology, funding, and engineering for the artificial mountain. The four huge sculptures and interior temple were then placed on this mountain and pieced back together, made to look as they had at the time of Ramses II. Inside the temple were columns shaped in the pharaoh's likeness, and all along the interior walls were paintings depicting his victories in battle. The amazing thing about Ramses II was that he, unlike many other pharaohs, had fought with his men on the front lines. He went all the way to Syria and returned home alive. He fought many battles and lived into his nineties, outliving his father, Seti I, by nearly forty years. The scenes painted on Abu Simbel's walls were from his war escapades as well as his conflict with the Hittites. This was an important event in history, because not only was an account discovered that had been written from the Egyptian point of view, but also an account written by the Hittites about the same conflict. As one can imagine, the two accounts were quite different—each history was written from the vantage point of its writer. In this instance, Ramses II was depicted as the hero by the Egyptian artist, and it appeared from the paintings that the Egyptian army had won. However, the account as recorded by the Hittites depicted the battle as a draw; according to them, Ramses II and his army had turned around, left their land, and returned to Egypt. This was an unusual case because it enables us to see both versions. Some scholars believe that the encounter may have been a diplomatic solution, or that it may have ended a draw.

At that time in history, the pharaohs had several wives, as Ramses II did. The temple built next to Abu Simbel was erected for his favorite wife, Nefertari, and it had six sculptures on the exterior as well as paintings on the interior. Of the six sculptures on the exterior, two were of the queen, and the other four were of the pharaoh himself. Much later, when the Aswan Dam was built, Nefertari's temple was moved along with Abu Simbel and placed on an artificial mountain.

The temple of Queen Hatshepsut, circa 1450 B.C., is located near the Valley of the Kings and has sometimes been referred to as a temple carved out of living rock. This temple has several levels as well as a massive ramp at the entrance and was originally constructed as a royal mortuary temple. Because no legitimate male heir was alive to take the throne, Hatshepsut inherited the throne and is reported to have become a pharaoh. "Reliefs are carved on the interior walls which represent Hatshepsut's birth, coronation and great deeds" (Gardner). According to tour guides, in some of the restored areas of the temple, relief carvings on the walls have the portion of her face that would make her identifiable, but it has been mutilated and chiseled out. This most likely occurred shortly after her reign at the command of her step-son, who inherited her throne after her death.

The tomb of the child pharaoh, King Tutankhamen, was found in 1922 by British archeologist Howard Carter. This tomb was significant, because the mummified body of the pharaoh was actually intact in the tomb, making this find the rarest and most valuable in the Valley of the Kings in the twentieth century. At the time of this discovery, Lord Carnarvon had been supplying financial assistance to Carter for several years. He was ready to give up on the project when Carter finally noticed part of a vase that helped him locate the tomb. It must have been quite a shock for Lord Carnarvon, arriving back in Great Britain, to receive a telegram from Howard Carter from Egypt, asking him to turn around and return to Egypt at once. Howard Carter had finally located the entrance to the tomb of King Tutankhamen, and he wanted Lord Carnarvon to be present when he opened the door of the tomb. This tomb had been sealed since ancient times, and Howard Carter and his workmen patiently waited until Lord Carnarvon and his daughter arrived back from England by ship. The treasures discovered in the tomb have been considered the most exquisite gold work from the ancient world and have never been surpassed by any treasures from any other tombs in that area. Howard Carter painstakingly numbered and catalogued each object located in that tomb and had them delivered to the Cairo Museum.

Ancient Egyptian Civilization Accomplishments

Architecture: building pyramids for their pharaohs and queens to place their body in a mummified form in order to go to their afterlife

Calendar: developed names for their seasons which helped them know when to plant their crops

Irrigation: developed a sophisticated system of irrigation to water their crops using water from the Nile River

Life after death: prepared mummies for their belief in the afterlife and if the body was a mummy (embalmed) it would be preserved

Mathematics: advanced use of geometry in their building of huge structures; they built pyramids during the Old Pyramid Age and they built temples during the New Pyramid Age

Post-and-lintel construction: used this type of architectural structure in their building of complexes near pyramids and also during the New Pyramid Age

Shipping: used their ship-building capability to travel the Nile River delivering goods and taking part in ceremonial events such as funerals; devised a major transportation and communication system in their known world

Language: use of hieroglyphics by scribes who wrote detailed accounts in the tombs of the pharaohs and the queens in the Valley of the Kings and the Valley of the Queens

Abu Simbel: a temple erected during the time of Ramses II who wanted this temple to represent his power and strength (When the Aswan Dam was built, this temple was moved piece by piece and block by block to higher ground in order to save the temple from being under water when a lake formed. The lake is Nasar Lake.)

GREEK CIVILIZATION

One of the authors whom I admired while in Art History class was Gene Mittler, who said that "Greece was the birthplace of Western civilization and that the Ancient Greeks had a profound impact on artists up to the present day" (*Art in Focus* 87.) The first group of people living in the area known as modern-day Greece were the Mycenaeans. The Mycenaeans' culture thrived for several hundreds of years and Mycenaeans fought in the famous battle of Troy with the Trojans and won.

The world's terrain—e.g., mountains—kept some areas more isolated than others, leaving some city-states to fend for themselves. The city-states were unable to join together and create a unified nation. Therefore, when they were bombarded by enemy forces, safety was a major concern. History tells the story of the Persian invasion during the fifth century B.C.E. when several city-states finally felt the need to band together. Since there is always a need for funds during times of war, the name of the group that joined together was called the Delian League. The island of Delos was the location of the treasury. Due to the organizational structure of the Delian League and the amount of money that Athens contributed to the fleet, Athens became powerful and gained the authority to collect money. Since Athens had been destroyed by the Persians and had to be rebuilt, a new climate developed.

Democracy was founded at this time and Pericles came to power. Athens's brand of democracy dealt with the concept of community awareness and strove to make communities better places to live by allowing male citizens the opportunity to vote. It focused on community interests as opposed to individual interests (Sporre, *Creative Impulse* 91). This was only the beginning of democracy. At that time, during the fifth century B.C.E., a democratic form of government was very new and membership in that type of system was reserved for property owners and men. Therefore, this was not a *true democracy*, it was just the foundation. "Nonetheless, the central factor in Greek politics remained the concept and sanctity of the *polis* or city. More than an organized conglomeration of people, the polis was a community, a body of men aware of the interest of the community as opposed to the individual interest" (Sporre, *Creative Impulse* 91).

By the fifth century B.C.E., Athens had become a very rich city-state and is cited by historians as a time of richness—the golden age of the Classical era—for the Greeks. It can be called the Classical fifth-century period or the Golden Age of Athens. This time period is also referred to as the age of Pericles and the time when Athens was the powerful economic and political center in that region. Pericles (495?–429 B.C.E.) was an orator and statesman at that time, and Athens remained powerful during his life. That era lasted less than one hundred years because, eventually, the Romans conquered the Greeks by occupying their lands.

Athens

In Athens, during the Golden Age, attention was given to the study of sculpture, architecture, theater, poetry, fencing, philosophy, and music. Athens is a remarkable city because it still has some of the most significant structures that represent the best architecture in the Western world. The main structure in Athens is the Parthenon, which was built during the time of Pericles and is on a high hill called the acropolis.

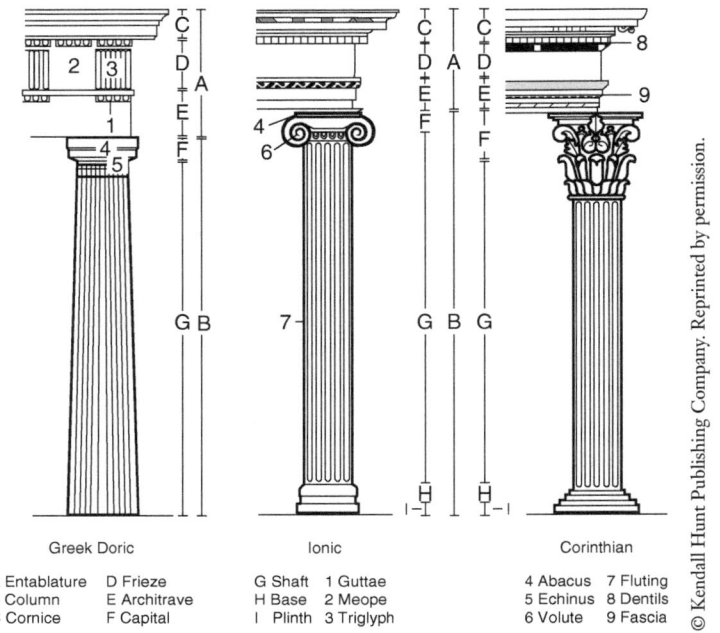

Greek columns and capitals: (*left*) Doric, (*center*) Ionic, (*right*) Corinthian.

Greek Philosophy

"Early Greek philosophy pursued an inquiry into the nature of the physical universe along both materialist and idealist paths. The sophists turned their attention to human affairs, examining such issues as morality and law. The Athenian Socrates adapted the Sophists' methods but rejected their relativism. Socrates' exemplary life and death inspired his student Plato to write the dialogues that elaborated Western philosophy's first great philosophical system. Plato's idealism culminated in his utopian description of the ideal city-state, *The Republic*. The thought of Aristotle, Plato's student, was equally influential encompassing every realm of human knowledge from ethics and poetics to science and logic" (Bishop 69).

Some historians say that Herodotus was the father of history. Herodotus traveled throughout the area around the Mediterranean world during the late fifth century B.C.E. He was born in 480 B.C.E. in Halicarnassus, a Greek town on the coast of Asia Minor, according to the *Quest for the Past* (Reader's Digest, 107). When he was a young man, his family moved to the island of Samos for political reasons. From there, Herodotus wandered around the Mediterranean region asking questions. He ultimately traveled to about thirty countries and wrote about his impressions. Surviving records of his travels have helped historians better understand the past and have informed historians over the years. His information and collections have been the subject of many scholarly writings, even though questions have been raised about some stories being more or less filled with fiction as well as fact.

Thus far, no one has successfully determined the exact date of Herodotus' death. Some scholars surmise that he died around 429 B.C.E., after the start of the Peloponnesian War, which began in 431 B.C.E. In his writings about the battles of Marathon, Thermopylae, and Salamis, the accounts have personal touches and are written in a manner that reflects his view of the "nobility of war." He discussed the disasters of war, the touching nature of war's devastation, and the vast numbers of soldiers who died.

Greek music served the purpose of expressing emotions and telling stories. The theater was a place where instruments were used to help tell the stories about the war heroes and their gods and goddesses. The way in which stories were told helped the people understand their culture and helped them know who the gods were. Certain names and ideas presented in the theater were common to most people who lived in the area—these are called conventions. Sometimes conventions are called traditions and refer to ways of doing things or thinking about things.

People could listen to music by attending outdoor amphitheaters. At these amphitheatres they could watch actors perform their parts—parts that were always played by men, even if they were playing female characters. In Classical Greek dramas, the male actors wore stock masks to portray particular emotions. Because these masks were customary, the audience could understand the mood and emotion being portrayed. The music was usually set to a beat and accompanied by sound or set to a beat without sound accompaniment. The music was patterned so words could be memorized in a rhyme. This was done to make memorization easier.

The instruments utilized by the ancient Greek era can be studied today by looking at Greek vases, such as the black figure and the red figure vases. Many vases depict ceremonies where a musician plays a harp or a flute-type instrument, called an aulos.

The difference between a black figure and a red figure piece of pottery is that the main image or figure on the vase is either black or red. The clay that is used to make the pottery is red in both the black figure and the red figure pottery.

Black Figure	Red Figure
Red Clay	Red Clay
Positive Shape is Black	Positive Shape is Red
The image appears black since the image is glazed with black	The image is red and left red

amphora, pelike, volute krater, krater, hydria, lekythos

amphora, kylix, skyphos, kantharos, aryballos

Many times, the subject of the pottery will depict gods and goddesses and show ceremonies where musicians play a kithera, aulos, harp, or lyre.

"The principal instruments were the lyre, a larger version of the lyre called the kithera, and the aulos. According to mythology the infant Hermes, son of Zeus, killed a turtle and strung gut strings across the hollow shell. That the strings were made from intestines of oxen stolen from his brother Apollo complicated the situation. Hermes craftily avoided further trouble by permitting Apollo to play his lyre. Thus that was the beginning of the legendary lyre and with it that was the lyre-playing tradition of the cult of Apollo" (Lamm and Cross 197).

During the sixth century through the fifth century, the shapes of the vases were created by potters and then painted by painters; these vases were of high quality. The pottery styles and designs were copied over and over by artisans, and there was a large demand for that type of work. Even today, that type of Greek pottery is considered quite elegant and a fine example from that time period. Some of these vases have survived in spite of earthquakes, fires, storms, and violent conflicts, and they are able to be seen in museums. Some of them have been pieced back together by art restorers who have painstakingly put the pieces back together and otherwise restored the containers for the public to see. Visit a museum, if possible, and view the work closely with your own eyes.

There are also websites that allow one to view these vases located in other parts of the world. Websites allow the viewer to appreciate the beauty and craftsmanship of Greek containers and vases. Nevertheless, going to a museum and actually seeing these vases is very helpful, and it can be an exiting experience.

Shapes of Vases

Kylix

This is shaped like a large bowl that one can see into, which the artist paints inside. These bowls were used to hold libations (drinks) that would be passed around. It was used for ritual, celebration, or ceremony.

Krater

This has a large opening on top and is usually very large. It has decorative painting on the sides and also has two handles.

Author		Date	Title
Sophocles	author	496?–406 B.C.E.	*Oedipus the King*
Aeschylus	author	525–456 B.C.E.	*Agamemnon*
Euripides	author	480?–406? B.C.E.	*The Trojan Women*

Amphora

This has a bulb-type shape on the sides and an opening at the top. It is a very feminine and gracefully shaped vase that has two long handles on each side.

Familiar scenes from Greek plays were often painted on Greek vases. Also, vases were sometimes placed in burial chambers.

Attending the theater was an extremely important event for those living in Athens during the fifth century. Even though very few plays remain in their entirety, three major playwrights from that era are remembered: Sophocles, Aeschylus, and Euripides.

During the Dionysus festival each year, a contest was held. (*Reader's Digest*, 110).

Oedipus the King by Sophocles

The play is about Oedipus, who is not aware that he is going to do something that he cannot help. The act is quite dreadful and most readers do not want to believe it will happen. The story invites the reader to question whether fate is in control or if Oedipus could have done something differently to change his lot in life.

Throughout the play, the audience becomes increasingly involved in the storyline and desperately wants to do something to change the course of events. This is a great example of writing. When the play is over, the audience feels for the main character—even though the audience is very disappointed at the same time. It is a rollercoaster of emotions that forms a skeletal structure for many future plays. For this reason, it is remembered as one of the best plays ever written.

In the play, Oedipus quickly leaves home after he hears a story at dinner from a drunken man who says he is going to marry his mother. Then he goes to an intersection of three roads and encounters a carriage. Oedipus becomes upset and an altercation ensues, which results in the death of an old man. Then, in his madness, he kills the other people in the carriage. He then forgets about his actions and goes down the road where he meets an ugly, sphinx-like creature guarding a city. The creature asks him to solve a riddle. If he can solve the riddle then he will be the winner of a contest. He is a very witty young man and he solves the riddle. The riddle is: Who first walks in the morning on four at noon with two and at night with three? If he can figure out the answer he will not be eaten by the sphinx, he will become the king, and he will be able to marry the queen who is very beautiful and who happens to be a recent widow. He solves the riddle by answering, "Man."

When he goes to the town he does not know that the woman he marries is his mother. Students may have to see the play to really understand it. It sounds like a dreadful play, but it is not. It is a play that, actually, is not about a man marrying his mother. It goes beyond that. The play has the basic elements of tragedy built into it, and it has been considered the model for all tragic plays. The tragic elements that Sophocles employed are still used by film script writers today when writing tragedy. For example, the idea of someone who has everything and then falls from glory has long been a common theme.

There are other interesting topics noticeable to the viewer and reader when time is taken to look at or read *Oedipus the King*. The play is still one of the most-read pieces of literature in the world by college students.

Oedipus the King by Sophocles

Translated by F. Storr

Sophocles' *Oedipus the King* is the most famous tragedy of antiquity. When first staged (about 430 B.C.) it was awarded top prize—the civic honor voted by judges for reasons as political and social as they were aesthetic. In the fourth century B.C. it was used by Aristotle as the ground for his analysis of tragedy in the Poetics, the West's earliest book of literary criticism. In modern times, it has come to mean the perfect tragedy.

Tragedy (Greek, "goat song") developed from the choral odes sung to the rural god Dionysus. In sixth-century B.C. Athens, a tyrant introduced this god's cult to the city and made the staging of tragedies part of the Great Dionysia. The coming of democracy to Athens (after 508 B.C.) made these plays even more popular, as people of all classes formed the audience (though it is uncertain if women were present). The Hellenic Age—with Persia in retreat and Athens as the center of Greece—saw the flowering of the genre in the works of three native Athenian: Aeschylus (ca. 525–456 B.C.), Sophocles (ca. 496–406 B.C.), and Euripides (ca. 480–406 B.C.).

Tragedy was basically political in that it addressed the city-state, or its metaphorical equivalent in the audience at the Great Dionysia. Tragedians wrote for this community, speaking as citizens to citizens. A city leader chose three dramatists to present four plays each, and other officials appointed wealthy citizens to pay production costs. The spectators were seated according to tribes, thus mapping the city's political structure. A panel of ten judges was chosen, one from each tribe. Before the plays, the city scored propaganda points by parading orphans of soldiers killed in service and welcoming foreign emissaries. In sum, the drama was the centerpiece of a rite devoted to reinforcing community cohesion.

At first, tragedy (like comedy) had two distinct elements, the actors and the chorus, symbolic of opposing forces in the city-state. In political terms, the actors symbolized individualism (a democratic idea), and the chorus stood for community values (an aristocratic idea). As tragedy evolved, the chorus waned in importance until it disappeared in the fourth century B.C., leaving the actors supreme. This event paralleled the decline of both the city-state and tragic drama.

Reading the Selection

Oedipus the King is typical of what became known as Sophoclean tragedy in that it has two themes: the relation between humans and gods, and the hero's moral dilemmas. These themes converge in the character Oedipus, a king destroyed by the gods as he tries to act morally. Highly ironic, the plot shows Oedipus unleashing new catastrophes despite good intentions. Warned by an oracle that he will kill his father and marry his mother, the well-meaning Oedipus flees from Corinth to Thebes, only to learn that his efforts to escape his dreaded fate have been in vain. Oedipus's downfall is the result of good motives, for he discovers his true identity after ordering an investigation into the old king's murder, so that a plague may be driven from the city.

Above all else, this tragedy is about the unbridgeable gulf between gods and humans. Oedipus repeatedly shows arrogance in his desire to credit himself and deny the truth of oracles ("the world knows my fame"; "I count myself the son of Chance"). Struck down, he finally recognizes that humans, even kings, are fated to suffer. The chorus makes this harsh vision the moral of the tragedy: "[L]ook on Oedipus...[C]ount no man happy till he dies, free of pain at last."

Characters

OEDIPUS king of Thebes
A PRIEST of Zeus
CREON brother of Jocasta
CHORUS of Theban citizens and their LEADER
TEIRESIAS a blind prophet
JOCASTA the queen, wife of Oedipus
MESSENGER from Corinth
HERDSMAN
A MESSENGER from inside the palace
ANTIGONE, ISMENE daughters of Oedipus and Jocasta
Guards and attendants
Priests of Thebes

TIME AND SCENE: The royal house of Thebes. Double doors dominate the façade; a stone altar stands at the center of the stage.

Many years have passed since OEDIPUS solved the riddle of the Sphinx and ascended the throne of Thebes, and now a plague has struck the city. A procession of priests enters; supplicants, broken and despondent, they carry branches wound in wool and lay them on the altar.

The doors open. Guards assemble. OEDIPUS comes forward, majestic but for a telltale limp, and slowly views the condition of his people.

OEDIPUS: My children, latest born to Cadmus old,
Why sit ye here as suppliants, in your hands
Branches of olive filleted with wool?
What means this reek of incense everywhere,
And everywhere laments and litanies?
Children, it were not meet that I should learn
From others, and am hither come, myself,
I Oedipus, your world-renowned king.
Ho! aged sire, whose venerable locks
Proclaim thee spokesman of this company,
Explain your mood and purport. Is it dread
Of ill that moves you or a boon ye crave?
My zeal in your behalf ye cannot doubt;
Ruthless indeed were I and obdurate
If such petitioners as you I spurned.

PRIEST: Yea, Oedipus, my sovereign lord and king,
Thou seest how both extremes of age besiege
Thy palace altars--fledglings hardly winged,
And greybeards bowed with years, priests, as am I
Of Zeus, and these the flower of our youth.
Meanwhile, the common folk, with wreathed boughs
Crowd our two market-places, or before
Both shrines of Pallas congregate, or where
Ismenus gives his oracles by fire.
For, as thou seest thyself, our ship of State,
Sore buffeted, can no more lift her head,
Foundered beneath a weltering surge of blood.
A blight is on our harvest in the ear,
A blight upon the grazing flocks and herds,
A blight on wives in travail; and withal
Armed with his blazing torch the God of Plague
Hath swooped upon our city emptying
The house of Cadmus, and the murky realm
Of Pluto is full fed with groans and tears.

Therefore, O King, here at thy hearth we sit,
I and these children; not as deeming thee
A new divinity, but the first of men;
First in the common accidents of life,
And first in visitations of the Gods.
Art thou not he who coming to the town
Of Cadmus freed us from the tax we paid
To the fell songstress? Nor hadst thou received
Prompting from us or been by others schooled;

No, by a god inspired (so all men deem,
And testify) didst thou renew our life.
And now, O Oedipus, our peerless king,
All we thy votaries beseech thee, find
Some succor, whether by a voice from heaven
Whispered, or haply known by human wit.
Tried counselors, methinks, are aptest found
To furnish for the future pregnant rede.
Upraise, O chief of men, upraise our State!
Look to thy laurels! for thy zeal of yore
Our country's savior thou art justly hailed:
O never may we thus record thy reign:--
"He raised us up only to cast us down."
Uplift us, build our city on a rock.
Thy happy star ascendant brought us luck,
O let it not decline! If thou wouldst rule
This land, as now thou reignest, better sure
To rule a peopled than a desert realm.
Nor battlements nor galleys aught avail,
If men to man and guards to guard them tail.

OEDIPUS: Ah! my poor children, known, ah, known too well,

The quest that brings you hither and your need.
Ye sicken all, well wot I, yet my pain,
How great soever yours, outtops it all.
Your sorrow touches each man severally,
Him and none other, but I grieve at once
Both for the general and myself and you.
Therefore ye rouse no sluggard from day-dreams.
Many, my children, are the tears I've wept,
And threaded many a maze of weary thought.
Thus pondering one clue of hope I caught,
And tracked it up; I have sent Menoeceus' son,
Creon, my consort's brother, to inquire
Of Pythian Phoebus at his Delphic shrine,
How I might save the State by act or word.
And now I reckon up the tale of days
Since he set forth, and marvel how he fares.
'Tis strange, this endless tarrying, passing strange.
But when he comes, then I were base indeed,
If I perform not all the god declares.

PRIEST: Thy words are well timed; even as thou speakest
That shouting tells me Creon is at hand.

OEDIPUS: O King Apollo! may his joyous looks
Be presage of the joyous news he brings!

PRIEST: As I surmise, 'tis welcome; else his head
Had scarce been crowned with berry-laden bays.
OEDIPUS: We soon shall know; he's now in earshot range.

Enter CREON.

My royal cousin, say, Menoeceus' child,
What message hast thou brought us from the god?

CREON: Good news, for e'en intolerable ills,
Finding right issue, tend to naught but good.

OEDIPUS: How runs the oracle? thus far thy words
Give me no ground for confidence or fear.

CREON: If thou wouldst hear my message publicly,
I'll tell thee straight, or with thee pass within.

OEDIPUS: Speak before all; the burden that I bear
Is more for these my subjects than myself.

CREON: Let me report then all the god declared.
King Phoebus bids us straitly extirpate
A fell pollution that infests the land,
And no more harbor an inveterate sore.

OEDIPUS: What expiation means he? What's amiss?

CREON: Banishment, or the shedding blood for blood.
This stain of blood makes shipwreck of our state.

OEDIPUS: Whom can he mean, the miscreant thus denounced?

CREON: Before thou didst assume the helm of State,
The sovereign of this land was Laius.

OEDIPUS: I heard as much, but never saw the man.

CREON: He fell; and now the god's command is plain:
Punish his takers-off, whoe'er they be.

OEDIPUS: Where are they? Where in the wide world to find
The far, faint traces of a bygone crime?

CREON: In this land, said the god; "who seeks shall find;
Who sits with folded hands or sleeps is blind."

OEDIPUS: Was he within his palace, or afield,
Or traveling, when Laius met his fate?

CREON: Abroad; he started, so he told us, bound
For Delphi, but he never thence returned.

OEDIPUS: Came there no news, no fellow-traveler
To give some clue that might be followed up?

CREON: But one escape, who flying for dear life,
Could tell of all he saw but one thing sure.

OEDIPUS: And what was that? One clue might lead us far,
With but a spark of hope to guide our quest.

CREON: Robbers, he told us, not one bandit but
A troop of knaves, attacked and murdered him.

OEDIPUS: Did any bandit dare so bold a stroke,
Unless indeed he were suborned from Thebes?

CREON: So 'twas surmised, but none was found to avenge
His murder mid the trouble that ensued.

OEDIPUS: What trouble can have hindered a full quest,
When royalty had fallen thus miserably?

CREON: The riddling Sphinx compelled us to let slide
The dim past and attend to instant needs.

OEDIPUS: Well, I will start afresh and once again
Make dark things clear. Right worthy the concern
Of Phoebus, worthy thine too, for the dead;
I also, as is meet, will lend my aid
To avenge this wrong to Thebes and to the god.
Not for some far-off kinsman, but myself,
Shall I expel this poison in the blood;
For whoso slew that king might have a mind
To strike me too with his assassin hand.
Therefore in righting him I serve myself.
Up, children, haste ye, quit these altar stairs,
Take hence your suppliant wands, go summon hither
The Theban commons. With the god's good help
Success is sure; 'tis ruin if we fail.

Exeunt OEDIPUS and CREON.

PRIEST: Come, children, let us hence; these gracious words
Forestall the very purpose of our suit.
And may the god who sent this oracle
Save us withal and rid us of this pest.

Exeunt PRIEST and SUPPLIANTS.

CHORUS (strophe 1):

Sweet-voiced daughter of Zeus from thy gold-paved Pythian shrine

Wafted to Thebes divine,
What dost thou bring me? My soul is racked and shivers with fear.

Healer of Delos, hear!
Hast thou some pain unknown before,
Or with the circling years renewest a penance of yore?
Offspring of golden Hope, thou voice immortal, O tell me.

(antistrophe 1)

First on Athene I call; O Zeus-born goddess, defend!
Goddess and sister, befriend,
Artemis, Lady of Thebes, high-throned in the midst of our mart!

Lord of the death-winged dart!
Your threefold aid I crave
From death and ruin our city to save.
If in the days of old when we nigh had perished, ye drave

From our land the fiery plague, be near us now and defend us!

(strophe 2)

Ah me, what countless woes are mine!
All our host is in decline;
Weaponless my spirit lies.
Earth her gracious fruits denies;
Women wail in barren throes;
Life on life downstriken goes,
Swifter than the wind bird's flight,
Swifter than the Fire-God's might,
To the westering shores of Night.

(antistrophe 2)

Wasted thus by death on death

All our city perisheth.
Corpses spread infection round;
None to tend or mourn is found.
Wailing on the altar stair
Wives and grandams rend the air--
Long-drawn moans and piercing cries
Blent with prayers and litanies.
Golden child of Zeus, O hear
Let thine angel face appear!

(strophe 3)

And grant that Ares whose hot breath I feel,
Though without targe or steel
He stalks, whose voice is as the battle shout,
May turn in sudden rout,
To the unharbored Thracian waters sped,
Or Amphitrite's bed.
For what night leaves undone,
Smit by the morrow's sun
Perisheth. Father Zeus, whose hand
Doth wield the lightning brand,
Slay him beneath thy levin bold, we pray,
Slay him, O slay!

(antistrophe 3)

O that thine arrows too, Lycean King,
From that taut bow's gold string,
Might fly abroad, the champions of our rights;
Yea, and the flashing lights
Of Artemis, wherewith the huntress sweeps
Across the Lycian steeps.
Thee too I call with golden-snooded hair,
Whose name our land doth bear,
Bacchus to whom thy Maenads Evoe shout;
Come with thy bright torch, rout,
Blithe god whom we adore,
The god whom gods abhor.

Enter OEDIPUS.

OEDIPUS: Ye pray; 'tis well, but would ye hear my words
And heed them and apply the remedy,
Ye might perchance find comfort and relief.
Mind you, I speak as one who comes a stranger
To this report, no less than to the crime;
For how unaided could I track it far
Without a clue? Which lacking (for too late
Was I enrolled a citizen of Thebes)
This proclamation I address to all:--
Thebans, if any knows the man by whom
Laius, son of Labdacus, was slain,
I summon him to make clean shrift to me.
And if he shrinks, let him reflect that thus
Confessing he shall 'scape the capital charge;
For the worst penalty that shall befall him
Is banishment--unscathed he shall depart.
But if an alien from a foreign land
Be known to any as the murderer,
Let him who knows speak out, and he shall have
Due recompense from me and thanks to boot.
But if ye still keep silence, if through fear
For self or friends ye disregard my hest,
Hear what I then resolve; I lay my ban
On the assassin whosoe'er he be.
Let no man in this land, whereof I hold
The sovereign rule, harbor or speak to him;
Give him no part in prayer or sacrifice
Or lustral rites, but hound him from your homes.
For this is our defilement, so the god
Hath lately shown to me by oracles.
Thus as their champion I maintain the cause
Both of the god and of the murdered King.
And on the murderer this curse I lay
(On him and all the partners in his guilt):--
Wretch, may he pine in utter wretchedness!
And for myself, if with my privity
He gain admittance to my hearth, I pray
The curse I laid on others fall on me.
See that ye give effect to all my hest,
For my sake and the god's and for our land,
A desert blasted by the wrath of heaven.
For, let alone the god's express command,
It were a scandal ye should leave unpurged
The murder of a great man and your king,
Nor track it home. And now that I am lord,
Successor to his throne, his bed, his wife,
(And had he not been frustrate in the hope
Of issue, common children of one womb
Had forced a closer bond twixt him and me,
But Fate swooped down upon him), therefore I
His blood-avenger will maintain his cause
As though he were my sire, and leave no stone
Unturned to track the assassin or avenge
The son of Labdacus, of Polydore,
Of Cadmus, and Agenor first of the race.
And for the disobedient thus I pray:
May the gods send them neither timely fruits
Of earth, nor teeming increase of the womb,
But may they waste and pine, as now they waste,
Aye and worse stricken; but to all of you,
My loyal subjects who approve my acts,
May Justice, our ally, and all the gods

Be gracious and attend you evermore.
CHORUS: The oath thou profferest, sire, I take and swear.

I slew him not myself, nor can I name
The slayer. For the quest, 'twere well, methinks
That Phoebus, who proposed the riddle, himself
Should give the answer--who the murderer was.

OEDIPUS: Well argued; but no living man can hope
To force the gods to speak against their will.

CHORUS: May I then say what seems next best to me?

OEDIPUS: Aye, if there be a third best, tell it too.

CHORUS: My liege, if any man sees eye to eye
With our lord Phoebus, 'tis our prophet, lord
Teiresias; he of all men best might guide
A searcher of this matter to the light.

OEDIPUS: Here too my zeal has nothing lagged, for twice
At Creon's instance have I sent to fetch him,
And long I marvel why he is not here.

CHORUS: I mind me too of rumors long ago--
Mere gossip.

OEDIPUS: Tell them, I would fain know all.

CHORUS: 'Twas said he fell by travelers.

OEDIPUS: So I heard,
But none has seen the man who saw him fall.

CHORUS: Well, if he knows what fear is, he will quail
And flee before the terror of thy curse.

OEDIPUS: Words scare not him who blenches not at deeds.

CHORUS: But here is one to arraign him. Lo, at length
They bring the god-inspired seer in whom
Above all other men is truth inborn.

Enter TEIRESIAS, led by a boy.

OEDIPUS: Teiresias, seer who comprehendest all,
Lore of the wise and hidden mysteries,
High things of heaven and low things of the earth,
Thou knowest, though thy blinded eyes see naught,
What plague infects our city; and we turn
To thee, O seer, our one defense and shield.
The purport of the answer that the God
Returned to us who sought his oracle,
The messengers have doubtless told thee--how
One course alone could rid us of the pest,
To find the murderers of Laius,
And slay them or expel them from the land.
Therefore begrudging neither augury
Nor other divination that is thine,
O save thyself, thy country, and thy king,
Save all from this defilement of blood shed.
On thee we rest. This is man's highest end,
To others' service all his powers to lend.

TEIRESIAS: Alas, alas, what misery to be wise
When wisdom profits nothing! This old lore
I had forgotten; else I were not here.

OEDIPUS: What ails thee? Why this melancholy mood?

TEIRESIAS: Let me go home; prevent me not; 'twere best
That thou shouldst bear thy burden and I mine.

OEDIPUS: For shame! no true-born Theban patriot
Would thus withhold the word of prophecy.

TEIRESIAS: Thy words, O king, are wide of the mark, and I

For fear lest I too trip like thee...

OEDIPUS: Oh speak,
Withhold not, I adjure thee, if thou know'st,
Thy knowledge. We are all thy suppliants.

TEIRESIAS: Aye, for ye all are witless, but my voice
Will ne'er reveal my miseries--or thine.

OEDIPUS: What then, thou knowest, and yet willst not speak!
Wouldst thou betray us and destroy the State?

TEIRESIAS: I will not vex myself nor thee. Why ask
Thus idly what from me thou shalt not learn?

OEDIPUS: Monster! thy silence would incense a flint.
Will nothing loose thy tongue? Can nothing melt thee,
Or shake thy dogged taciturnity?

TEIRESIAS: Thou blam'st my mood and seest not thine own
Wherewith thou art mated; no, thou taxest me.

OEDIPUS: And who could stay his choler when he heard
How insolently thou dost flout the State?

TEIRESIAS: Well, it will come what will, though I be mute.

OEDIPUS: Since come it must, thy duty is to tell me.

TEIRESIAS: I have no more to say; storm as thou willst,
And give the rein to all thy pent-up rage.

OEDIPUS: Yea, I am wroth, and will not stint my words,
But speak my whole mind. Thou methinks thou art he,
Who planned the crime, aye, and performed it too,
All save the assassination; and if thou
Hadst not been blind, I had been sworn to boot
That thou alone didst do the bloody deed.

TEIRESIAS: Is it so? Then I charge thee to abide
By thine own proclamation; from this day
Speak not to these or me. Thou art the man,
Thou the accursed polluter of this land.

OEDIPUS: Vile slanderer, thou blurtest forth these taunts,
And think'st forsooth as seer to go scot free.

TEIRESIAS: Yea, I am free, strong in the strength of truth.

OEDIPUS: Who was thy teacher? not methinks thy art.

TEIRESIAS: Thou, goading me against my will to speak.

OEDIPUS: What speech? repeat it and resolve my doubt.

TEIRESIAS: Didst miss my sense wouldst thou goad me on?

OEDIPUS: I but half caught thy meaning; say it again.

TEIRESIAS: I say thou art the murderer of the man
Whose murderer thou pursuest.

OEDIPUS: Thou shalt rue it
Twice to repeat so gross a calumny.

TEIRESIAS: Must I say more to aggravate thy rage?

OEDIPUS: Say all thou wilt; it will be but waste of breath.

TEIRESIAS: I say thou livest with thy nearest kin
In infamy, unwitting in thy shame.

OEDIPUS: Think'st thou for aye unscathed to wag thy tongue?

TEIRESIAS: Yea, if the might of truth can aught prevail.

OEDIPUS: With other men, but not with thee, for thou
In ear, wit, eye, in everything art blind.

TEIRESIAS: Poor fool to utter gibes at me which all
Here present will cast back on thee ere long.

OEDIPUS: Offspring of endless Night, thou hast no power
O'er me or any man who sees the sun.

TEIRESIAS: No, for thy weird is not to fall by me.
I leave to Apollo what concerns the god.

OEDIPUS: Is this a plot of Creon, or thine own?

TEIRESIAS: Not Creon, thou thyself art thine own bane.

OEDIPUS: O wealth and empiry and skill by skill
Outwitted in the battlefield of life,
What spite and envy follow in your train!
See, for this crown the State conferred on me.
A gift, a thing I sought not, for this crown
The trusty Creon, my familiar friend,
Hath lain in wait to oust me and suborned
This mountebank, this juggling charlatan,
This tricksy beggar-priest, for gain alone
Keen-eyed, but in his proper art stone-blind.
Say, sirrah, hast thou ever proved thyself
A prophet? When the riddling Sphinx was here
Why hadst thou no deliverance for this folk?
And yet the riddle was not to be solved
By guess-work but required the prophet's art;
Wherein thou wast found lacking; neither birds

Nor sign from heaven helped thee, but I came,
The simple Oedipus; I stopped her mouth
By mother wit, untaught of auguries.
This is the man whom thou wouldst undermine,
In hope to reign with Creon in my stead.
Methinks that thou and thine abettor soon
Will rue your plot to drive the scapegoat out.
Thank thy grey hairs that thou hast still to learn
What chastisement such arrogance deserves.

CHORUS: To us it seems that both the seer and thou,
O Oedipus, have spoken angry words.
This is no time to wrangle but consult
How best we may fulfill the oracle.

TEIRESIAS: King as thou art, free speech at least is mine

To make reply; in this I am thy peer.
I own no lord but Loxias; him I serve
And ne'er can stand enrolled as Creon's man.
Thus then I answer: since thou hast not spared
To twit me with my blindness--thou hast eyes,
Yet see'st not in what misery thou art fallen,
Nor where thou dwellest nor with whom for mate.
Dost know thy lineage? Nay, thou know'st it not,
And all unwitting art a double foe
To thine own kin, the living and the dead;
Aye and the dogging curse of mother and sire
One day shall drive thee, like a two-edged sword,
Beyond our borders, and the eyes that now
See clear shall henceforward endless night.
Ah whither shall thy bitter cry not reach,
What crag in all Cithaeron but shall then
Reverberate thy wail, when thou hast found
With what a hymeneal thou wast borne
Home, but to no fair haven, on the gale!
Aye, and a flood of ills thou guessest not
Shall set thyself and children in one line.
Flout then both Creon and my words, for none
Of mortals shall be striken worse than thou.

OEDIPUS: Must I endure this fellow's insolence?
A murrain on thee! Get thee hence! Begone
Avaunt! and never cross my threshold more.

TEIRESIAS: I ne'er had come hadst thou not bidden me.

OEDIPUS: I know not thou wouldst utter folly, else
Long hadst thou waited to be summoned here.

TEIRESIAS: Such am I--as it seems to thee a fool,
But to the parents who begat thee, wise.

OEDIPUS: What sayest thou--"parents"? Who begat me, speak?

TEIRESIAS: This day shall be thy birth-day, and thy grave.

OEDIPUS: Thou lov'st to speak in riddles and dark words.

TEIRESIAS: In reading riddles who so skilled as thou?

OEDIPUS: Twit me with that wherein my greatness lies.

TEIRESIAS: And yet this very greatness proved thy bane.

OEDIPUS: No matter if I saved the commonwealth.

TEIRESIAS: 'Tis time I left thee. Come, boy, take me home.

OEDIPUS: Aye, take him quickly, for his presence irks
And lets me; gone, thou canst not plague me more.

TEIRESIAS: I go, but first will tell thee why I came.
Thy frown I dread not, for thou canst not harm me.
Hear then: this man whom thou hast sought to arrest
With threats and warrants this long while, the wretch
Who murdered Laius--that man is here.
He passes for an alien in the land
But soon shall prove a Theban, native born.
And yet his fortune brings him little joy;
For blind of seeing, clad in beggar's weeds,
For purple robes, and leaning on his staff,
To a strange land he soon shall grope his way.
And of the children, inmates of his home,
He shall be proved the brother and the sire,
Of her who bare him son and husband both,
Co-partner, and assassin of his sire.
Go in and ponder this, and if thou find
That I have missed the mark, henceforth declare
I have no wit nor skill in prophecy.

Exeunt TEIRESIAS and OEDIPUS.

CHORUS (strophe 1):

Who is he by voice immortal named from Pythia's rocky cell,

Doer of foul deeds of bloodshed, horrors that no tongue

can tell?
A foot for flight he needs
Fleeter than storm-swift steeds,
For on his heels doth follow,
Armed with the lightnings of his Sire, Apollo.
Like sleuth-hounds too
The Fates pursue.

(antistrophe 1)

Yea, but now flashed forth the summons from Parnassus' snowy peak,

"Near and far the undiscovered doer of this murder seek!"

Now like a sullen bull he roves
Through forest brakes and upland groves,
And vainly seeks to fly
The doom that ever nigh
Flits o'er his head,
Still by the avenging Phoebus sped,
The voice divine,
From Earth's mid shrine.

(strophe 2)

Sore perplexed am I by the words of the master seer.
Are they true, are they false? I know not and bridle my tongue for fear,
Fluttered with vague surmise; nor present nor future is clear.

Quarrel of ancient date or in days still near know I none

Twixt the Labdacidan house and our ruler, Polybus' son.
Proof is there none: how then can I challenge our King's good name,

How in a blood-feud join for an untracked deed of shame?

(antistrophe 2)

All wise are Zeus and Apollo, and nothing is hid from their ken;

They are gods; and in wits a man may surpass his fellow men;

But that a mortal seer knows more than I know--where
Hath this been proven? Or how without sign assured, can I blame
Him who saved our State when the winged songstress came,

Tested and tried in the light of us all, like gold assayed?

How can I now assent when a crime is on Oedipus laid?

CREON: Friends, countrymen, I learn King Oedipus
Hath laid against me a most grievous charge,
And come to you protesting. If he deems
That I have harmed or injured him in aught
By word or deed in this our present trouble,
I care not to prolong the span of life,
Thus ill-reputed; for the calumny
Hits not a single blot, but blasts my name,
If by the general voice I am denounced
False to the State and false by you my friends.

CHORUS: This taunt, it well may be, was blurted out
In petulance, not spoken advisedly.

CREON: Did any dare pretend that it was I
Prompted the seer to utter a forged charge?

CHORUS: Such things were said; with what intent I know not.

CREON: Were not his wits and vision all astray
When upon me he fixed this monstrous charge?

CHORUS: I know not; to my sovereign's acts I am blind.
But lo, he comes to answer for himself.

Enter OEDIPUS.

OEDIPUS: Sirrah, what mak'st thou here? Dost thou presume

To approach my doors, thou brazen-faced rogue,
My murderer and the filcher of my crown?
Come, answer this, didst thou detect in me
Some touch of cowardice or witlessness,
That made thee undertake this enterprise?
I seemed forsooth too simple to perceive
The serpent stealing on me in the dark,
Or else too weak to scotch it when I saw.
This thou art witless seeking to possess
Without a following or friends the crown,
A prize that followers and wealth must win.

CREON: Attend me. Thou hast spoken, 'tis my turn
To make reply. Then having heard me, judge.

OEDIPUS: Thou art glib of tongue, but I am slow to learn
Of thee; I know too well thy venomous hate.

CREON: First I would argue out this very point.

OEDIPUS: O argue not that thou art not a rogue.

CREON: If thou dost count a virtue stubbornness,
Unschooled by reason, thou art much astray.

OEDIPUS: If thou dost hold a kinsman may be wronged,
And no pains follow, thou art much to seek.

CREON: Therein thou judgest rightly, but this wrong
That thou allegest--tell me what it is.

OEDIPUS: Didst thou or didst thou not advise that I
Should call the priest?

CREON: Yes, and I stand to it.

OEDIPUS: Tell me how long is it since Laius...

CREON: Since Laius...? I follow not thy drift.

OEDIPUS: By violent hands was spirited away.

CREON: In the dim past, a many years agone.

OEDIPUS: Did the same prophet then pursue his craft?

CREON: Yes, skilled as now and in no less repute.

OEDIPUS: Did he at that time ever glance at me?

CREON: Not to my knowledge, not when I was by.

OEDIPUS: But was no search and inquisition made?

CREON: Surely full quest was made, but nothing learnt.

OEDIPUS: Why failed the seer to tell his story then?

CREON: I know not, and not knowing hold my tongue.

OEDIPUS: This much thou knowest and canst surely tell.

CREON: What's mean'st thou? All I know I will declare.

OEDIPUS: But for thy prompting never had the seer
Ascribed to me the death of Laius.

CREON: If so he thou knowest best; but I
Would put thee to the question in my turn.

OEDIPUS: Question and prove me murderer if thou canst.

CREON: Then let me ask thee, didst thou wed my sister?

OEDIPUS: A fact so plain I cannot well deny.

CREON: And as thy consort queen she shares the throne?

OEDIPUS: I grant her freely all her heart desires.

CREON: And with you twain I share the triple rule?

OEDIPUS: Yea, and it is that proves thee a false friend.

CREON: Not so, if thou wouldst reason with thyself,
As I with myself. First, I bid thee think,
Would any mortal choose a troubled reign
Of terrors rather than secure repose,
If the same power were given him? As for me,
I have no natural craving for the name
Of king, preferring to do kingly deeds,
And so thinks every sober-minded man.
Now all my needs are satisfied through thee,
And I have naught to fear; but were I king,
My acts would oft run counter to my will.
How could a title then have charms for me
Above the sweets of boundless influence?
I am not so infatuate as to grasp
The shadow when I hold the substance fast.
Now all men cry me Godspeed! wish me well,
And every suitor seeks to gain my ear,
If he would hope to win a grace from thee.
Why should I leave the better, choose the worse?
That were sheer madness, and I am not mad.
No such ambition ever tempted me,
Nor would I have a share in such intrigue.
And if thou doubt me, first to Delphi go,
There ascertain if my report was true
Of the god's answer; next investigate
If with the seer I plotted or conspired,
And if it prove so, sentence me to death,

Not by thy voice alone, but mine and thine.
But O condemn me not, without appeal,
On bare suspicion. 'Tis not right to adjudge
Bad men at random good, or good men bad.
I would as lief a man should cast away
The thing he counts most precious, his own life,
As spurn a true friend. Thou wilt learn in time
The truth, for time alone reveals the just;
A villain is detected in a day.

CHORUS: To one who walketh warily his words
Commend themselves; swift counsels are not sure.

OEDIPUS: When with swift strides the stealthy plotter stalks
I must be quick too with my counterplot.
To wait his onset passively, for him
Is sure success, for me assured defeat.

CREON: What then's thy will? To banish me the land?

OEDIPUS: I would not have thee banished, no, but dead,
That men may mark the wages envy reaps.

CREON: I see thou wilt not yield, nor credit me.

OEDIPUS: None but a fool would credit such as thou.

CREON: Thou art not wise.

OEDIPUS: Wise for myself at least.

CREON: Why not for me too?

OEDIPUS: Why for such a knave?

CREON: Suppose thou lackest sense.

OEDIPUS: Yet kings must rule.

CREON: Not if they rule ill.

OEDIPUS: Oh my Thebans, hear him!

CREON: Thy Thebans? am not I a Theban too?

CHORUS: Cease, princes; lo there comes, and none too soon,

Jocasta from the palace. Who so fit
As peacemaker to reconcile your feud?

Enter JOCASTA.

JOCASTA: Misguided princes, why have ye upraised
This wordy wrangle? Are ye not ashamed,
While the whole land lies striken, thus to voice
Your private injuries? Go in, my lord;
Go home, my brother, and forebear to make
A public scandal of a petty grief.

CREON: My royal sister, Oedipus, thy lord,
Hath bid me choose (O dread alternative!)
An outlaw's exile or a felon's death.

OEDIPUS: Yes, lady; I have caught him practicing
Against my royal person his vile arts.

CREON: May I ne'er speed but die accursed, if I
In any way am guilty of this charge.

JOCASTA Believe him, I adjure thee, Oedipus,
First for his solemn oath's sake, then for mine,
And for thine elders' sake who wait on thee.

CHORUS (strophe 1):

Hearken, King, reflect, we pray thee, but not stubborn but relent.

OEDIPUS: Say to what should I consent?

CHORUS: Respect a man whose probity and troth
Are known to all and now confirmed by oath.

OEDIPUS: Dost know what grace thou cravest?

CHORUS: Yea, I know.

OEDIPUS: Declare it then and make thy meaning plain.

CHORUS: Brand not a friend whom babbling tongues assail;
Let not suspicion 'gainst his oath prevail.

OEDIPUS: Bethink you that in seeking this ye seek
In very sooth my death or banishment?

CHORUS: No, by the leader of the host divine!

(strophe 2)

Witness, thou Sun, such thought was never mine,
Unblest, unfriended may I perish,
If ever I such wish did cherish!
But O my heart is desolate
Musing on our striken State,
Doubly fall'n should discord grow
Twixt you twain, to crown our woe.

OEDIPUS: Well, let him go, no matter what it cost me,
Or certain death or shameful banishment,
For your sake I relent, not his; and him,
Where'er he be, my heart shall still abhor.

CREON: Thou art as sullen in thy yielding mood
As in thine anger thou wast truculent.
Such tempers justly plague themselves the most.

OEDIPUS: Leave me in peace and get thee gone.

CREON: I go,
By thee misjudged, but justified by these.

Exeunt CREON.

CHORUS (antistrophe 1):

Lady, lead indoors thy consort; wherefore longer here delay?

JOCASTA: Tell me first how rose the fray.

CHORUS: Rumors bred unjust suspicious and injustice rankles sore.

JOCASTA: Were both at fault?

CHORUS: Both.

JOCASTA: What was the tale?

CHORUS: Ask me no more. The land is sore distressed;
'Twere better
sleeping ills to leave at rest.

OEDIPUS: Strange counsel, friend! I know thou mean'st me well,
And yet would'st mitigate and blunt my zeal.

CHORUS (antistrophe 2):

King, I say it once again,

Witless were I proved, insane,
If I lightly put away
Thee my country's prop and stay,
Pilot who, in danger sought,
To a quiet haven brought
Our distracted State; and now
Who can guide us right but thou?

JOCASTA: Let me too, I adjure thee, know, O king,
What cause has stirred this unrelenting wrath.

OEDIPUS: I will, for thou art more to me than these.
Lady, the cause is Creon and his plots.

JOCASTA: But what provoked the quarrel? make this clear.

OEDIPUS: He points me out as Laius' murderer.

JOCASTA: Of his own knowledge or upon report?

OEDIPUS: He is too cunning to commit himself,
And makes a mouthpiece of a knavish seer.

JOCASTA: Then thou mayest ease thy conscience on that score.

Listen and I'll convince thee that no man
Hath scot or lot in the prophetic art.
Here is the proof in brief. An oracle
Once came to Laius (I will not say
'Twas from the Delphic god himself, but from
His ministers) declaring he was doomed
To perish by the hand of his own son,
A child that should be born to him by me.
Now Laius--so at least report affirmed--
Was murdered on a day by highwaymen,
No natives, at a spot where three roads meet.
As for the child, it was but three days old,
When Laius, its ankles pierced and pinned
Together, gave it to be cast away
By others on the trackless mountain side.
So then Apollo brought it not to pass
The child should be his father's murderer,
Or the dread terror find accomplishment,
And Laius be slain by his own son.
Such was the prophet's horoscope. O king,
Regard it not. Whate'er the god deems fit
To search, himself unaided will reveal.

OEDIPUS: What memories, what wild tumult of the soul

Came o'er me, lady, as I heard thee speak!

JOCASTA: What mean'st thou? What has shocked and startled thee?

OEDIPUS: Methought I heard thee say that Laius
Was murdered at the meeting of three roads.

JOCASTA: So ran the story that is current still.

OEDIPUS: Where did this happen? Dost thou know the place?

JOCASTA: Phocis the land is called; the spot is where
Branch roads from Delphi and from Daulis meet.

OEDIPUS: And how long is it since these things befell?

JOCASTA: 'Twas but a brief while were thou wast proclaimed
Our country's ruler that the news was brought.

OEDIPUS: O Zeus, what hast thou willed to do with me!

JOCASTA: What is it, Oedipus, that moves thee so?

OEDIPUS: Ask me not yet; tell me the build and height
Of Laius? Was he still in manhood's prime?

JOCASTA: Tall was he, and his hair was lightly strewn
With silver; and not unlike thee in form.

OEDIPUS: O woe is me! Mehtinks unwittingly
I laid but now a dread curse on myself.

JOCASTA: What say'st thou? When I look upon thee, my king,
I tremble.

OEDIPUS: 'Tis a dread presentiment
That in the end the seer will prove not blind.
One further question to resolve my doubt.

JOCASTA: I quail; but ask, and I will answer all.

OEDIPUS: Had he but few attendants or a train
Of armed retainers with him, like a prince?

JOCASTA: They were but five in all, and one of them
A herald; Laius in a mule-car rode.

OEDIPUS: Alas! 'tis clear as noonday now. But say, Lady, who carried this report to Thebes?

JOCASTA: A serf, the sole survivor who returned.

OEDIPUS: Haply he is at hand or in the house?

JOCASTA: No, for as soon as he returned and found
Thee reigning in the stead of Laius slain,
He clasped my hand and supplicated me
To send him to the alps and pastures, where
He might be farthest from the sight of Thebes.
And so I sent him. 'Twas an honest slave
And well deserved some better recompense.

OEDIPUS: Fetch him at once. I fain would see the man.

JOCASTA: He shall be brought; but wherefore summon him?

OEDIPUS: Lady, I fear my tongue has overrun
Discretion; therefore I would question him.

JOCASTA: Well, he shall come, but may not I too claim
To share the burden of thy heart, my king?

OEDIPUS: And thou shalt not be frustrate of thy wish.
Now my imaginings have gone so far.
Who has a higher claim that thou to hear
My tale of dire adventures? Listen then.
My sire was Polybus of Corinth, and
My mother Merope, a Dorian;
And I was held the foremost citizen,
Till a strange thing befell me, strange indeed,
Yet scarce deserving all the heat it stirred.
A roisterer at some banquet, flown with wine,
Shouted "Thou art not true son of thy sire."
It irked me, but I stomached for the nonce
The insult; on the morrow I sought out
My mother and my sire and questioned them.
They were indignant at the random slur
Cast on my parentage and did their best
To comfort me, but still the venomed barb
Rankled, for still the scandal spread and grew.
So privily without their leave I went
To Delphi, and Apollo sent me back
Baulked of the knowledge that I came to seek.
But other grievous things he prophesied,
Woes, lamentations, mourning, portents dire;
To wit I should defile my mother's bed
And raise up seed too loathsome to behold,

And slay the father from whose loins I sprang.
Then, lady,--thou shalt hear the very truth--
As I drew near the triple-branching roads,
A herald met me and a man who sat
In a car drawn by colts--as in thy tale--
The man in front and the old man himself
Threatened to thrust me rudely from the path,
Then jostled by the charioteer in wrath
I struck him, and the old man, seeing this,
Watched till I passed and from his car brought down
Full on my head the double-pointed goad.
Yet was I quits with him and more; one stroke
Of my good staff sufficed to fling him clean
Out of the chariot seat and laid him prone.
And so I slew them every one. But if
Betwixt this stranger there was aught in common
With Laius, who more miserable than I,
What mortal could you find more god-abhorred?
Wretch whom no sojourner, no citizen
May harbor or address, whom all are bound
To harry from their homes. And this same curse
Was laid on me, and laid by none but me.
Yea with these hands all gory I pollute
The bed of him I slew. Say, am I vile?
Am I not utterly unclean, a wretch
Doomed to be banished, and in banishment
Forgo the sight of all my dearest ones,
And never tread again my native earth;
Or else to wed my mother and slay my sire,
Polybus, who begat me and upreared?
If one should say, this is the handiwork
Of some inhuman power, who could blame
His judgment? But, ye pure and awful gods,
Forbid, forbid that I should see that day!
May I be blotted out from living men
Ere such a plague spot set on me its brand!

CHORUS: We too, O king, are troubled; but till thou
Hast questioned the survivor, still hope on.

OEDIPUS: My hope is faint, but still enough survives
To bid me bide the coming of this herd.

JOCASTA: Suppose him here, what wouldst thou learn of him?

OEDIPUS: I'll tell thee, lady; if his tale agrees
With thine, I shall have 'scaped calamity.

JOCASTA: And what of special import did I say?

OEDIPUS: In thy report of what the herdsman said
Laius was slain by robbers; now if he
Still speaks of robbers, not a robber, I
Slew him not; "one" with "many" cannot square.
But if he says one lonely wayfarer,
The last link wanting to my guilt is forged.

JOCASTA: Well, rest assured, his tale ran thus at first,

Nor can he now retract what then he said;
Not I alone but all our townsfolk heard it.
E'en should he vary somewhat in his story,
He cannot make the death of Laius
In any wise jump with the oracle.
For Loxias said expressly he was doomed
To die by my child's hand, but he, poor babe,
He shed no blood, but perished first himself.
So much for divination. Henceforth I
Will look for signs neither to right nor left.

OEDIPUS: Thou reasonest well. Still I would have thee send
And fetch the bondsman hither. See to it.

JOCASTA: That will I straightway. Come, let us within.
I would do nothing that my lord mislikes.

Exeunt OEDIPUS and JOCASTA.

CHORUS (strophe 1):

My lot be still to lead
The life of innocence and fly
Irreverence in word or deed,
To follow still those laws ordained on high
Whose birthplace is the bright ethereal sky
No mortal birth they own,
Olympus their progenitor alone:
Ne'er shall they slumber in oblivion cold,
The god in them is strong and grows not old.

(antistrophe 1)

Of insolence is bred
The tyrant; insolence full blown,
With empty riches surfeited,
Scales the precipitous height and grasps the throne.
Then topples o'er and lies in ruin prone;
No foothold on that dizzy steep.
But O may Heaven the true patriot keep
Who burns with emulous zeal to serve the State.
God is my help and hope, on him I wait.

(strophe 2)

But the proud sinner, or in word or deed,
That will not Justice heed,
Nor reverence the shrine
Of images divine,
Perdition seize his vain imaginings,
If, urged by greed profane,
He grasps at ill-got gain,
And lays an impious hand on holiest things.
Who when such deeds are done
Can hope heaven's bolts to shun?
If sin like this to honor can aspire,
Why dance I still and lead the sacred choir?

(antistrophe 2)

No more I'll seek earth's central oracle,
Or Abae's hallowed cell,
Nor to Olympia bring
My votive offering.
If before all God's truth be not bade plain.
O Zeus, reveal thy might,
King, if thou'rt named aright
Omnipotent, all-seeing, as of old;
For Laius is forgot;
His weird, men heed it not;
Apollo is forsook and faith grows cold.

Enter JOCASTA.

JOCASTA: My lords, ye look amazed to see your queen
With wreaths and gifts of incense in her hands.
I had a mind to visit the high shrines,
For Oedipus is overwrought, alarmed
With terrors manifold. He will not use
His past experience, like a man of sense,
To judge the present need, but lends an ear
To any croaker if he augurs ill.
Since then my counsels naught avail, I turn
To thee, our present help in time of trouble,
Apollo, Lord Lycean, and to thee
My prayers and supplications here I bring.
Lighten us, lord, and cleanse us from this curse!
For now we all are cowed like mariners
Who see their helmsman dumbstruck in the storm.

Enter Corinthian MESSENGER.

MESSENGER: My masters, tell me where the palace is
Of Oedipus; or better, where's the king.

CHORUS: Here is the palace and he bides within;
This is his queen the mother of his children.

MESSENGER: All happiness attend her and the house,
Blessed is her husband and her marriage-bed.

JOCASTA: My greetings to thee, stranger; thy fair words
Deserve a like response. But tell me why
Thou comest--what thy need or what thy news.

MESSENGER: Good for thy consort and the royal house.

JOCASTA: What may it be? Whose messenger art thou?

MESSENGER: The Isthmian commons have resolved to make
Thy husband king--so 'twas reported there.

JOCASTA: What! is not aged Polybus still king?

MESSENGER: No, verily; he's dead and in his grave.

JOCASTA: What! is he dead, the sire of Oedipus?

MESSENGER: If I speak falsely, may I die myself.

JOCASTA: Quick, maiden, bear these tidings to my lord.
Ye god-sent oracles, where stand ye now!
This is the man whom Oedipus long shunned,
In dread to prove his murderer; and now
He dies in nature's course, not by his hand.

Enter OEDIPUS.

OEDIPUS: My wife, my queen, Jocasta, why hast thou
Summoned me from my palace?

JOCASTA: Hear this man,
And as thou hearest judge what has become
Of all those awe-inspiring oracles.

OEDIPUS: Who is this man, and what his news for me?

JOCASTA: He comes from Corinth and his message this:
Thy father Polybus hath passed away.

OEDIPUS: What? let me have it, stranger, from thy mouth.

MESSENGER: If I must first make plain beyond a doubt
My message, know that Polybus is dead.

OEDIPUS: By treachery, or by sickness visited?

MESSENGER: One touch will send an old man to his rest.

OEDIPUS: So of some malady he died, poor man.

MESSENGER: Yes, having measured the full span of years.

OEDIPUS: Out on it, lady! why should one regard
The Pythian hearth or birds that scream i' the air?
Did they not point at me as doomed to slay
My father? but he's dead and in his grave
And here am I who ne'er unsheathed a sword;
Unless the longing for his absent son
Killed him and so I slew him in a sense.
But, as they stand, the oracles are dead--
Dust, ashes, nothing, dead as Polybus.

JOCASTA: Say, did not I foretell this long ago?

OEDIPUS: Thou didst: but I was misled by my fear.

JOCASTA: Then let I no more weigh upon thy soul.

OEDIPUS: Must I not fear my mother's marriage bed.

JOCASTA: Why should a mortal man, the sport of chance,
With no assured foreknowledge, be afraid?
Best live a careless life from hand to mouth.
This wedlock with thy mother fear not thou.
How oft it chances that in dreams a man
Has wed his mother! He who least regards
Such brainsick phantasies lives most at ease.

OEDIPUS: I should have shared in full thy confidence,
Were not my mother living; since she lives
Though half convinced I still must live in dread.

JOCASTA: And yet thy sire's death lights out darkness much.

OEDIPUS: Much, but my fear is touching her who lives.

MESSENGER: Who may this woman be whom thus you fear?

OEDIPUS: Merope, stranger, wife of Polybus.

MESSENGER: And what of her can cause you any fear?

OEDIPUS: A heaven-sent oracle of dread import.

MESSENGER: A mystery, or may a stranger hear it?

OEDIPUS: Aye, 'tis no secret. Loxias once foretold
That I should mate with mine own mother, and shed
With my own hands the blood of my own sire.
Hence Corinth was for many a year to me
A home distant; and I trove abroad,
But missed the sweetest sight, my parents' face.

MESSENGER: Was this the fear that exiled thee from home?

OEDIPUS: Yea, and the dread of slaying my own sire.

MESSENGER: Why, since I came to give thee pleasure, King,
Have I not rid thee of this second fear?

OEDIPUS: Well, thou shalt have due guerdon for thy pains.

MESSENGER: Well, I confess what chiefly made me come
Was hope to profit by thy coming home.

OEDIPUS: Nay, I will ne'er go near my parents more.

MESSENGER: My son, 'tis plain, thou know'st not what thou doest.

OEDIPUS: How so, old man? For heaven's sake tell me all.

MESSENGER: If this is why thou dreadest to return.

OEDIPUS: Yea, lest the god's word be fulfilled in me.

MESSENGER: Lest through thy parents thou shouldst be accursed?

OEDIPUS: This and none other is my constant dread.

MESSENGER: Dost thou not know thy fears are baseless all?

OEDIPUS: How baseless, if I am their very son?

MESSENGER: Since Polybus was naught to thee in blood.

OEDIPUS: What say'st thou? was not Polybus my sire?

MESSENGER: As much thy sire as I am, and no more.

OEDIPUS: My sire no more to me than one who is naught?

MESSENGER: Since I begat thee not, no more did he.

OEDIPUS: What reason had he then to call me son?

MESSENGER: Know that he took thee from my hands, a gift.

OEDIPUS: Yet, if no child of his, he loved me well.

MESSENGER: A childless man till then, he warmed to thee.

OEDIPUS: A foundling or a purchased slave, this child?

MESSENGER: I found thee in Cithaeron's wooded glens.

OEDIPUS: What led thee to explore those upland glades?

MESSENGER: My business was to tend the mountain flocks.

OEDIPUS: A vagrant shepherd journeying for hire?

MESSENGER: True, but thy savior in that hour, my son.

OEDIPUS: My savior? from what harm? what ailed me then?

MESSENGER: Those ankle joints are evidence enow.

OEDIPUS: Ah, why remind me of that ancient sore?

MESSENGER: I loosed the pin that riveted thy feet.

OEDIPUS: Yes, from my cradle that dread brand I bore.

MESSENGER: Whence thou deriv'st the name that still is thine.

OEDIPUS: Who did it? I adjure thee, tell me who
Say, was it father, mother?

MESSENGER: I know not.
The man from whom I had thee may know more.

OEDIPUS: What, did another find me, not thyself?

MESSENGER: Not I; another shepherd gave thee me.

OEDIPUS: Who was he? Would'st thou know again the man?

MESSENGER: He passed indeed for one of Laius' house.

OEDIPUS: The king who ruled the country long ago?

MESSENGER: The same: he was a herdsman of the king.

OEDIPUS: And is he living still for me to see him?

MESSENGER: His fellow-countrymen should best know that.

OEDIPUS: Doth any bystander among you know
The herd he speaks of, or by seeing him
Afield or in the city? answer straight!
The hour hath come to clear this business up.

CHORUS: Methinks he means none other than the hind
Whom thou anon wert fain to see; but that
Our queen Jocasta best of all could tell.

OEDIPUS: Madam, dost know the man we sent to fetch?
Is the same of whom the stranger speaks?

JOCASTA: Who is the man? What matter? Let it be.
'Twere waste of thought to weigh such idle words.

OEDIPUS: No, with such guiding clues I cannot fail
To bring to light the secret of my birth.

JOCASTA: Oh, as thou carest for thy life, give o'er
This quest. Enough the anguish I endure.

OEDIPUS: Be of good cheer; though I be proved the son
Of a bondwoman, aye, through three descents
Triply a slave, thy honor is unsmirched.

JOCASTA: Yet humor me, I pray thee; do not this.

OEDIPUS: I cannot; I must probe this matter home.

JOCASTA: 'Tis for thy sake I advise thee for the best.

OEDIPUS: I grow impatient of this best advice.

JOCASTA: Ah mayst thou ne'er discover who thou art!

OEDIPUS: Go, fetch me here the herd, and leave yon woman
To glory in her pride of ancestry.

JOCASTA: O woe is thee, poor wretch! With that last word
I leave thee, henceforth silent evermore.

Exit JOCASTA.

CHORUS: Why, Oedipus, why stung with passionate grief
Hath the queen thus departed? Much I fear
From this dead calm will burst a storm of woes.

OEDIPUS: Let the storm burst, my fixed resolve still holds,

To learn my lineage, be it ne'er so low.
It may be she with all a woman's pride
Thinks scorn of my base parentage. But I
Who rank myself as Fortune's favorite child,
The giver of good gifts, shall not be shamed.
She is my mother and the changing moons
My brethren, and with them I wax and wane.
Thus sprung why should I fear to trace my birth?
Nothing can make me other than I am.

CHORUS (strophe):

If my soul prophetic err not, if my wisdom aught avail,

Thee, Cithaeron, I shall hail,
As the nurse and foster-mother of our Oedipus shall greet

Ere tomorrow's full moon rises, and exalt thee as is meet.

Dance and song shall hymn thy praises, lover of our royal race.

Phoebus, may my words find grace!

(antistrophe)

Child, who bare thee, nymph or goddess? sure thy sure was more than man,
Haply the hill-roamer Pan.
Of did Loxias beget thee, for he haunts the upland wold;
Or Cyllene's lord, or Bacchus, dweller on the hilltops cold?
Did some Heliconian Oread give him thee, a new-born joy?
Nymphs with whom he love to toy?

OEDIPUS: Elders, if I, who never yet before
Have met the man, may make a guess, methinks
I see the herdsman who we long have sought;
His time-worn aspect matches with the years
Of yonder aged messenger; besides
I seem to recognize the men who bring him
As servants of my own. But you, perchance,
Having in past days known or seen the herd,
May better by sure knowledge my surmise.

CHORUS: I recognize him; one of Laius' house;
A simple hind, but true as any man.

Enter HERDSMAN.

OEDIPUS: Corinthian, stranger, I address thee first,
Is this the man thou meanest!

MESSENGER: This is he.

OEDIPUS: And now old man, look up and answer all
I ask thee. Wast thou once of Laius' house?

HERDSMAN: I was, a thrall, not purchased but home-bred.

OEDIPUS: What was thy business? how wast thou employed?

HERDSMAN: The best part of my life I tended sheep.

OEDIPUS: What were the pastures thou didst most frequent?

HERDSMAN: Cithaeron and the neighboring alps.

OEDIPUS: Then there
Thou must have known yon man, at least by fame?

HERDSMAN: Yon man? in what way? what man dost thou mean?

OEDIPUS: The man here, having met him in past times...

HERDSMAN: Off-hand I cannot call him well to mind.

MESSENGER: No wonder, master. But I will revive
His blunted memories. Sure he can recall
What time together both we drove our flocks,
He two, I one, on the Cithaeron range,
For three long summers; I his mate from spring
Till rose Arcturus; then in winter time
I led mine home, he his to Laius' folds.
Did these things happen as I say, or no?

HERDSMAN: 'Tis long ago, but all thou say'st is true.

MESSENGER: Well, thou mast then remember giving me
A child to rear as my own foster-son?

HERDSMAN: Why dost thou ask this question? What of that?

MESSENGER: Friend, he that stands before thee was that child.

HERDSMAN: A plague upon thee! Hold thy wanton tongue!

OEDIPUS: Softly, old man, rebuke him not; thy words
Are more deserving chastisement than his.

HERDSMAN: O best of masters, what is my offense?

OEDIPUS: Not answering what he asks about the child.

HERDSMAN: He speaks at random, babbles like a fool.

OEDIPUS: If thou lack'st grace to speak, I'll loose thy tongue.

HERDSMAN: For mercy's sake abuse not an old man.

OEDIPUS: Arrest the villain, seize and pinion him!

HERDSMAN: Alack, alack!
What have I done? what wouldst thou further learn?

OEDIPUS: Didst give this man the child of whom he asks?

HERDSMAN: I did; and would that I had died that day!

OEDIPUS: And die thou shalt unless thou tell the truth.

HERDSMAN: But, if I tell it, I am doubly lost.

OEDIPUS: The knave methinks will still prevaricate.

HERDSMAN: Nay, I confessed I gave it long ago.

OEDIPUS: Whence came it? was it thine, or given to thee?

HERDSMAN: I had it from another, 'twas not mine.

OEDIPUS: From whom of these our townsmen, and what house?

HERDSMAN: Forbear for God's sake, master, ask no more.

OEDIPUS: If I must question thee again, thou'rt lost.

HERDSMAN: Well then--it was a child of Laius' house.

OEDIPUS: Slave-born or one of Laius' own race?

HERDSMAN: Ah me!
I stand upon the perilous edge of speech.

OEDIPUS: And I of hearing, but I still must hear.

HERDSMAN Know then the child was by repute his own,
But she within, thy consort best could tell.

OEDIPUS: What! she, she gave it thee?

HERDSMAN: 'Tis so, my king.

OEDIPUS: With what intent?

HERDSMAN: To make away with it.

OEDIPUS: What, she its mother.

HERDSMAN: Fearing a dread weird.

OEDIPUS: What weird?

HERDSMAN: 'Twas told that he should slay his sire.

OEDIPUS: What didst thou give it then to this old man?

HERDSMAN: Through pity, master, for the babe. I thought
He'd take it to the country whence he came;
But he preserved it for the worst of woes.
For if thou art in sooth what this man saith,
God pity thee! thou wast to misery born.

OEDIPUS: Ah me! ah me! all brought to pass, all true!
O light, may I behold thee nevermore!
I stand a wretch, in birth, in wedlock cursed,
A parricide, incestuously, triply cursed!

Exit OEDIPUS.

CHORUS (strophe 1):

Races of mortal man
Whose life is but a span,
I count ye but the shadow of a shade!
For he who most doth know
Of bliss, hath but the show;
A moment, and the visions pale and fade.
Thy fall, O Oedipus, thy piteous fall
Warns me none born of women blest to call.

(antistrophe 1)

For he of marksmen best,
O Zeus, outshot the rest,
And won the prize supreme of wealth and power.
By him the vulture maid
Was quelled, her witchery laid;
He rose our savior and the land's strong tower.
We hailed thee king and from that day adored
Of mighty Thebes the universal lord.

(strophe 2)

O heavy hand of fate!
Who now more desolate,
Whose tale more sad than thine, whose lot more dire?
O Oedipus, discrowned head,
Thy cradle was thy marriage bed;
One harborage sufficed for son and sire.
How could the soil thy father eared so long
Endure to bear in silence such a wrong?

(antistrophe 2)

All-seeing Time hath caught
Guilt, and to justice brought
The son and sire commingled in one bed.
O child of Laius' ill-starred race
Would I had ne'er beheld thy face;
I raise for thee a dirge as o'er the dead.
Yet, sooth to say, through thee I drew new breath,
And now through thee I feel a second death.

Enter SECOND MESSENGER.

SECOND MESSENGER: Most grave and reverend senators of Thebes,

What Deeds ye soon must hear, what sights behold
How will ye mourn, if, true-born patriots,
Ye reverence still the race of Labdacus!
Not Ister nor all Phasis' flood, I ween,
Could wash away the blood-stains from this house,
The ills it shrouds or soon will bring to light,
Ills wrought of malice, not unwittingly.
The worst to bear are self-inflicted wounds.

CHORUS: Grievous enough for all our tears and groans
Our past calamities; what canst thou add?

SECOND MESSENGER: My tale is quickly told and quickly heard.
Our sovereign lady queen Jocasta's dead.

CHORUS: Alas, poor queen! how came she by her death?

SECOND MESSENGER: By her own hand. And all the horror of it,
Not having seen, yet cannot comprehend.
Nathless, as far as my poor memory serves,
I will relate the unhappy lady's woe.
When in her frenzy she had passed inside
The vestibule, she hurried straight to win
The bridal-chamber, clutching at her hair
With both her hands, and, once within the room,
She shut the doors behind her with a crash.
"Laius," she cried, and called her husband dead
Long, long ago; her thought was of that child

By him begot, the son by whom the sire
Was murdered and the mother left to breed
With her own seed, a monstrous progeny.
Then she bewailed the marriage bed whereon
Poor wretch, she had conceived a double brood,
Husband by husband, children by her child.
What happened after that I cannot tell,
Nor how the end befell, for with a shriek
Burst on us Oedipus; all eyes were fixed
On Oedipus, as up and down he strode,
Nor could we mark her agony to the end.
For stalking to and fro "A sword!" he cried,
"Where is the wife, no wife, the teeming womb
That bore a double harvest, me and mine?"
And in his frenzy some supernal power
(No mortal, surely, none of us who watched him)
Guided his footsteps; with a terrible shriek,
As though one beckoned him, he crashed against
The folding doors, and from their staples forced
The wrenched bolts and hurled himself within.
Then we beheld the woman hanging there,
A running noose entwined about her neck.
But when he saw her, with a maddened roar
He loosed the cord; and when her wretched corpse
Lay stretched on earth, what followed--O 'twas dread!
He tore the golden brooches that upheld
Her queenly robes, upraised them high and smote
Full on his eye-balls, uttering words like these:
"No more shall ye behold such sights of woe,
Deeds I have suffered and myself have wrought;
Henceforward quenched in darkness shall ye see
Those ye should ne'er have seen; now blind to those
Whom, when I saw, I vainly yearned to know."
Such was the burden of his moan, whereto,
Not once but oft, he struck with his hand uplift
His eyes, and at each stroke the ensanguined orbs
Bedewed his beard, not oozing drop by drop,
But one black gory downpour, thick as hail.
Such evils, issuing from the double source,
Have whelmed them both, confounding man and wife.
Till now the storied fortune of this house
Was fortunate indeed; but from this day
Woe, lamentation, ruin, death, disgrace,
All ills that can be named, all, all are theirs.

CHORUS: But hath he still no respite from his pain?

SECOND MESSENGER: He cries, "Unbar the doors
and let all Thebes
Behold the slayer of his sire, his mother's--"
That shameful word my lips may not repeat.
He vows to fly self-banished from the land,
Nor stay to bring upon his house the curse
Himself had uttered; but he has no strength
Nor one to guide him, and his torture's more
Than man can suffer, as yourselves will see.
For lo, the palace portals are unbarred,
And soon ye shall behold a sight so sad
That he who must abhorred would pity it.

Enter OEDIPUS blinded.

CHORUS: Woeful sight! more woeful none
These sad eyes have looked upon.
Whence this madness? None can tell
Who did cast on thee his spell, prowling all thy life around,

Leaping with a demon bound.
Hapless wretch! how can I brook
On thy misery to look?
Though to gaze on thee I yearn,
Much to question, much to learn,
Horror-struck away I turn.

OEDIPUS: Ah me! ah woe is me!
Ah whither am I borne!
How like a ghost forlorn
My voice flits from me on the air!
On, on the demon goads. The end, ah where?

CHORUS: An end too dread to tell, too dark to see.

OEDIPUS (strophe 1):

Dark, dark! The horror of darkness, like a shroud,
Wraps me and bears me on through mist and cloud.
Ah me, ah me! What spasms athwart me shoot,
What pangs of agonizing memory?

CHORUS: No marvel if in such a plight thou feel'st
The double weight of past and present woes.

OEDIPUS (antistrophe 1)

Ah friend, still loyal, constant still and kind,
Thou carest for the blind.
I know thee near, and though bereft of eyes,
Thy voice I recognize.

CHORUS: O doer of dread deeds, how couldst thou mar
Thy vision thus? What demon goaded thee?

OEDIPUS (strophe 2):

Apollo, friend, Apollo, he it was
That brought these ills to pass;
But the right hand that dealt the blow
Was mine, none other. How,
How, could I longer see when sight
Brought no delight?

CHORUS: Alas! 'tis as thou sayest.

OEDIPUS: Say, friends, can any look or voice
Or touch of love henceforth my heart rejoice?
Haste, friends, no fond delay,
Take the twice cursed away
Far from all ken,
The man abhorred of gods, accursed of men.

CHORUS: O thy despair well suits thy desperate case.
Would I had never looked upon thy face!

OEDIPUS (antistrophe 2):

My curse on him whoe'er unrived
The waif's fell fetters and my life revived!
He meant me well, yet had he left me there,
He had saved my friends and me a world of care.

CHORUS: I too had wished it so.

OEDIPUS: Then had I never come to shed
My father's blood nor climbed my mother's bed;
The monstrous offspring of a womb defiled,
Co-mate of him who gendered me, and child.
Was ever man before afflicted thus,
Like Oedipus.

CHORUS: I cannot say that thou hast counseled well,
For thou wert better dead than living blind.

OEDIPUS: What's done was well done. Thou canst never shake
My firm belief. A truce to argument.
For, had I sight, I know not with what eyes
I could have met my father in the shades,
Or my poor mother, since against the twain
I sinned, a sin no gallows could atone.
Aye, but, ye say, the sight of children joys
A parent's eyes. What, born as mine were born?
No, such a sight could never bring me joy;
Nor this fair city with its battlements,
Its temples and the statues of its gods,
Sights from which I, now wretchedst of all,
Once ranked the foremost Theban in all Thebes,
By my own sentence am cut off, condemned
By my own proclamation 'gainst the wretch,
The miscreant by heaven itself declared
Unclean--and of the race of Laius.
Thus branded as a felon by myself,
How had I dared to look you in the face?
Nay, had I known a way to choke the springs
Of hearing, I had never shrunk to make
A dungeon of this miserable frame,
Cut off from sight and hearing; for 'tis bliss to bide in
regions sorrow cannot reach.
Why didst thou harbor me, Cithaeron, why
Didst thou not take and slay me? Then I never
Had shown to men the secret of my birth.
O Polybus, O Corinth, O my home,
Home of my ancestors (so wast thou called)
How fair a nursling then I seemed, how foul
The canker that lay festering in the bud!
Now is the blight revealed of root and fruit.
Ye triple high-roads, and thou hidden glen,
Coppice, and pass where meet the three-branched ways,
Ye drank my blood, the life-blood these hands spilt,
My father's; do ye call to mind perchance
Those deeds of mine ye witnessed and the work
I wrought thereafter when I came to Thebes?
O fatal wedlock, thou didst give me birth,
And, having borne me, sowed again my seed,
Mingling the blood of fathers, brothers, children,
Brides, wives and mothers, an incestuous brood,
All horrors that are wrought beneath the sun,
Horrors so foul to name them were unmeet.
O, I adjure you, hide me anywhere
Far from this land, or slay me straight, or cast me
Down to the depths of ocean out of sight.
Come hither, deign to touch an abject wretch;
Draw near and fear not; I myself must bear
The load of guilt that none but I can share.

Enter CREON.

CREON: Lo, here is Creon, the one man to grant
Thy prayer by action or advice, for he
Is left the State's sole guardian in thy stead.

OEDIPUS: Ah me! what words to accost him can I find?
What cause has he to trust me? In the past
I have bee proved his rancorous enemy.

CREON: Not in derision, Oedipus, I come
Nor to upbraid thee with thy past misdeeds.

To BYSTANDERS.

But shame upon you! if ye feel no sense
Of human decencies, at least revere
The Sun whose light beholds and nurtures all.
Leave not thus nakedly for all to gaze at
A horror neither earth nor rain from heaven
Nor light will suffer. Lead him straight within,
For it is seemly that a kinsman's woes
Be heard by kin and seen by kin alone.

OEDIPUS: O listen, since thy presence comes to me
A shock of glad surprise--so noble thou,
And I so vile--O grant me one small boon.
I ask it not on my behalf, but thine.

CREON: And what the favor thou wouldst crave of me?

OEDIPUS: Forth from thy borders thrust me with all speed;
Set me within some vasty desert where
No mortal voice shall greet me any more.

CREON: This had I done already, but I deemed
It first behooved me to consult the god.

OEDIPUS: His will was set forth fully--to destroy
The parricide, the scoundrel; and I am he.

CREON: Yea, so he spake, but in our present plight
'Twere better to consult the god anew.

OEDIPUS: Dare ye inquire concerning such a wretch?

CREON: Yea, for thyself wouldst credit now his word.

OEDIPUS: Aye, and on thee in all humility
I lay this charge: let her who lies within
Receive such burial as thou shalt ordain;
Such rites 'tis thine, as brother, to perform.
But for myself, O never let my Thebes,
The city of my sires, be doomed to bear
The burden of my presence while I live.
No, let me be a dweller on the hills,
On yonder mount Cithaeron, famed as mine,
My tomb predestined for me by my sire
And mother, while they lived, that I may die
Slain as they sought to slay me, when alive.

This much I know full surely, nor disease
Shall end my days, nor any common chance;
For I had ne'er been snatched from death, unless
I was predestined to some awful doom.
So be it. I reck not how Fate deals with me
But my unhappy children--for my sons
Be not concerned, O Creon, they are men,
And for themselves, where'er they be, can fend.
But for my daughters twain, poor innocent maids,
Who ever sat beside me at the board
Sharing my viands, drinking of my cup,
For them, I pray thee, care, and, if thou willst,
O might I feel their touch and make my moan.
Hear me, O prince, my noble-hearted prince!
Could I but blindly touch them with my hands
I'd think they still were mine, as when I saw.

ANTIGONE and ISMENE are led in.

What say I? can it be my pretty ones
Whose sobs I hear? Has Creon pitied me
And sent me my two darlings? Can this be?

CREON: 'Tis true; 'twas I procured thee this delight,
Knowing the joy they were to thee of old.

OEDIPUS: God speed thee! and as meed for bringing them
May Providence deal with thee kindlier
Than it has dealt with me! O children mine,
Where are ye? Let me clasp you with these hands,
A brother's hands, a father's; hands that made
Lack-luster sockets of his once bright eyes;
Hands of a man who blindly, recklessly,
Became your sire by her from whom he sprang.
Though I cannot behold you, I must weep
In thinking of the evil days to come,
The slights and wrongs that men will put upon you.
Where'er ye go to feast or festival,
No merrymaking will it prove for you,
But oft abashed in tears ye will return.
And when ye come to marriageable years,
Where's the bold wooers who will jeopardize
To take unto himself such disrepute
As to my children's children still must cling,
For what of infamy is lacking here?
"Their father slew his father, sowed the seed
Where he himself was gendered, and begat
These maidens at the source wherefrom he sprang."
Such are the gibes that men will cast at you.
Who then will wed you? None, I ween, but ye
Must pine, poor maids, in single barrenness.

O Prince, Menoeceus' son, to thee, I turn,
With the it rests to father them, for we
Their natural parents, both of us, are lost.
O leave them not to wander poor, unwed,
Thy kin, nor let them share my low estate.
O pity them so young, and but for thee
All destitute. Thy hand upon it, Prince.
To you, my children I had much to say,
Were ye but ripe to hear. Let this suffice:
Pray ye may find some home and live content,
And may your lot prove happier than your sire's.

CREON: Thou hast had enough of weeping; pass within.

OEDIPUS: I must obey,
Though 'tis grievous.

CREON: Weep not, everything must have its day.

OEDIPUS: Well I go, but on conditions.

CREON: What thy terms for going, say.

OEDIPUS: Send me from the land an exile.

CREON: Ask this of the gods, not me.

OEDIPUS: But I am the gods' abhorrence.

CREON: Then they soon will grant thy plea.

OEDIPUS: Lead me hence, then, I am willing.

CREON: Come, but let thy children go.

OEDIPUS: Rob me not of these my children!

CREON: Crave not mastery in all,
For the mastery that raised thee was thy bane and wrought thy fall.

CHORUS: Look ye, countrymen and Thebans, this is Oedipus the great,

He who knew the Sphinx's riddle and was mightiest in our state.

Who of all our townsmen gazed not on his fame with envious eyes?

Now, in what a sea of troubles sunk and overwhelmed he lies!

Therefore wait to see life's ending ere thou count one mortal blest;

Wait till free from pain and sorrow he has gained his final rest.

THE END

Agamemnon by Aeschylus

The play was written by Aeschylus about a hero who fought in the Trojan War. He was the hero from Greece (Mycenae), and he was coming home as the hero. Unbeknown to him, he was actually going to be murdered by Clytemnestra, his wife. She was waiting for him to come home, but she would not forgive him for sacrificing their daughter for the sake of the country. Their daughter, Iphigenia, had to be sacrificed or terrible things would happen, such as Greece losing the war or the entire navy perishing due to a lack of wind for sailing. Agamemnon chose the country over his own flesh and blood. Other accounts are in the myth that Iphigenia was sent for by deception and chose to be sacrificed but at first she thought that she was going to be married to Achilles. Some accounts say that she first thought that she was being sent for to become the wife of Achilles, but instead she ended up giving up her own life for her country.

Ultimately, the play is about Agamemnon as he comes home to his wife, and what he has to confront. His wife does not forgive him for having their daughter sacrificed. To some he was a hero who won the war. To others he was not a hero at all. The play is supposed to raise questions. The reader or viewer knows that Agamemnon lost his daughter, but he or she does not know Agamemnon's role in the entire scenario. What could he have done? What is the role of a leader in a situation where one must defend one's country? This play also raises issues and asks questions which are universal and, partly due to this fact, the *Agamemnon* continues to be read and performed over and over again.

The Trojan Women by Euripides

Why did Euripides write the play *The Trojan Women*? It is said that Euripides may have been influenced by an actual attack on innocent people. In 416 B.C.E., the Athenians attacked the tiny, neutral island of Melos on the general principle that "if you are not with us, you must be against us." Athens won in one day. The women and children were sold into slavery and all the men were killed. Euripides opposed war and, supposedly, when he heard of this incident it influenced him to write the play.

The play raises questions, such as when it is proper to attack, who is allowed to attack during war, and what the rules of war should be, etc.

Archaic Greece

The Archaic Greek period lasted from about 800–480 B.C.E. At this time, in the Western world, a god was portrayed as a male, nude human for the first time. It was a form not to be portrayed as a human. It was not to be imaged as a human male object. It was a form that in today's standard would be hard to imagine. However, it is to be imaged as a god. It is a form that for the first time in known Western history it was considered to be a "perfect being" that was to become at that time during the seventh century a representation of athleticism. That represented the perfection of orderly life and a godlike image. It represented balance and perfection, and it was called a *kouros*. The plural of kouros is *kouroi*, and the female version of kouros is *kore*.

During this time the temples became known as post-and-lintel structures and the music performed in ceremonies consisted of modes, which sound somewhat like modern-day scales (i.e., a progression of tones). According to Dennis Sporre, the Greeks held that the Dorian mode possessed a warlike feeling (*Reality* 114).

Greek Classical Sculpture

The sculpture of the Classical period was more representational than the archaic style. To many students, the Archaic-style smile looks unassuming. In short, Classical sculptures do not have emotional expressions, a characteristic that supposedly indicates perfection, extreme grace, and an orderly, balanced pattern called *kanon* (i.e., "rule" or "law"). This lack of emotional expression was used by sculptors during the Classical era with the hope of granting sculptures ideal proportions. Also, the features were idealized in Classical sculpture, which means that the sculptures looked perfect in shape and form—the figure looked better than any real human could actually look (Sporre).

Another feature seen in Classic Greek sculptures is the bent knee, which forces the body's weight to rest on one leg. There appears to be a slight curve—sometimes referred to as an s-shaped curve—when one looks at the shape of a sculpture from the Classical time frame. This s-shaped stance is a termed *Contrapposto*.

The *Iliad* by Homer

Set in twenty-four books, and exploring the *heroic ideal* with all its contradictions, the *Iliad* begins with an explanation of the quarrel between King Agamemnon (ad-uh-MEM-nahn), commander of the Greek army, and Achilles, the Greeks' greatest warrior. When the action opens, the Greeks have been besieging Troy for nine years, trying to rescue Helen, wife of Agamemnon's brother Menelaus (mehn-uh-LAY-uhs), from Paris, one of the sons of the Trojan King Priam (PRY-uhm). As a result of his quarrel with Agamemnon, Achilles leaves the Greek forces, taking his followers with him. Without Achilles, the Greeks suffer many losses. Unable to bear it when the Trojans set fire to the Greek fleet, one of Achilles' close friends asks permission to rejoin the fight. Achilles agrees and lends him his armor. When his friend is killed by the Trojan hero Hector, Achilles exacts revenge by killing Hector. Hector's father, King Priam, asks Achilles for his son's body so that it can be properly buried. Achilles agrees, and his anger is assuaged. The work ends with Hector's funeral.

Homer develops events on the battlefield and behind the lines of both adversaries. From his descriptions, an elaborate evocation emerges of the splendor and tragedy of war and the inconsistencies of mortals and gods. The heroes are types, not real people, and their characters were established in legend long before they were described in the epic poem. In the poem we find a careful structure that alternates between individual encounters and mass movements of opposing armies. The battle poetry uses recurring elements and motifs, but it has subtle variety resulting from the highly individualized episodes. Even in translation we witness the elevated language style, highly formal poetry we see again in the next chapter, for example, in the dramatic verse of the classical tragedian Aeschylus. Here is a brief extract from Book XX:

> So these now, the Achaians, beside the curved ships were arming
> around you, son of Peleus, insatieate of battle, while on the other side
> at the break of the plain the Trojans armed. But Zeus, from the many-
> folded peak of Olympos, told Themis to summon all the gods into
> assembly. She went everywhere, and told them to make their way to
> Zeus' house. There was no river who was not there, except only Ocean,
> there was not any one of the nymphs who live in the lovely graves, and
> the springs of rivers and grass of the meadow, who came not.
>
> These all assembling into the house of Zeus cloud gathering
> took places among the smooth-stone cloister walks which Hephaestus
> had built for Zeus the father by his craftsmanship and contrivance.
> So they were assembled within Zeus' house; and the shaker
> of the earth did not fail to hear the goddess, but came up among them
> from the sea, and sat in the midst of them, and asked Zeus of this
>   counsel:
> "Why, lord of the shining bolt, have you called the gods to assembly
> once more? Are you deliberating Achaians and Trojans? For the onset
>   of battle is almost broken to flame between them."
> In turn Zeus who gathers the clouds spoke to him in answer:
> "You have seen, shaker of the earth, the counsel within me,
> and why I gathered you. I think of these men though they are dying.
> Even so, I shall stay here upon the fold of Olympos sitting still, watch,
>   to pleasure my heart. Meanwhile all you others

> go down, wherever you may go among the Achaians and Trojans
> and give help to either side, as your own pleasure directs you,
> for if we leave Achilles alone to fight with the Trojans they will not
> even for a little hold off swift-footed Peleion.
> For even before now they would tremble whenever they saw him,
> and now, when his heart if grieved and angered for his companion's
> death, I fear against destiny he may storm their fortress."

So spoke the son of Kronos and woke the incessant battle.

Greek Hellenistic Sculpture

Sculpture from the Classical Hellenistic period, though it came later, was similar to Classical Greek sculpture. The Hellenistic style expressed more emotion than Classical style, and sculptures in this style appeared to move and show action. At times, the subject matter was violent and conveyed warlike themes.

Sculpture of Laocoön and Sons (a famous work considered to be Hellenistic)

Hellenistic sculptures also sometimes differ from Classical sculptures since they may tell a story about an incident. One famous story by Homer—supposed author of *The Iliad* and *The Odyssey*—about the Trojan War and its heroes, inspired a sculpture that captures the moment when a serpent is sent by the god Poseidon to destroy his two sons and the priest Laocoön. One of the most well-known Hellenistic sculptures is this one which has been called the *Laocoön and Sons*. This eight-foot marble sculpture was created in the early first century A.D. and is now housed in the Vatican Museums in Rome at the Vatican Museum Agesander, Athenodoru, and Polydorus of Rhodes.

Characteristics of the Greek Types of Sculptures:

Archaic	Classical	Hellenistic
Stationary	S-shape curve	Motion
Stance feet side by side	Contrapposto stance	Active and moving
Lacking expression	Emotional retraint	Expressive

This is also called the Laocoön Group (Gilbert and McCarter). Allegedly, when traveling to the Vatican, Michelangelo was influenced by this particular sculpture—in fact, this sculpture provided the inspiration to sculpt his *Pieta*, which is in the chapel area of St. Peter's at the Vatican.

> **QUESTIONS**
>
> **Questions to Contemplate**
>
> What are some of the reasons why it is easier to remember poems and songs that rhyme and have melodies than words and phrases that do not?
>
> Are there any parallels between modern music and the Greeks' utilization of rhythm and poetry in their performances?

Characteristics

- Theater such as their Greek plays of tragedy and comedy
- Shapes of vases
- Names given to vases of the glazed figures (black and red figure)
- Mathematics especially geometry and Pythagorean theorem
- Physical form as a perfect being representing a godlike figure

Terms

Contrapposto stance: the way a sculptor designed Greek Classical sculpture during that time, which shows one foot in front of the other, a bent knee, and weight bearing on the opposite leg

Festival of Dionysus: held in ancient Greek times in Athens to honor the god of wine, through festivities such as plays

Idealized: in Greek art, during the Classical Period, the artist would portray the artist as perfect without flaws

Iphigenia: daughter of Agamemnon

Agamemnon: play written about the King of Mycenae whose name was Agamemnon, the brother of Menelaus who was Helen's husband

Kore: in Greek art starting with the Archaic Greek Period, this is a female form

Kouros: the term in the Ancient Greek Period to represent the male form

Sophocles: author who wrote the play *Oedipus the King*

Ancient Greek Accomplishments

In architecture: the ancient Greeks developed three major orders of columns, the Doric, Ionic, and Corinthian.

Democracy: the idea that democratic government would be considered to have started here.

Theater: inspired future generations and writers about Shakespeare and others

Geometry and the use of the golden mean (also referred to the perfect rectangle): used in construction of the Parthenon and other sites

Ceramics: provide a glimpse of ancient paintings

The writings of Homer: *Iliad* and *Odyssey*

The Parthenon: considered to be one of the best designed structures of the ancient world

Myths: stories about gods

Black and red figure pottery of shapes: kylix, amphora, and Krater

ANCIENT ROMAN PERIOD

Modern-day Rome is where the ancient city of Rome was, and some buildings from that great city such as the Pantheon and the Colosseum still remain. In order to fully understand how Rome came to be such an enormous and powerful empire in the ancient world, it is important to begin with the seventh century B.C.E. At that time, the Etruscan people inhabited the Italian peninsula (Gilbert and Mc-Carter 371). The Italian peninsula would eventually be part of the Roman Empire. The Romans would become the most powerful culture on the Mediterranean Sea, and their empire would stretch from modern-day Scotland to the Sahara Desert. Whether or not the early inhabitants, known as the Etruscans, came from the Near East is up for speculation. However, the Etruscans certainly influenced the development of Roman culture. The Etruscans were known for their mineral resources, and by the seventh and sixth centuries B.C.E. they were major exporters of fine painted pottery and black ceramic ware. Much of what is known about the Etruscans has come down to us from their art works and from their terra cotta burial coffins. The Etruscan sarcophagi, or coffins, are artifacts that serve as indicators of their lifestyle. At least they can give us a glimpse into the nature of Etruscan marriage relationships and how they felt about burying the dead. They left behind burial sites and decorated coffins, which were made of a clay-type material called terra cotta. Archaeologists have discovered that husbands and wives were placed in coffins side by side, and that in death they were reclining together in a single burial sarcophagas (Sayre 236).

Roman culture was partially influenced by the ways of the Etruscan culture. A few of the influences were street, masonry, and arch designs. The Etruscans also shaped Roman sanitation, engineering, and construction. The Roman practices of burying the dead in cemeteries and using terra cotta for coffins were borrowed from the Etruscans (Lamm and Cross 211).

The Greeks influenced the Romans. In the eighth century B.C.E., colonies developed in the southern part of modern-day Italy. A tourist can still observe some of the Greek architectural influences on ancient temples in the areas of Naples and Paestum. The temple of Hera at Paestum stands as a testament to that period. The Romans copied the orders, such as the Doric order, that were used in the Greek construction. On the Colosseum, one sees the use of all three orders as decorative elements on the building's exterior. The orders are utilized on many temples throughout Greece. The three orders are the Doric, the Ionic, and the Corinthian. The Doric order is the simplest of the three and has no base. The Ionic order has swirls on each side at the top and has a base. The Corinthian order is the most elaborate and has many curves and swirls. It also has a base. The Corinthian order is used on the Temple of Zeus. The Romans and the

Greeks shared the same pantheon of gods. But since the Romans and the Greeks spoke different languages, they had different names for the gods. For example, the Roman name for Zeus was Jupiter. An illustration of the Temple of Jupiter may also be labeled as the Temple of Zeus. The name that is used depends upon whether the text uses the Greek or the Latin terms. The Romans are said to have admired Greek art, and they imported many Greek works of art. They acquired the art from Greek merchants who transported sculptures by ship across the Mediterranean Sea from Greece to Rome. Many Greek artists were taken to Rome, where they produced sculpture en masse. Military leaders were represented in sculptures as symbols of power. The Roman leaders knew how to use art for their own political purposes.

The Romans established a republic and conquered the ancient Greeks. Julius Caesar (100–44 B.C.E.) became emperor, but he was assassinated. The republic then fell.

After Caesar's death, Emperor Augustus (63 B.C.E.–14 C.E.) initiated a short-lived period of peace. During this time, Rome became a center for architecture, city planning, transportation, and militarization. His period of rule marked a time of relative stability.

With the *Aenied* having been written by Virgil, Augustus had established for himself a propagandistic aim of justifying imperial power. Just as the *Aeneid* told the story of Aeneas the warrior who was a hero for the Roman people, the story was an attempt to parallel the Roman culture's *Iliad* and the *Odyssey* from the Greeks. Just like Homer's *Iliad* and the *Odyssey* had established the conventions of the day and laid out the basic cultural ties and commonalities, the Romans would have their own identity with the stories in the *Aeneid* (Bishop 92). "He kept the provinces under control and established strong defenses along the frontiers of the Roman Empire. He began to develop a civil service staffed by skilled administrators to help govern the empire. Trade flourished, and art and literature reached a high point during what has been called the Augustan Age" (*World Book Encyclopdia*).

The expanding Roman Empire conquered Egypt and brought an end to Ptolemaic rule in that region in 31 B.C.E. His huge empire flourished until Emperor Constantine moved the capital from Rome to Constantinople (modern-day Istanbul, Turkey). That ended the days of the Latin Empire (Dixon and Fleming 39).

The Romans dominated the Greeks militarily, but they were fascinated with the Greek theater, gods, sculpture, and architecture. For that reason, many of the Greek works come down through history from the Romans. Some of the sculptures that remain are only Roman copies of Greek originals. Original Greek sculptures were usually made of bronze, and the Romans copied them in stone. The Romans were very organized in their methods of city planning and used poured concrete to build monuments. They also pioneered an efficient road system and engineered an efficient system of aqueducts and sewers (Dixon and Fleming 40).

Sculptures demonstrated power. Augustus had supreme power and, in a well-known sculpture now in the Vatican Museum, "He portrayed himself as a near-deity" (Sayre 245). In this sculpture he is showing his obligation to the country. The sculpture is unusual in that his face is idealized. In most other Roman sculptures created at that time the face would have looked more like the individual it portrayed. In other words, the work would have been representational. In this work, the face appeared to be similar to a Greek sculpture, the Doryphoros (Spear-Bearer). The original sculpture of the Doryphorus was created around 450–440 B.C.E.

Augustus also wanted to be remembered and respected. Therefore he knew that he must have the people think of him as a ruler who was endowed with the right to rule from the gods. If he was to rule effectively and maintain his authority Augustus knew that he needed a plan. Therefore he sought to create a myth, or legend, which would idealize him in a Greek manner and portray him as a noble ruler. To accomplish this goal, he commissioned Virgil to write *The Aeneid*. It was written with many of the same elements as the Greek stories found in Homer's *Iliad*. Careful analysis of Augustus's sculpture from the Vatican Museum reveals that Virgil's ideas about Augustus' royal lineage are symbolically represented. Virgil traced his ancestry to Aeneas, the founder of Rome. Augustus' divine origin was represented in the sculpture by Cupid and Venus. Venus was said to be the mother of Aeneas. She was symbolized by the images of both the dolphin and Cupid as seen under the right leg of Augustus' sculpture. These symbols communicated the emperor's royal linage (Lamm and Cross 265). It is important to realize how Augustus used sculptures and literature to influence public opinion. He placed his sculpture in strategic locations around the city. He also represented himself in the likeness of a Greek and a ruler. That image helped him to achieve his leadership style. The public learned to honor and respect his leadership.

The Romans developed a water transport system using aqueducts. Parts of these aqueducts remain standing in France and are in excellent condition. Roads and bridges built by the Romans in the first and second centuries still stand and some even remain in use. At the time, it was said that all roads lead to Rome. Their transportation system set the modern-day standard. They invented a type of poured concrete, which was used on the construction of the Pantheon in Rome. The building was so revolutionary that an artist from the Renaissance studied the Pantheon's structure and design. The Romans have influenced future generations of builders. Many architects and engineers have studied Roman designs and domes over the centuries, and they have developed new ideas based on Roman plans and structures. The Romans left behind an important legacy.

The story of the founding of Rome was based on the traditional Etruscan legend of twin brothers named Romulus and Remus. The boys were abandoned on the shores of the Tiber River by their uncle, and rescued by a she-wolf. The she-wolf protected and fed them until a shepherd came along and brought them home to his wife to raise. When they became teenagers they often got into arguments. One day, during a heated argument, one of them was killed accidentally. Rome was named after Romulus, the one who lived. According to legend, Remus died around 753 B.C.E., and Romulus became the first King of Rome.

Roman sculpture tends to look more like the actual individual being portrayed than does Classical Greek sculpture. The Greek Hellenistic style, which was more decorative and sometimes told a story, was utilized more by the Romans. The Romans also mass-produced sculptures. Often they placed sculptures of their leaders in strategic areas around the city in order to commemorate a victory or to improve the leader's reputation. When a military leader returned from a victory, the conqueror would commission artwork, such as a triumphal arch, to be erected in his honor. Artists would also produce busts of a ruler's likeness with scars on his face to represent his bravery. This showed the public that it was important to fight for Rome and to be a good citizen.

Augustus of Prima Porta is the famous sculpture of Augustus in which he is shown in his role as commander in chief. "Riding a dolphin at his feet is a small Cupid, son of the goddess Venus, laying claim to the Julian family's divine descent from Venus and Aeneas." Though Augustus was over seventy years old when he died, he was always depicted as young and vigorous, choosing to portray himself, apparently, as the ideal leader rather than the wise, older *pater*.

Augustus was careful to maintain at least the trappings of the Republic. The Senate stayed in place, but Augustus soon eliminated the distinction between patricians and *equites* and fostered the careers of all capable individuals, whatever their origin. Some he made provincial governors, others administrators in the city, and he encouraged still others to enter political life. Soon the Senate was populated with many men who had never dreamed of politician-owed everything to Augustus. Their loyalty further solidified his power (Sayre 246).

Augustus was the adopted son of Julius Caesar, and became the first emperor of Rome when Caesar was assassinated on March 15, 44 B.C.E. Before Caesar, Rome had been a republic. Augustus restored peace and gained control of parts of modern-day Europe, North Africa, and the Near East.

Augustus (also known as Octavian) was a patron of the arts and he arranged for artistic patronage to pass through his office. Augustus also supported the construction of baths, theaters, triumphal arches, and a colonnaded main road leading to an administrative center in the middle of the city of Rome (Sayre 252). The time period of stability under Augustus became known as the *Pax Romana* or Roman Peace.

"Roman society was divided into citizens and non-citizens. There were three classes of citizens—patricians, the richest aristocrat; equites, the wealthy merchants; and plebeians, the ordinary citizens. All citizens were allowed to vote in elections and to serve in the army. They were also allowed to wear togas" (*Encyclopedia of World History*).

The Roman Army was originally formed to protect the city of Rome. It was made up largely of volunteer soldiers. General Marius (155–86 B.C.E.) reorganized the army into a more disciplined and efficient fighting force. Soldiers were paid wages and enlisted for a period of 20 to 25 years. Ordinary soldiers were grouped into units called legions; each legion was made up of about 5,000 men. The legions, in turn, were made up of smaller units called centuries. Each century contained eighty men. These were commanded by soldiers called centurions (*Encyclopedia of World History*).

Roman soldiers were well trained and well organized. Wearing heavy armor and plumed bronze or iron helmets, they were capable of marching about twenty miles a day carrying weapons, food, and a camping kit (*Encyclopedia of World History*).

The Romans told stories about their interpretation of the universe, which included various interpretations and revisions of the Greek gods. The list below gives the Greek and Roman names for some of the major gods and describes their functions. The Roman name is in parentheses.

Olympian Gods

Aphrodite (Venus): Goddess of love and beauty

Apollo (Apollo): God of the sun, truth (reason), archery, music, medicine, and prophecy

Ares (Mars): God of war

Artemis (Diana): Goddess of the hunt, twin sister of Apollo, guardian of women

Demeter (Ceres): Goddess of the underworld/agriculture

Hades (Pluto): Ruler of the underworld

Hera (Juno): Goddess of marriages; wife of Zeus

Hermes (Mercury): Messenger of the gods

Hestia (Vesta): Goddess of the family and home

Pallas Athena (Minerva): Goddess of wisdom and war; patroness of artisans

Poseidon (Neptune): Ruler of the sea; carried a magic trident

Zeus (Jupiter): Ruler of the gods, god of the sky. Symbol: thunderbolt and lighting

Other Gods

Atlas: Superhuman strength; carried the world on his shoulders

Chronus (Saturn): God of time

Dionysus (Bacchus): God of wine

Nike (Victoria): Goddess of victory

Pandora: When she opened a certain box, she released evil into the world

Persephone (Prosperine): Goddess of the underworld

Priapus: God of fertility

Prometheus: Cousin of Zeus; clever

Psyche: Goddess of the soul

The Middle Ages followed the Roman period. Christianity was one of the new religions that spread across the Roman world. The Romans worshipped many gods and often adopted new religions from the people that they conquered. The teaching of Jesus Christ began to spread, but many of the people at that time were unaware of the meaning of those teachings. The Romans built huge structures, such as markets, businesses, and law courts, which were constructed using the vaulted arch. These public buildings were called basilicas. The basilica was an important architectural structure for the early Christians. John P. Sedgwick Jr., in his book *Art Appreciation Made Simple*, states, "This is most important when we regard what happened in the Early Christian basilica, designed as a church, a product that reflected spiritualism, mystery, other worldly, and a sense of being overpowered by something greater than oneself. Contrary to the classical and practical world of the Roman characteristics which were considered to be more functional, decorative and secular. The Middle Ages would become a civilization that according to some historians they could no longer consider it to belong to the ancient world" (Sedgwick 56).

According to Sedgwick, the Middle Ages ushered in a new type of attitude toward religion. Medieval architecture and culture would reflect that spiritual attitude. They placed emphasis on the next life, and believed that this life should be spent doing good works so that the next life would be better. After a person died, if he had done good deeds, such as helping to build a church, he would be able to live in heaven for eternity. Constantine's conversion to Christianity transformed the ancient world.

Cultural transformation is often reflected in art. There had been a shift in attitudes between the Classical Greek and Roman periods. Graceful, idealized forms were used to show ideas and represent truth and beauty during the Golden Age of Greece. During the later years of the Roman period, when art was used to dictate political rhetoric, the style became rigid and static. The early art of the Christian era may appear to be somewhat flat and decorative. The baby Jesus and his mother were the subjects of many works. The figures may have lines that are very noticeable, and the colors applied almost as if the artist was simply trying to paint inside the lines. That was the style then.

Many of the church leaders did not want to have sculptures or paintings of their religious figures in the style of the Classical Greek sculptures. They were not to appear to be from the natural world, but from the spiritual realm.

It was not until A.D. 391 that the Church in Rome had Christianity declared an official religion of Rome. In A.D. 333 Constantine the Great set up his capitol in the city of Constantinople (modern-day Istanbul, Turkey). When his mother became a Christian he set up Christianity as a state religion.

There have been volumes and volumes written about the Romans. They have fascinated historians for centuries and will continue to do so. The Romans were influenced by the Greeks especially in the areas of art and architecture. Greek gods were given Etruscan names, a belief in an afterlife, and mausoleums were constructed in the form of houses (an idea borrowed from Greek myths). The Romans built the Pantheon, which had an enormous dome with columns at the entrance. The Romans also built the Pont du Gard during the late first century. This aqueduct was used to carry water to towns in the region (Parrott 65).

Historians have long debated the reasons Rome fell and divided in the way that it did. There are clues to the causes in many primary sources. These records may be tapped by students. Some historians say that taxes became so high that they became unbearable and many people could not afford to pay them. Also, at times there was an absence of a centralized government.

One individual who was in the vicinity when a cataclysmic event took place in 70 C.E. was Pliny the Elder. He wrote accounts that have been helpful in understanding the history of the Roman people. His nephew, Pliny the Younger, was present on the day that Mt. Vesuvius erupted. He managed to stay away from the disaster. His uncle, Pliny the Elder, was commander of the navel fleet at Misenum. According to his nephew's account, he died because he was attempting to rescue others who were across the bay. They were unable to land anywhere close to the mountain because of the hot ash and lava coming from the mountain. An account written by an individual named Gaius reported that Pliny the Elder was trying to rescue people and collapsed the next day from breathing the toxic flumes. He was unable to get back onto a ship and died. Gaius heard the story from witnesses who verbally reported it to him. That is how it has been passed down in history. Pliny the Younger wrote a very touching account about how he and his mother ran through an open field before they escaped on a ship. He also expressed deep sadness for the loss of his beloved uncle.

Town of Pompeii

After the eruption in 79 C.E., Pompeii was covered in volcanic ash and many feet of volcanic material. In the late 1800s excavation teams managed to uncover parts of the town. The town was incredibly well preserved. Researchers could walk on Pompeii's streets, complete with pavement and stepping stones. They could also examine houses and shops. The artifacts and features found at Pompeii can provide valuable insight into the way of life of first-century Romans.

The walls in many of the buildings were covered with exquisite paintings. Many of them depicted ceremonies, in addition to landscapes and still lifes. Many representational paintings were on walls, and the artists' use of perspective made it look as though you were looking out a window. The reddish-orange color that was used was very bright and intense, and was often used in murals in that area.

Much of what is known today about the way people lived during the first century in this Italian coastal town is known only because of the Vesuvius eruption. Many of the wealthy escaped, but the workers did not. Firsthand accounts, like Pliny the Younger's, help researchers understand the past better (Sayre, *Discover* 93–94).

For about sixteen centuries Pompeii was covered with ash and lava. In 1748 excavations were undertaken by German archaeologist Joachim Winckelmann. The archaeologists soon uncovered businesses and homes. The buildings revealed many frescoes, which were surprisingly in excellent condition. Some historians think that the paintings in the homes at Pompeii may have been painted by Greeks who had immigrated to Pompeii. However, this has not been proven. One reason some scholars argue for Greek involvement is that the subject of a series of paintings in the "Villa of Mysteries" was a ritual associated with Dionysus, the Greek god of wine (Gilbert and McCarter 372).

Accomplishments of the Ancient Roman Civilization Period

- A transportation system of roads
- The use of the aqueduct as a successful water system
- Military Science
- Use of the dome in architecture - An example which is still standing in tact is the Pantheon which is in Rome, Italy
- The use of the Greek gods and goddesses as their gods and goddesses
- The Romans did not invent the arch however, they used it in construction
- Used poured concrete in architecture

MIDDLE AGES (THE MEDIEVAL PERIOD)

The Middle Ages is the period from around the fifth century to the fifteenth century. The time period was named the Middle Ages because it occurred between the Roman period and the Renaissance period. There are not exact dates to mark the end of the Roman Empire. Bryce Lyon, a western European author, argues that the medieval civilization was influenced by Muslims in Spain and the Middle East and by the Byzantine Empire in southern Europe. There were many architectural and cultural developments made during those 1,000 years, even though some books refer to this period as the Dark Ages.

The reason some people call this period the Dark Ages may be because there were some groups of single-minded people who stifled many of the thinkers of their day. For that reason scientific advancement was at a stand still. There was less law and order since there was no longer a strong Roman central government. The Roman system of laws that had protected the citizens had nearly vanished, and the safety of the public was in jeopardy. Barbarians were invading the area from the regions of the Danube and the Rhine. Guilt or innocence was not determined by trial but rather by ordeal. For example, under this system, the accused might place his hand on a red-hot iron, and if his hand healed quickly he was considered innocent (*World Book Encyclopedia*).

Barbarian invasions wrought havoc on the trade routes that had been established by the Romans, and eventually the road system broke down. The economy was destroyed, and most people were forced to make a living by moving to the country and living off the land. Later, a class of hundreds of vassals developed. The individuals who led the vassals were princes, barons, dukes, and counts, and they became independent rulers of their own fiefs. That would then develop into a system called manorialism (*World Book Encyclopedia*).

The noblemen collected taxes and fines and acted as the judge in legal disputes. They also maintained the army for their own territory. A nobleman was a nobleman merely because he was born into the noble class. The various positions at that time of feudalism were nobleman, knight, vassal, and lord—all at the same time. He was a nobleman because he had been born into the noble class. He became a knight when he decided to spend his life as a professional warrior. He became a vassal when he promised to serve a king or other important person in return for a fief. Finally, he became a lord when he gave part of his own land to persons who promised to serve him (*World Book Encyclopedia*).

The feudal states during the twelfth and thirteenth centuries in some of the central European countries helped to establish some peace and security for their people. However, in Italy and Germany that system of government was not able to unite their countries. The Church became the driving force to help unite the masses. Led by clergy, Christians built monasteries and church structures in the centers of their towns. The power of the Church can be seen today in the large Romanesque and Gothic architectural structures that remain in regions of France, Germany, and Italy.

Monks wrote down chants, which were used in the church services. The written notations were called neumes; they are the equivalent of modern-day notes. The language during the Middle Ages was Latin, and the compositions that were part of the service were called plainsongs or chants. They developed from the chants found originally in Greek music and from Hebrew verses. Plainsongs would have been sung in unison, which means that only one melody is sung at a time. In musical terms, that music was referred to as monophonic.

Spiritual and educational strength was an important commodity for the Church to sell to the medieval townspeople. Local church leaders had to raise money, and one way to do that was to build a shrine at their church to attract visitors. Many of the cathedrals began to gather reliquaries (decorative objects that contained one or more relics). It was important to try to have the body of a saint, or at least a portion of one. For example, even a bone fragment from a disciple of Jesus Christ or one of the saints would help attract more visitors to the church. Many visitors believed that they could be healed or blessed if they made a pilgrimage to see a reliquary. Pilgrims often made donations to the churches that they visited. This helped the churches raise money for their building projects.

During the eleventh and twelfth centuries, the church became the most stabilizing force in Europe. Centers of commerce, banking, and manufacturing emerged. Guilds, organizations of workers in a particular craft, also developed during this period. As the organizations grew, so did the population in the cities. New farming techniques emerged and some cities began to prosper. Cities began to compete with one another to build great cathedrals. Morality plays were performed in the city to show the townspeople how to be good and to portray the struggle between good and evil. Plays that were about themes from the Bible were called mystery plays.

Large monasteries developed and became powerful in the Church. Two of the important monastic orders were the Cluniacs and the Benedictines. The members of the Cluniac order expressed their beliefs by composing music and writing illuminated manuscripts. Many of the churches and monasteries became stopping places along the pilgrimage routes that were traveled by thousands of penitents in search of salvation (Parrottt 100).

"Women, especially those from aristocratic homes, were able to commission psalm books called psalters. There was an increase of literacy among certain women and some of the women were privileged to become patrons of the arts. A well-known religious woman of the twelfth century was the German mystic, Hildegard of Bingen (1098–1179). She composed music to accompany hymns and wrote Latin poetry and treatises on herbs and medicine" (Parrott 100).

A church that exemplifies the Romanesque style of architecture is Sainte Marie Madeleine at Vézelay. Like most Christian churches, it is oriented with its apse to the east and the main entrance to the west. This expresses the idea that the church building is a metaphor of the Christian world, with the Holy Land in the east and Europe to the west. The church at Vézelay was also involved in supporting the Crusades. The church actively encouraged the first two of the eight Crusades against the Muslims that were undertaken by the Church between 1095 and 1291 (Parrott 100).

Middle Ages Period

The Middle Ages developed innovations in architectural structures. The use of the Roman arch was utilized in the construction of the Romanesque churches, castles, and monasteries. Some still exist today for us to see and visit.

The use of the Latin cross as a floor plan is noticeable in both Romanesque and Gothic church plans. This was done for symbolic reasons. The Gothic cathedrals became taller than the Romanesque style. The Gothic style had pointed arches and they used a support system referred to as "flying buttresses." These flying buttresses can be seen since they appear as extensions coming out of the sides of the building. Notre Dame Cathedral in Paris was one of the first Gothic cathedrals to add this system due to cracking. However, it became more common in other Gothic construction to help increase the height of the building. Gothic architecture also utilized the stain glass window which was made with colored glass pieces assembled together into a window of a "glass picture" or work of art. These images would be a subject or story from the Bible to help worshippers understand the religion.

The floor plan of the Gothic cathedrals were of the Latin cross which has one stem longer than the other.

The Byzantine style of architecture was in the more eastern area of Europe and in other parts more towards modern-day Greece and Russia.

This construction utilized paintings of saints and Jesus along with mosaics.

The floor plan was a Greek cross which has stems of the cross the same length. In the interior of the church were paintings and mosaics of subject matter to tell worshippers about the Bible and beliefs of the Orthodox beliefs.

The paintings have flat areas of gold paint behind the images of the figures of saints or the works of Jesus. There are also icons throughout the cathedral which are sacred images to the believer of that faith.

The Byzantine cathedrals have domes constructed on pendentive.

Source: https://www.britannica.com/technology/pendentive

Characteristics of Middles Age Construction (Architecture)

Romanesque Architecture Characteristics   800-1100 C.E. *approximately*

Clear small windows, round use of the arch, small clear windows, cut precise stone, Latin cross-shaped floor plan, use of the barrel vault system construction

Gothic Architecture Characteristics   1100-1300 C.E. *approximately*
Big stained glass windows, pointed arches, flying buttresses, tall structures, Latin cross-shaped floor plan

Byzantine Architecture Characteristics   600-1600 C.E. *approximately*
Domes used on pendentive, Greek cross-shaped floor plan, icons, mosaics
Source: http://www.visual-arts-cork.com/history-of-art/byzantine.htm

Terms to Consider

Byzantine characteristics—domes, mosaics, icons, shape of a Greek cross
Romanesque characteristics—rounded arches, small clear windows, heavy use of stone work
Gothic characteristics—pointed arches, stained glass windows, flying butteresses, very tall structures

QUESTION

Question to Contemplate

Why did Rome fall?

Accomplishments of Middle Ages

During the 1200's people in towns used cobblestones in their streets and stopped throwing garbage in the streets. Stone and brick began to be used in architecture in towns instead of wood in order to prevent fires in towns. The church built huge cathedrals which housed hundreds of townspeople and served as the religious and social center of the town. The monks wrote down manuscripts for religious services and wrote them down. Monks copied down chants that were written down with images called neumes which are similar to what we now call notes. There were accomplishments in architectural work such as stone masonry and stained glass windows. Developments were made in agriculture improving the tools such as the plough.

RENAISSANCE 9

The Renaissance refers to the birth of culture in Italy during the 1400s (fifteenth century) and lasting until the Baroque Period of the 1600s (seventeenth century). There were innovations in science, the fine arts, new creations in technologies, architecture, religious ideas, political institutions, and banking at this time. There was a new way of looking at the arts of the Greeks and at their myths and trying to locate their buried sculptures and find out about their gods. There was also an interest in what the Romans believed in and what their architecture was like; how they copied from the Greek gods; how their Latin language was used in their everyday life; and how they brought legends to life through the arts. The Renaissance has been called a rebirth of learning from the Greeks and the Roman way of life.
Source: http://petrarch.petersadlon.com/bio.html

Petrarch was born in Arezzo, Italy on July 20, 1304 in the beginning of the early Renaissance during the time of the Black Death (bubonic plague). He and his brother were both spending time in service to the Catholic Church as monks. They both became leaders in the Church and advanced in position to diplomats.

Petrarch became an ambassador to rural areas of Italy which helped bring unity to these areas and eventully was asked to travel to France and the Netherlands as well. In his journeys he encountered a woman named Laura who would die from the plague. Laura became his inspiration to write many of his enduring poems. Petrarch's speaking and writing skills reflected his human nature so much so that they evolved into the modern-day ideas called humanism.
Source: http://petrarch.petersadlon.com/bio.html

The Renaissance in Europe began in the fifteenth century; it followed the crippling bubonic plague that ravaged Sicily in 1347 and then proceeded to spread northward. Francesco Petrarca, a poet known as Petrarch, left behind accounts of his anguish and the loss of family members. Petrarch's poem about Laura, who died from the bubonic plague, is touching. He wrote this poem as a sonnet, which is a poem written with fourteen lines. Another writer who can help increase one's understanding of the fourteenth century is Geoffrey Chaucer. He wrote with descriptive words and phrases that bring the characters to life. Chaucer translated Petrarch's work, and from those writings the reader gets a sense of the feelings and the ideas surrounding each poet's life (Sayre, *Discover* 183). Petrarch wrote "Sonnet 134."

Geoffrey Chaucer (1340–1400) wrote *Canterbury Tales*. The *Canterbury Tales* was a series of stories told by pilgrims who were on their way to the shrine where Thomas Becket had been murdered. The thirty pilgrims each tell stories on their way to the shrine and on their way back. The stories are very telling, and Chaucer conveys the flavor of the time through his exquisite writing style, which is natural and down to earth. For example, the story told by the Wife of Bath, who is portrayed as a woman of questionable character, proceeds to tell a moral tale about character (Van de Bogart).

The Renaissance can be called a rebirth of learning. It has also been referred to as a revival. What was it renewing? There was a new interest in the Greek Classical era and the Roman Forum was being excavated. Allegedly, some of the individuals interested in supporting the arts and the excavations were important church leaders. Henry Sayre describes one important individual who helped promote the turn of events that spurred on the Renaissance. That person was Cosimo from the wealthy Medici family. Cosimo de'Medici (1389–1464) went from being a banker to being the pope. At this time, there was not a separation between the church and the state; they were connected. When one reads about Michelangelo's life and his commissions, one finds the connection of many of his works to the Medici family. Michelangelo was commissioned by some of the princes of the Medici family when they became involved with the papacy. When Michelangelo was a young boy he went to the sculpture school that was run by the Medici family and he met the boys there.

During the Renaissance wealthy families of Florence, such as the Medici family, wanted to turn their cities into attractive and workable environments. They were civic-minded people who started to take pride in their city. Like Cosimo Medici, many of the wealthy were bankers and had enough funds to contribute to the community. The idea of building libraries, hospitals, and other places to help the community began to take shape. That idea was called humanism, because of the focus on human beings and their value. The study of humanism, in a formal sense, also includes the study of the ancient art of Greece and Rome and the study of the arts, music, theater, and literature.

When one examines paintings from this time period, beginning with artists such as Giotto, one detects a change from flat, decorative forms to realistic, human, emotional beings. Giotto paved the way for other artists and subsequent paintings to begin placing figures within an environment, such as a background of trees and lakes, to show that the person lived in the real world. That was a reflection of the humanistic spirit emerging.

Cities began to prosper in some areas with the spread of a humanistic attitude and fewer health problems. To study the Renaissance most effectively, one would need to travel to various locations, because the Renaissance differed in various areas around the world. Most noteworthy, however, was Florence, Italy, which became the hub of all activity. Even today, the huge orange dome can be seen over the top of most other buildings around Florence. The Santa Maria del Fiore cathedral's dome is magnificent. The art of some of the most famous artists from the Renaissance lived in Florence.

Florence was a center for the arts, and the Medici family had an art competition in 1401 to design large doors on a building next to the cathedral of the Santa Maria del Fiore, or the Florence Cathedral. It may not seem like anything today to have a competition; however, during the Middle Ages, an artist was rarely given credit for his or her work individually, but rather artists were expected to do the work strictly for the "glory of God." The competition was held and the two finalists were Ghiberti and Brunelleschi. The winner was Ghiberti.

The entries for the competition were to include a panel about the subject of Abraham in the moment when he was about to sacrifice his son. Of course, that did not happen because Abraham was told not to sacrifice his son, and in the contest both artists depicted an angel giving Abraham the message. In Brunelleschi's version, the angel grabs Abraham's arm to stop him right before he takes the knife to his son. Both panels were superb; however, historians say that Ghiberti's design and handling of the human form was ahead of his time. His style had an impact on contemporary artists.

Ghiberti's doors are still standing and used today. The building is still used for baptisms. However, a replica of one set named the "Gates of Paradise" is no longer outside—it has been moved to the museum down the street from the site. Ghiberti's father was a goldsmith, and Ghiberti had been trained to create detailed work and cast. Working on these massive doors for the Baptistery building was a long and tedious process and it took him the rest of his life to complete. When Michelangelo saw the doors, he was so taken by their beauty and elegance that he called them the "Gates of Paradise," the name that remains today.

Meanwhile, Brunelleschi, the artist who lost, was extremely upset and humiliated, so he left Florence and moved to Rome. During his time in Rome he studied the ancient buildings of the Romans, saw their excavations, and studied the Pantheon. Though he lost the contest, his life was better for it—though he did not yet realize that fact. His big break was yet to come. He had become fascinated with how the Romans built structures using arches and how they poured concrete and buttresses, and he spent several years studying architecture and engineering. He was intrigued with the design of the dome of the Pantheon. He knew that he could build a dome as an addition to the Florence Cathedral if given the opportunity.

As the story goes, Brunelleschi went back a number of years later after he lost the competition to Ghiberti. Brunelleschi obtained an appointment with the church fathers because they needed to finish a large portion of the cathedral of Florence (Santa Maria del Fiore). They asked to see his drawings. He sat down and said, "I don't have any." Then he said to an errand boy, "Run fetch me an egg at the market, but you have to hurry," and he gave him some money. The boy came back in a flash and Brunelleschi in the meantime obtained a bowl.

Brunelleschi looked at each one of the gentlemen sitting around the table, ensuring that he had their attention.

Then he took the egg, clicked it against the bowl so that it cracked perfectly into halves. He poured the yolk into the bowl and put the clean half—straight edge down—in the middle of the table. The perfectly shaped half egg shell sat there on the table for all to see, and Brunelleschi said, "That is what I am going to build for you."

What do think their reaction was? They must have been rather surprised; but, amazingly, they all agreed to trust him and they accepted his offer. The dome was built and stands as a crowning achievement of Renaissance architecture.

QUESTIONS

Questions to Contemplate

Why do you think Brunelleschi did not want anyone to see his plans?

Or do you think he did not have any drawn plans?

You may want to do your own research about the construction of the dome.

Question

Why didn't Brunelleschi show his drawings?

Answer

Some say that Brunelleschi was afraid that someone would steal them.

The dome by Filippo Brunelleschi was built from 1420 to 1434. The dome of the Santa Maria del Fiore (St. Mary of the Flower) was built during this same time period. This dome influenced Michelangelo, who was the architect of the St. Peter's dome. St. Peter's is where the pope has his headquarters at the Vatican. Both the doors of the Baptistery at Santa Maria del Fiore and the outstanding dome are popular attractions for visitors from around the world when they travel to Florence, Italy.

Santa Maria del Fiore's Baptistery, where people are baptized, is one of the oldest buildings in Florence. It was built in the twelfth century and is of Romanesque construction.

Florence was a significant player in the Italian Renaissance and it has left its mark. It paved the way for other cities, and it helped establish the concept of being civic minded. For the people of Florence, being civic minded meant placing sculptures and art works in public places for all the citizens to enjoy. Some wealthy Florentine families felt that it was their duty to provide a better environment for their citizens, so they commissioned artists to produce works. One of the commissioned works was *David*, a sculpture by a young artist named Michelangelo, which symbolized the city of Florence as an up and coming power gaining momentum. *David* was inspired by the story of the shepherd boy, David, who killed the giant, Goliath. Michelangelo chose to sculpt *David* in marble, and the sculpture was placed in the square outside the Piazza della Signoria.

Story of David and Goliath

Once upon a time there was a family who had several sons and the father was named Jesse. David was the youngest of the sons and was a talented musician who played a harp. He had been summoned by King Saul to play for him, so that evil spirits would vacate the king's premise, which brought the king great joy.

A conflict occurred and the young men were called upon to fight. David wanted to go but his father would not allow him. Instead his father told him that he was too young and he needed to take care of the sheep. David was not happy that he was not able to go to fight in the conflict with his brothers. Every day he would ask his father if he could go see his brothers and bring them some food. Day after day David tended the sheep, but continued to ask his father when he would be old enough to go fight. Finally one day Jesse said that he could go take his brothers some loaves and corn. This was because Jesse was worried about the length of time his other sons had been gone. David left home and when he arrived at the campsite, he found the Philistine army all lined up on one side of a mountain. Each day the ten-foot Goliath would come out and threaten any one of the Israelites to fight. Goliath would shout to the crowd of men about how he would make them their servants if he prevailed. He asked if anyone wanted to fight.

Some days the men just stayed in their tents in hopes that the giant would eventually go away. David's brothers were happy to see David. When David saluted his brothers in the trench, Goliath strode right over to David and his brothers. Everyone else ran away in fear. At that point David went to King Saul and told him that no one had to worry because he would fight the giant. King Saul did not think that David was old enough for the task. David told the King how he saved his sheep from a lion and another time from a bear, killing each predator with his own hands. The king eventually gave David his blessing, along with his armor and helmet. The gear was too large, however, so David appeared defenseless. David went over to the river and found five smooth stones. He prepared his sling and approached the Philistine giant. The Philistines cursed David and made fun of him The giant even yelled at David making all types of strange comments. David calmly stated that he was there in the name of his god. David placed a single stone in his sling and hurled it toward Goliath, hitting him in the forehead. The giant fell dead to the ground.

The little shepherd boy was able to kill the big giant. That is where the phrase comes from about the David and Goliath story that has been told over and over again.

Martin Luther (1483–1546) was a cleric in the Catholic Church who disagreed with Pope Julius II's policies. Pope Julius II allowed the selling of indulgences in order to pay for his building projects and raise money. The German people did not benefit directly from those funds, and a revolt led by Martin Luther became known as Protestantism. The Protestants did not believe that admittance to heaven could be obtained by selling indulgences and doing good works. They also believed that one could establish a one-on-one relationship with God by doing away with the priesthood, saints, and intercessors.

This gave way to a powerful new method of art: printmaking. Martin Luther also wrote music and translated the Bible into German from Greek. As a result of more translations and the art of printmaking itself, the Bible became more accessible to people. In 1521, Martin Luther was excommunicated by Pope Leo X. Nevertheless, Martin Luther is remembered as a major figure in the history of Christianity and he initiated the split within Christianity between Protestants and Roman Catholics (*World Book Encyclopedia* 532). The Lutheran Church was named after Martin Luther.

The Renaissance in Italy and other southern areas of Europe were not experiencing the same circumstances culturally as the northern parts of Europe. When one examines the styles of both regions, the differences are noticeable. The Hundred Years' War, caused by the supremacy of Burgundy, created problems for France and England. The area known as modern-day Belgium and Holland was under the rule of a French king. The conditions in which artists were living were much like the feudal system from the Middle Ages.

"With the death in 1477 of Duke Charles the Bold son of Philip the Good, the Habsburg empire in Germany moved into the cultural ascendancy. Early in the 16th century, the tensions that had been simmering for years between feudal lords and middle classes, the Church of Rome and the Holy Roman Empire, and the northern countries and Italy, broke forth in the form of the commercial revolution and the Protestant Reformation. As much for economic reasons as religious ones, the northern countries severed their financial and ideological ties to the Pope in Rome, causing repercussions that are still felt to this day. At about the same time, the court of Henry VIII in England did the same, albeit for different reason. In spite of or perhaps because of, this great conflict, the arts in both Germany and England flourished" (Dixon and Fleming 111).

Artists Give Us Insight into How People Lived

Artists such as Pieter Brueghel, the Elder from Flanders (modern Belgium), portrayed man's smallness in the world. His paintings of winter scenes and a wedding dance portray regular people in activities. Brueghel's paintings have a very different look than Michelangelo's use of dark and light and volume and perspective. The time period of Brueghel's unique work was 1525 to 1569. In the *Wedding Dance*, the folks dancing in the background wear the same value of red as the ones in the foreground. Without making that tint or tone of red lighter or darker, the scene tends to become more vibrant, which creates a sense of happiness and movement. However, it does not seem as representational, real, or natural as some of the Italian Renaissance artists who used chiaroscuro (light and dark) as a method or treatment by using more shadows for more contrast.

Brueghel's subject matter provides insight in terms of how the people of his day and time lived by showing the manners and customs of that time. This insight makes his work quite significant in the humanities.

Historical Events Affect the Arts

"The English dealt a severe blow to Spanish sea-power when they defeated the Armada in 1588. When Ferdinand Isabella married and united their kingdoms in 1492, they did not establish a unified country. Each of the great provinces had a separate administrative and financial organization. The Catholic Church was the only institution common to all parts of Spain. After the Moors were driven out of Spain in 1492, the Spaniards continued to expand and established a colonial empire with the religious and militant spirit of a crusade. This was the situation inherited by Philip II (1556–98), the son of the Holy Roman Emperor, Charles V. During Philip's reign, great quantities of gold and silver were brought to Spain from the New World (Americas)."

The Spanish citizens revolted against the Spanish government because they wanted to practice their own religion, Calvinism, which was part of the Protestant Reformation. Meanwhile, the Dutch felt that they did not have to contribute by paying taxes to Spain since they supported Spain and not the Dutch.

Gradually Spain declined in power due to oppressive taxation, their inability to promote an industrial society, and the defeat of the Armada in 1588 by England.

Printing Press

A major achievement in the northern Renaissance was the printing press. The printing press had a tremendous impact on this region in many ways. It helped create both a freer way of thinking, which caused some to question the Roman Catholic Church, and a means of mass producing art work. Printmaking became important to produce prints for the books that were being printed and sold.

One of the greatest engravers from Germany was Albrecht Durer. William Fleming in *Arts and Ideas* stated it this way, "In a few short years, northern Europe rose from feudalism to capitalism, from art in the service of the aristocracy to art as reflection of all classes of people" (Dixon and Fleming 111).

What the Renaissance ushered in was a sense of identity and the opportunity for an artist to be recognized. For the first time in many years, an artist was allowed to have his or her name on a work and obtain a commission. The artist at that time, however, was not a free-spirited individual compared to the Abstract-Expressionists of the twentieth century, for example. The artists of the Renaissance had to maintain positions within the Church and work on commission or work for an aristocrat. The subject matter was normally religious (sacred).

Some works were secular (not religious), but there were not as many commissioned pieces of secular topics as there were of topics about the saints and the disciples. Artists also began to include themselves in paintings and there are a few self-portraits from this time period. Oils also became available, and this new medium allowed for greater consumer access to oil on canvas paintings.

There is a story about Leonardo da Vinci which explains that he began writing with mirror imagery because others were reading his work, and if his ideas were to get into the wrong hands, it would be dangerous. Some say that he was ambidextrous. That makes sense when one sees his notebooks, which are written backward (for many people, a mirror is required to read them). Another interesting note is that some of the notebooks are housed in Windsor Castle in England and the *Mona Lisa* hangs in France in the Louvre—many pieces of art are no longer in their countries of origin. The mural the *Last Supper*, though, is on the wall in Milan, Italy, at the Santa Maria della Grazie.

Some time ago an artist friend of mine who taught Art History referred to the Renaissance as the time of the three greats. She meant the time when Michelangelo, Leonardo da Vinci, and Raphael all were living and creating art. Raphael (1483–1520) was the youngest of the three when he died. He painted a very famous work that was painted down a hall from the Sistine Chapel while Michelangelo was painting the ceiling of the chapel. One story (and this is only a story as told by a tour guide) explains that Michelangelo allowed Raphael to see his work and watch him paint. Then, one day, Michelangelo went down the hall and stepped into the room where Raphael was painting *The School of Athens*, and, lo and behold, there was a figure who had his elbow resting on his right leg and his head bent. It looked almost identical to one of the figures that Michelangelo had wrestled with, and he told Raphael how unhappy he was that his work had been copied. The next day, Michelangelo locked Raphael out of the chapel.

Raphael's *School of Athens* has a title that is not exactly helpful to its meaning. The word "school" can mean thought, so one should think about the painting in the following terms: Thinking of Athens—i.e., someone thinking that those people in the painting are actually standing in the old area of ancient Greece discussing philosophy and math. *The School of Athens* is a very large fresco (9' × 27'). Its composition consists of vivid colors, and the artist made excellent use of space by using perspective with great success.

The School of Athens has two central figures who resemble Raphael's competitors, Leonardo da Vinci and Michelangelo. The two central figures are positioned directly below the arch in the painting and reflect the pope's interest in the study of the Greeks. The figure with the longest hair on the left is Plato (Leonardo da Vinci) and the one on the right holding a book is thought to be Aristotle (Michelangelo). *The School of Athens* is located in the Vatican, down the hall from the Sistine Chapel in the Stanza della Segnatura, a room that was used for signing papers by Pope Julius II. Raphael was commissioned by Pope Julius II to paint the mural on wet plaster. There are other paintings by Raphael at the Vatican (Sayre 213).

Leonardo da Vinci (1452–1519)

In Leonardo da Vinci's *The Last Supper*, he was able to expressively capture the moment when Jesus Christ, who sits at the very center of the table, says, "One of you will betray me." The room looks spacious, and all the disciples are seated beside Jesus. They are grouped and it almost appears that the painting was created from an old film's freeze frame. It seems so real. Da Vinci tried a new concoction of paint material on a dry plastered wall when he painted it. The paint did not hold up as well as he would have liked. Some artists had to repair parts of it a few years after he did the work.

During World War II, the church, the Santa Maria della Grazie, was heavily damaged by a bomb. The wall with the mural of *The Last Supper* remained intact, but it was subjected to rain for awhile so the painting incurred even more damage. Since then it has been repaired, and the building has been remodeled. The wall and the painting are now in good condition.

As one walks into the refectory of the Santa Maria della Grazie and sees *The Last Supper*, it seems possible to walk up into the painting and join them. The painting is absolutely outstanding and spectacular. The painting engrosses the viewer by drawing him or her into the painting through the use of perspective. Da Vinci was able to accomplish a moment in time in his painting by using value, light and dark colors, and rectangular and rounded shapes arranged to complement each other in the composition.

The Renaissance marked a time when painters were considered important people in society who had risen from craftsmen to intellectuals. Da Vinci was a multitalented individual who was able to draw and come up with many ideas related to city planning, architecture, and transportation, to list a few. There was a profound change in the role of the artist in culture during the Renaissance (Sedgwick). Da Vinci was respected not only for his seventeen paintings, but also for his drawings, his intellect, and his scientific writings.

Michelangelo

Michelangelo's sculpture of David is said to represent the spirit of the Renaissance in that it represents the humanistic spirit, individualism, and a defiance toward the enemy (Sedgwick). When the sculpture was first shown to the public it was not well received and some people threw stones at it. *David* was placed outside in front of the town hall of Florence (Palazzo Vecchio).

During the Renaissance, the Medici family, who had been acquainted with Michelangelo since his father sent him to the Medici family sculpture school, became popes. Pope Julius II died in 1513, right after Michelangelo had completed the Sistine Chapel ceiling.

Niccolò Machiavelli was an important thinker and diplomat who lived at the time of the Italian Renaissance. Historians consider him a leading Florentine statesman and writer who "sought to explain politics realistically" (*World Book Encyclopedia*).

In his book, *The Prince*, Machiavelli wrote that, in politics, a healthy environment should be orderly and unified, and if the leader finds that the state is in disarray, the leader must resort to almost any means to restore order. In some cases those measures may be cruel (*World Book Encyclopedia*).

The Renaissance was a time of discovery, renewed interest in the Greco-Roman world, the new world of the Americas, the Protestant Reformation, and the growth of cities. Many artists went to Florence and Rome to find work, and artists were hired to paint and decorate churches.

Michelangelo worked on the ceiling from 1508 to 1512. He was commissioned by Pope Julius II. This pope had previously commissioned Michelangelo to sculpt his tomb, a task Michelangelo was asked to complete by many people over the course of his life. Michelangelo considered himself a sculptor and preferred to sculpt. He was not interested in executing the ceiling but began with a design that included figures of disciples. When he had worked on it for quite some time, however, he looked at it from below and realized that the figures were not large enough. He also gave up his first theme for a new plan. He painted a large area of the ceiling fresco, and when he came down from the scaffolding seventy feet above, he looked up and, to his dismay, realized that the work did not look correct. When he was up close to the figures that he painted they looked fine. When he stepped down they looked way too small. He covered them up again with plaster and started fresh.

For his new painting, Michelangelo decided to use the first book of the Bible and focus on the Creation story. The frescos depict Separation of Light from Darkness, Creation of Sun, Moon Planets, Separation of Land from Water, Creation of Adam, Temptation and Expulsion from the Garden of Eden, Sacrifice of Noah, The Flood, and Drunkenness of Noah. Those are the paintings down the center of the ceiling and the sides portray Sibyls and prophets.

Michelangelo was a sculptor who worked on the *Pieta* and *David* when he was in his early twenties. Michelangelo also designed tombs for Giuliano and Lorenzo de' Medici in the Medici Chapel in the church of San Lorenzo (Hale 106).

Michelangelo worked on the *Last Judgment*, which is also in the Sistine Chapel, from 1534 to 1541. He was commissioned under Pope Paul III. *Last Judgment* possesses an emerging style that historians called Mannerism. Mannerism emphasizes the use of light and dark and elongated forms to express ideas. *Last Judgment* depicts Judgment Day—the day when God comes back on the last day and each person is judged.

Shakespeare

In England, plays such as *Henry V*, *Hamlet*, *A Winter's Tale*, and *Othello* were being performed. Shakespeare wrote those plays and many more. In general, Shakespeare wrote plays with themes that deal with universal feelings and ideas. The plays deal with heavy themes that raise deep questions about life and death. The issues that Shakespeare wrote about dealt with how men and women had the capability to make up their own minds and think freely. In *Hamlet* when the main character, Hamlet, talks to his friend he notes that "man is noble in reason and infinite in faculty." Think about how Shakespeare represented and reflected the time in which he lived, and yet how his plays remain meaningful in the world today. How is that possible? What makes a play remain meaningful and have the capacity to be performed over and over again?

> **QUESTIONS**
>
> **Questions to Contemplate**
>
> What does the term *Renaissance* mean?
>
> What type of paintings did Michelangelo create?
>
> What is a fresco?
>
> What was the Reformation?
>
> Who was Martin Luther?
>
> Why do paintings from the area called Flanders look different than those from Florence?
>
> What impact did the printing press have on European life?
>
> How is it possible for Shakespeare's *Hamlet* and *A Winter's Tale* to remain meaningful even to today's audiences? What makes a play remain meaningful and have the capacity to be performed over and over again?

Accomplishments of the Renaissance

Renaissance major accomplishments were many:

Modern commercial infrastructure developed

Trade between countries in their known world (modern Europe) became possible

Florence became the center of this financial industry

The idea of man being the center of the universe (humanism developed)

A decline of feudalism

Change from a land-based society to more enterprises

Great artworks such as fresco paintings by the "three greats," Michelangelo, Raphael, Leonardo da Vinci

Use of perspective—the illusion of depth (in paintings such as *School of Athens* and *Last Supper*)

The great marble sculptures of Michelangelo's *David* and *Pieta*

The renewed interest in Greek art which was being excavated

BAROQUE 10

The Baroque Period roughly stretched from 1650 to 1750. Loosely speaking, the art and music were elaborate and ornate. In some areas during this period, especially in Northern Europe, the Protestant Reformation enabled the emergence of the middle class. Also during this time, the Catholic Church had to deal with unrest within itself, from a movement known as the Counter-Reformation.

The Baroque style can be seen at St. Peters at Vatican City. The architect Maderno added the balcony and the new facade to St. Peter's. Gianlorenzo Bernini (1598–1680) designed the large square and the colonnade. Bernini was an architect as well as a sculptor. Bernini represents the hero at the moment that he threw the stone against the giant Goliath (Parrott 155).

Baroque paintings made use of dramatic lighting, to intensify emotion, and sharp contrasts between light and dark, which seemed to make many of the forms move. The use of curves and swirls can also be noticed in the typical Baroque painting.

Some of the leading painters of this time period are discussed in this section.

Rembrandt van Rijn (1606–1669), Dutch artist

Rembrandt was a portrait painter, landscape artist, and printmaker who perfected the art of etching. He also did many self-portraits at various ages throughout his life. These have given us a glimpse into his life from when he was a young man on the threshold of his career, through his later years, when he was alone and bankrupt. To appreciate his use of light/dark and chiaroscuro, and to see the textures and colors, you need to visit a museum and view his work with your own eyes—a photograph does not do justice to his paintings. Seeing a Rembrandt portrait is a life-changing experience, which will make one less tolerant of inferior art.

Peter Paul Rubens (1577–1640), Flemish artist

Rubens lived in Flanders (modern-day Belgium). He painted commissions for royalty such as Maria de Medici (Louis XIII's mother), Philip IV of Spain, and

Charles I of England. He painted huge canvases and covered them with swirling, brightly covered figures in the Baroque flavor.

Johannes Vermeer (1632–1675), Dutch artist

Johannes Vermeer is said to have "composed his pictures with a camera obscura which was a popular 17th century" optical device. To see this feature of his style, look at some of his paintings and note that some areas seem to be blurred in the background, similar to how snapshot photos appear when taken (Bishop 289).

Vermeer exemplifies painting of the period of art known as Baroque. Much of the subject matter of his art concerned the middle-class household and daily tasks of women in their homes of individuals taking and giving music lessons. Vermeer did not create as many paintings as other famous master painters throughout history; however, the work that he left behind has given us an idea about what everyday life may have been like for some individuals in the middle class during his lifetime.

Source: Lawrence S. Cunningham, John J. Reich, and Lois Fichner-Rathus, *Culture and Values, Volume 1.*

Diego Velasquez (1599–1660), Spain artist

Velasquez was a court painter of Philip IV of Spain. His paintings are considered to be some of the best of the period and can be studied to understand his time period in the history in Spain. They are representative of and show vivid details of the Baroque style. His portraits, which capture the character of the individuals he painted, are extremely telling. The Meadows Museum at Southern Methodist University has a couple examples of his work, but his most famous works are in Spain. Once you have seen a Velasquez portrait in person, you will never again be satisfied with mediocre portrait painting. No painting can be truly captured by a photograph. To appreciate the textures, colors, and brush strokes you must see the work for yourself. In one of his most famous paintings, in which he painted the king and queen posing in a standing position, he places himself in the background, painting a canvas. This work, known as *The Maids of Honor*, resides in a famous museum called the Prado in Madrid, Spain (Van de Bogart 165–167).

When a Flemish artist, Peter Paul Rubens, visited Spain and met Diego Velasquez, he obtained a leave of absence for Velasquez to study in Rome. Velasquez had only seen copies and reproductions of Italian painters such as work by Caravaggio painted by imitators. These works had an impact on Velasquez's work; however, having the actual firsthand experience to see the art of the great Italian masters helped Velasquez understand how to transform his portraits into paintings that became his unique style. These works are ranked as some of the best portraits ever painted by any artist.

Velasquez lived from 1599 to 1660 and spent most of his life in Madrid, Spain, as a court painter for King Philip IV. Many of the subjects of his paintings were portraits of the king's family, the children of the king and queen, and other members of the royal family.

Lorenzo Bernini (1598-1680), Italian sculptor

In contrast to the Renaissance, Baroque period sculpture looked like it forgot to use straight lines and instead subsituted curves. An example of this is Bernini's sculpture of David. Bernini chose a subject that Michelangelo had already sculpted—David killing the Philistine giant Goliath—but with a completely different interpretation. Bernini's David is depicted in the middle of throwing a stone at the giant. In contrast to Michelangelo's statute, Bernini's David is twisted and in the process of swinging and hurling a stone. The facial expression is also much more troubled in Bernini's David. The Greek influence characterizes Michelangelo's David, and comparing the two Davids is quite interesting.

Bernini lived in Rome and another of his masterpieces was the baldacchino (canopy) which was placed directly under the dome of St. Peter's that had been designed by Michelangelo in the last years of his life. The baldacchino stands nearly 100 feet high and carved into it on the top is an ornate crown. The purpose of this canopy is to shelter the altar in St. Peter's. That entire work is very detailed and can be seen in person or when Vatican ceremonies at the Basilica of St. Peter are televised.

Another of Bernini's famous, swirling, moving Baroque works of sculpture is the *Ecstasy of St. Theresa*, where an angel is sculpted piercing the heart of St. Theresa. This statute is in the Cornaro Chapel in Rome.

El Greco (1541-1614), Greek artist

El Greco is considered Spanish, although he was born on the island of Crete which was part of Greece. He moved to Spain and remained there and was loved by the King of Spain and the people so he is an exception to the rule. Most of the time in art the rule is if you are born in the country and even if you move to another country you are called the name of where you were born. So he would be called Cretan but he is not. He is Spanish. El Greco, however, means "the Greek."

El Greco's use of elongated figures shows his idea of spiritualism. His paintings of the Madonna are striking and some are very different in style from what was then the norm, as they are elongated and very unique. Sometimes they are referred to as *Mannerist* in style. Mannerism was a rebellion against the Renaissance that did not fit into the Baroque style. Once, so goes the story, El Greco visited the Sistine Chapel and he said that he did not like *The Last Judgement* of Michelangelo. The statement made the Pope so angry that he was not allowed to work in Rome. For that reason El Greco had to look for work elsewhere and he found it in Toledo, Spain, where he became a well-known altar-piece painter. El Greco was commissioned by King Philip IV to work on the palace that was being built called the Escorial, but El Greco never painted on that structure. He painted for churches instead.

El Greco's given name was Domenikos Theotokopoulos. His canvas and altar pieces were bold works that had distorted images of holy figures. The figures were decorated with symbols and halos. The imagery and symbolism were represented by means of mysterious lighting using light and dark shadows. He had a unique style that was revitalized and renewed many years later by another Spanish artist by the name of Pablo Picasso.

Baroque Period Painters

Rembrandt van Rijn
Peter Paul Rubens
Diego Velasquez
Johannes Vermeer
Lorenzo Bernini

Baroque Period Musicians

George Frederic Handel
Johann Sebastian Bach
Antonio Vivaldi

Mannerist Period Artists

El Greco

Classical Period Artists

Jacque-Louis David
Architect of Monticello (his home)
  Thomas Jefferson

Classical Composers of Music

Wolfgang Amadeus Mozart
Ludwig Van Beethoven
Franz Joseph Haydn

Opera began during the Baroque Period

George Frederic Handel (1685-1759), German composer

George Frederic Handel was a violinist and wrote many harpsichord suites, cantatas, and ceremonial orchestral music for royal performances. A famous work still performed today is *The Messiah*, which includes the renown Hallelujah Chorus as part of that oratorio.

Johann Sebastian Bach (1685-1750), German composer

Handel, along with Johann Sebastian Bach, influenced European music more than any other Baroque composers. Bach was born to a Lutheran family of musicians and was deeply religious. He wrote over 600 chorale preludes. Famous works include the *St. Matthew Passion* (1727) and the *Brandenburg Concertos* (1721) (Parrott 157).

As a result of the Counter-Reformation (or, the cleansing of the church) the art commissioned for the churches in Spain was different from art works commissioned by the church in other areas of Europe and Italy during the seventeenth century. There was a new spiritual movement of praying within the church, which was reflected in the art forms that involved a mystical and mysterious look, with saints and holy figures filling the altar walls. The mother of Christ, for example, was depicted with a long body and a small head and a flowing gown rising towards heaven (Parrott 157).

"During the 1660s, King Louis XIV moved his court from the Louvre in Paris, France to the small town of Versailles, France. That building was built and is considered Baroque in style. There were 4,000 servants and an army of 9,000 men. The palace ground at Versailles included around 1,400 fountains in the formal garden. King Louis XIV was interested in the arts, and during his reign, Jean-Baptiste Lully established the distinct style of opera that utilized a continuous melodic flow and a style that included short arias" (Parrott 156).

QUESTIONS

Questions to Contemplate

What similarities and contrasts can be noted about the "Davids" of Michelangelo and Bernini?

What factors influenced the lives of these artists (Michelangelo and Bernini)?

What factors influenced Rembrandt's life?

What is an oratorio?

What was the style of the palace at Versailles, France?

Why was Mannerism a form of art in Spain that was painted by El Greco?

Opera

Music during the Baroque Period brought to the fore the organ, the harpsichord, the violin, and opera. "During the Baroque period the type of modern tonality of major and minor keys emerged. Standard three-note chords became common. The baroque era has been given the dates from 1600 to 1750. Composers began to modulate and a new form of texture became popular. The musical genre of opera also emerged during the Baroque era. Typical subjects for operas were taken from Greek myths. The first great opera composer was the Italian Claudio Monteverdi. Antonio Vivaldi wrote about 80 concerti grossi and composed hundreds of solo concertos. Vivaldi was known for illustrating a sonnet. The most famous piece still performed today is 'Spring' from *The Four Seasons*. He wrote one section in *The Four Seasons* to represent each season" (Parrott 156).

The first opera house was built in Venice, Italy in 1637. By the end of the seventeenth century, there were many other theaters built around Italy. Opera began as an attempt to revive Greek theater and recreate the way in which plays were performed. Early on it was thought (by a group of men known as the Camerata) that Greek plays had been sung. Despite the fact that this was not correct, opera was nevertheless created as a new art form by artists who thought that they were recreating Greek drama (Fiero 286).

John Milton (1608-1674)

John Milton wrote *Paradise Lost*, an epic poem about Satan's rebellion against God that goes into detail about the fall of man. "He became Latin secretary in Cromwell's government and, in several important tracts, one of its defenders" (Lamm and Cross 320). *Paradise Lost* represented the grandeur of the Baroque Period and showed that the power that was deep within an individual is actually a paradise.

Terms and Important Individuals to Consider

Polyphonic texture—two or more melodies sounding together simultaneously

Giovanni Lorenzo Bernini—a great Baroque sculptor who created sculptures such as the *Ecstasy of Saint Teresa* and the Baroque sculpture of the *David*. He also sculpted the large circular Colonnade symbolizing the outstretched arms in front of Saint Peter's Basilica and the Baldachin (altar), which is inside the basilica, and many other sculptures on the exterior of the basilica.

Vivaldi—a Baroque composer known for a famous composition, "The Four Seasons," which uses a small Baroque orchestra playing the four seasons, Summer, Winter, Spring, and Autumn. Winter feels cold. You can hear the birds sing in Spring and hear the leaves fall in the Autumn portion.

Johann Sebastian Bach—a great teacher of the Boys Choir and the Boys School, writer of music for all the Lutheran churches in his town, organist, and composer. He has been said to have left and still influences musicians today about how to write music and understand harmony, composition, and music theory.

Rembrandt van Rijn—a great Baroque portrait painter who did many self-portraits and is known for his important portrait paintings and creative arrangement of space and use of diagonal space and composition. He captured the psychological aspects, deep emotions, and personality of the subjects he painted. He not only painted a representational work of each person, but also much more. He was interested in a deep meaning.

John Milton—a Baroque writer who felt that individuals can find a paradise inside themselves if they search for it. He wrote *Paradise Lost*.

El Greco—a great artist (painter) who was originally from Crete. His real name was Domenikos Theotokopoulous. In his spiritual (religious) work, El Greco created elongated figures for the purpose of showing which individuals were saints or the mother of Jesus Christ (the Madonna), Jesus Christ, or the disciples (followers of Jesus).
> Exception to the rule:
> El Greco was born in Crete (part of Greece) and textbooks like to consider him a Greek painter.
> In art history, artists are considered to be an artist from whichever country they were born; however, El Greco is called Spanish in many books even though he was born on the island of Crete. He is an exception to the rule.

King Louis XIV—a well-known king of France who had the Palace of Versailles built. This is also the time when he and his court lived in luxury, a factor which led to financial problems and eventually caused the French Revolution. During his reign he did support the arts as well as the artists and writers of his day. In 1660, he married the famous Maria Theresa from Spain.
Source: *World Book Encyclopedia*, vol. 12 (New York: Scott Fetzer Publisher, 1992), 478

Hallelujah Chorus—a musical composition called an oratorio. The four-part harmony, sung by vocalists, begins with either an organ playing (accompaniment) or a Baroque orchestra. The orchestra and vocals create a polyphonic texture in many portions of the work. The words, "Hallelujah, Hallelujah, Hallelujah" are repeated over and over. Then other words come in and the texture becomes more complicated (texture is the overlapping of the soprano, alto, tenor, and basses each singing "Hallelujah"). The portion entitled the "Hallelujah Chorus" is only a small portion of the entire length oratorio which contains many sections, but this one is the most well known.

Baldacchino—an altar inside a cathedral. A famous one with twisted columns (with decoration) (not straight) is inside St. Peter's Basilica in the Vatican and was carved by Bernini; it is named St. Peter's Baldachino.

Mannerism in painting—a style that displays some figures longer than others. The figures that are long and out of proportion are sacred individuals, including Jesus Christ, His mother, and His disciples.

Baroque Period Accomplishments

The architecture of the Baroque Period was more dramatic. One notices the use of more decorative and ornate shape and curved lines during the Baroque Period than one notices during the Renassance Period. The Renaissance Period was more emotionally restrained than the Baroque Period. The Baroque Period's architecture and paintings utilized rounded forms and elaborate decor. The Baroque paintings of the Baroque Period were often filled with contrast of light and dark. The muic of the Baroque Period was both secular and played in the courts for the royalty and also composed for the church. There was music created for both the Catholic Church and the Protestant Churches. Some of the great composers were Johann Sebastian Bach, George F. Handel and Antonio Vivaldi.

CLASSICAL PERIOD 11

Since Greek architecture was already referred to as Classic or Classical, eighteenth-century architecture was occasionally referred to as "Neo-Classical" so as not to be confused with that of the earlier period.

The Classical period followed the Baroque period. One of the French writers of the eighteenth century wrote, "God makes all thing good; man meddles with them and they become evil" (Bishop 303). Jean-Jacques Rousseau (1712–78) wrote about the concept that the individual has worth and that science and government can corrupt human goodness. Philosophers at that time went back and forth over issues that dealt with how to establish a society with safeguards to protect freedoms for individuals and …"yet provide an individual's right of a supreme right to freedom and autonomy" (Bishop 303).

The eighteenth century was a significant period that brought about the development of the Classical style of music and the development of the symphony orchestra. It was also during this century that the abolition movement began in France and its colonies. The monarchs gradually began to acknowledge some individual rights, including the beginning of free speech and expanded suffrage, but initially it was not done willingly (Parrott).

Following the lead of John Locke, other eighteenth-century thinkers advocated civil liberties such as basic judicial rights, the right to public assembly, and the freedom of the press. Social and political factors affecting these new ideas included the rise of the middle class and individual enterprise. These developments also contributed the opportunity for some individuals to select their own professions (Parrott).

After the death of Louis XIV in 1715, the cultural center of Europe moved from the Versailles court to Paris. The salons in Paris became gathering places for philosophical and intellectual discussions. The problems of the period were discussed and satire was used to express viewpoints defending the rights of individuals (Parrott).

Public concerts also gave a new group of people the opportunity to experience and appreciate music. During the Classical period, some of the greatest Western composers wrote music that had wide appeal. This music remains meaningful to us today. The three most recognized Classical composers were Franz Joseph Haydn, Wolfgang Amadeus Mozart, and Ludwig Van Beethoven (Parrott).

The thinkers and individuals who organized disciplines into classifications helped alter points of view. Because of these changes in ideas, the eighteenth century has been called the Age of Reason and the Age of Enlightenment (Parrott).

Toward the end of the eighteenth century, the notion that laws should be made with consent of the governed, rather than imposed upon them by royalty, became widespread in the minds of the people. This new mindset inspired two major upheavals. The American Revolution of 1776 and the French Revolution of 1789 shattered the old idea of the divine rights of kings in Western political life (Parrott).

During this period, the greater availability of printed material helped influence the people's opinions. One important work was *Common Sense* by Thomas Paine (1737–1809). Paine moved from England to America in 1774. He was a staunch believer in human rights and wrote anti-slavery tracts. He believed that legitimate laws were designed to protect individual citizens (Parrott).

In 1770, the grandson of Louis XIV was the ruler of Spain. He would be the last Hapsburg ruler of Spain. Louis XIV would be alive for fifteen more years. Britain and the Netherlands allied together in hopes of discouraging Spain and France from possibly uniting. The European powers fought several wars during the eighteenth century. One, the War of the Spanish Succession, was settled by the Treaty of Utrecht. Other wars, such as the conflict between Austria and Prussia, were struggles over the right to rule over hereditary Hapsburg territories. Hostilities between Austria and Prussia developed into a colonial struggle between France and Britain. In America, the conflict was known as the French and Indian War. After winning many of the eighteenth-century wars, Britain became the dominant European power—a position it held until World War I (1914–18).

The philosophers of the eighteenth century embraced the spirit of the Enlightenment. Catholic Austria under Maria Theresa and her son Joseph II enacted reforms. They included freedom for serfs and economic modernization. Peter the Great continued to reform Russia. Catherine II was a German princess. She gained support from the population despite favoring the nobility over the serfs. She believed in educating women and in patronizing the arts.

The thinkers of the Enlightenment, such as Thomas Paine and Benjamin Franklin, were inspired by science, but they believed that God created the universe. These individuals wanted an educational curriculum independent from the Church. The influential thinkers in the Parisian salons were authors such as Denis Diderot, François-Marie Arouet de Voltaire, and Jean-Jacques Rousseau. Their ideas spread to a wide audience in Europe and America through novels, essays, and political pamphlets.

Charles-Louis de Montesquieu, a member of the French nobility and a local judge, wrote satires and political essays. His work was designed as social commentary and intended to send a persuasive message. Montesquieu called for separate jurisdictions divided among executive, legislative, and judicial branches of government. His ideas were very influential and were used by the Framers of the American Constitution (Parrott).

German philosophers during the early seventeenth century were interested in metaphysics. Gottfried Wilhelm von Leibniz (1646–1716) argued that God had created a harmonious universe. Immanuel Kant believed that God existed even though we cannot see him or demonstrate his existence. One the most complex ideas attributed to Kant was transcendental metaphysics. His transcendentalism was adopted by the Romantic movement (Parrott).

Unlike Kant, David Hume, a Scottish philosopher and historian, was interested in the limits of reason and the distinction between inner and outer experience.

The main artistic style in France after Louis XIV died was the Rococo style. Rococo artists such as Jean-Antoine Watteau and François Boucher represented the frivolity, fine material possessions, and rich taste of that style. Artists in Britain produced their own version of the Rococo style. British artists focused on portraiture rather than the frivolity of Boucher's work.

The director of the Royal Academy of Arts was founded in London in 1768. Sir Joshua Reynolds (1723–92) was its first director. He advocated the study of Greek and Roman art and he introduced the idea of combining Classical and Rococo features.

Robert Adam, an architect from Scotland, combined Greek, Roman, and Etruscan designs with Rococo color schemes in his buildings.

William Hogarth was an English engraver who drew and etched the working class and used satire to expose the aristocrats' way of life. Still life and genre painting help viewers today understand eighteenth-century bourgeois style. The best-known painter of the bourgeois style was Jean-Baptiste-Siméon Chardin.

Virtuoso musicians traveled from city to city. Women learned to play the harp, and men tended to take up the violin or flute. Composers began to write music and perform for their own enjoyment rather than for a special occasion. The style of the eighteenth century is referred to as Classical. This is due to its structure, proportion, order, and formal organization. Mozart, Beethoven, and Haydn were major composers who wrote lengthy symphonies for orchestra. A major German composer of opera was Christoph Willibald Gluck. Gluck emphasized the chorus just like the Greeks had done in their performances of Greek tragedy.

The orchestra began to take on its standard form of four sections during the middle of the eighteenth century. The piano was an important instrument that also came into use toward the end of the eighteenth century. During the Classical Period, composers such as Mozart and Beethoven composed music that utilized the timbre unique to the individual instrument. They also began writing for all four sections of the orchestra, which created a new sound. The earliest symphonies performed at that time had three or four movements and were written in the sonata form. Franz Joseph Haydn was known as the fist major classical composer. Haydn's *The Creation* is an oratorio based on Milton's *Paradise Lost* (Parrott).

Wolfgang Amadeus Mozart was a child prodigy who wrote forty-one symphonies. He also wrote operas such as *The Marriage of Figaro*, *The Magic Flute*, and *Don Giovanni*. He was a master violinist and a highly skilled pianist.

Ludwig van Beethoven can be placed into the Romantic period toward the end of his life. Beethoven studied with Haydn and used the structure of the Classical style. However, Beethoven was a composer who expressed very intense emotions in his work. His music reflected a unique style, which was more free form, and had an extended musical range (Parrott).

When the British King George III needed funds to pay the debt he amassed during the Seven Years War, he forced the colonists to pay taxes. The Stamp Act of 1765 required the colonists to purchase a stamp or license for the right to read a newspaper, send a letter, or sign a contract. The king eventually repealed the tax, but the problem was not solved. In 1770, British troops fired on colonists in an incident known as the Boston Massacre. In 1773, colonists from Massachusetts protested a tax on tea by throwing tea from ships into Boston Harbor. The First Continental Congress met in Philadelphia. In 1776, the pamphleteer Thomas Paine published the tract *Common Sense* in which he declared that the American colonies were a new nation.

Thomas Paine and *Common Sense*

Thomas Paine was born in 1737 in England. He went to Philadelphia in 1774 and in 1776 he began the sale of his pamphlet known as *Common Sense*. This forty-seven-page book influenced the minds of many early settlers in America to become independent. It has been said that this pamphlet had one of the biggest impacts upon individuals in transforming their attitude from being the colonies to becoming independent and joining in the American Revolution.

Source: http://www.history.com/this-day-in-history/thomas-paine-publishes-common-sense

Thomas Paine served in the United States Army and was employed by the U.S. Commission of Foreign Affairs. He returned to Europe in 1787. He then wrote other pamphlets related to topics influencing the ideas of independence which helped persuade individuals to support the French Revolution. After that, Thomas Paine was arrested in Europe for his political opinions. For that reason, he fled to the United States in 1802. He died in 1809 in New York.

Source: http://www.history.com/this-day-in-history/thomas-paine-publishes-common-sense

The Second Continental Congress formed a committee to draft a statement of independence. The document, primarily drafted by Thomas Jefferson, was the Declaration of Independence.

Despite the Enlightenment views of the Framers of the Constitution, slavery was retained. In 1789 George Washington declined an offer to become king and instead accepted the office of president. Thomas Jefferson became the third president of the United States. He was also a musician and an architect. He founded the University of Virginia because he was a firm believer in public education and a humanist curriculum. The Rotunda at the University of Virginia reflects the shape and form of the Roman Pantheon (Parrott).

During the summer of 1789, 80,000 commoners, enraged at the high cost of grain and bread, stormed the Bastille prison in Paris in search of ammunition and weapons. In August, the National Assembly wrote the Declaration of the Rights of Man and of the Citizen. The clergy were reclassified as ordinary citizens, and the king was made chief executive but had no right to enact laws. Also, slavery was abolished in France. In June 1791, Louis XVI and his queen, the unpopular Marie-Antoinette, tried to escape, but they were captured and imprisoned. Marie-Antoinette was reported to have said, "Let them eat cake," when she was told that many people were starving because of bread shortages. The artist Elisabeth Vigée-Lebrun (1755–1842) captured this attitude in her portrait of the queen. The artist Jacques Louis David reflected his anger over injustice in his paintings. An example is *The Oath of the Tennis Court*.

In the United States, the rule of the monarchs was over. France was stabilized by Napoléon, but only temporarily (Parrott).

Terminology

Cadenza—part of a solo that displays extremely good technical skill.
Coda—the end of a section of music added on.
Development—the middle section of an orchestral or piano composition in sonata form.
Duet—two performers playing together.
Epistolary—type of novel that uses letters and diaries to reveal character.
Exposition—first section of a piece of music where the theme is stated.
Galant—elegant, light, and simple style of music popular during the eighteenth century.
Masque—a short dramatic composition of allegorical content usually performed as a mime, music, and dance for the court.
Metaphysics—type of philosophy dealing with existence and understanding.
Recapitulation—the third section of a movement in a composition in sonata form that is restated in the home key.

Rondo—musical form used in symphonies, sonatas, and chamber works that is based on a recurrent theme.
Sonata—musical composition that includes several movements for solo instruments.
Sonata form—used in the Classical period for symphony music, string quartets, and piano. It has the three movements: exposition, development, and recapitulation.
String quartet—an ensemble of instruments: two violins, a viola, and a cello.
Symphony—means "sounding together." An orchestral work with three or four movements.
Tonic—musical key that is the home key.

QUESTIONS

Questions to Contemplate

Why do you think the Framers of the American Constitution retained slavery?

Why did Thomas Jefferson design the University of Virginia to look like the Pantheon?

What were Thomas Jefferson's beliefs about a humanist curriculum and public education?

What was meant by Marie-Antoinette's comment, "Let them eat cake."

Who was an influential writer who started the University of Virginia? What were some of his main beliefs?

How were Montesquieu's ideas and his treatise *The Spirit of Laws* (1748) used by the Framers of the American Constitution?

What type of music did Beethoven write?

What type of music did Mozart write?

What are the characteristics of Classical music?

Describe the paintings of Jacques Louis David of France.

Accomplishments of the FINE Art Forms of the Classical Period and Neo-Classical Period

Rejection of the Baroque decorative type of sculpture and use of more formal and orderly arrangements and formal balance

Rejection of the use of strong diagonals in the overall arrangement of space in paintings

The use of formal balance and order by painters

The use of formal balance and order in the musical arrangements in compositions

The beginning of the symphony orchestra with four sections: Brass, Woodwinds, Strings, Percussion

The use of piano with the orchestra

The use of a conductor, because the orchestra is larger than a Baroque orchestra

The use of the sonata – allegro form in symphony orchestra compositions

The use of piano along with the symphony orchestra in compositions

The composition became popular: the concerto

In architecture: the use of the style which utilized the ancient Greek forms such as their columns and the Roman use of their dome

Source: http://www.visual-arts-cork.com/sculpture/neoclassical-sculptors.htm

ROMANTIC PERIOD 12

The Romantic period followed the Classical period. The period between 1760 and 1830 has been described as a time when the middle class began to win power from the aristocracy.

Liberalism and nationalism were two philosophical trends that had been inspired by the Enlightenment. Liberal thinkers advocated the rights of citizens. The nationalists affirmed the importance of national culture and independent statehood, and contributed to cultural distinctions between evolving nations. Classicism was appropriated by Napoléon to promote his power and image (Parrott).

An American author, Henry David Thoreau, espoused transcendentalism. Thoreau believed in the natural goodness of humanity, and concluded that people are capable of governing themselves. He thought that the best form of government is no government at all (Parrott).

In 1804, Napoléon Bonaparte proclaimed himself emperor and expanded French authority in Europe. Napoléon had attended military school in France and was a general by the time he was twenty-four. Napoléon governed France as a military dictator. In 1801, Napoléon's legal system codified the idea of the secular state and gave the state supremacy over the Catholic Church. Napoléon declared that Roman Catholicism was the primary religion of France. He also granted religious freedom to Protestants and Jews. Napoléon was not progressive in his thinking about the role of women. He maintained that women should remain home and take care of children. Napoléon died in 1821 after being exiled for the second time (Parrott).

The art and architecture of Napoléon's reign reflect his manipulation of power. Napoléon's building campaign adopted Roman architectural forms, such as the triumphal arch, that reflected his imperial status. The painting of Napoléon by Jacques-Louis David was done in the tradition of imperial equestrian portraits. David was a Classical painter who Napoléon used to promote himself. Sometimes historians referred to that type of art as propaganda art (Parrott).

After the Napoleonic period, the restoration of a constitutional monarchy under Louis XVIII followed. A bid to restore absolutism by King Charles X restricted the rights of citizens. Unrest followed and workers in Paris revolted. By 1848, a revolution sparked by workers and middle-class liberals overthrew the Chamber of Deputies. Two years later, the nephew of emperor Napoléon was elected president. He was defeated in the Franco-Prussian War and the French Third Republic began (Parrott).

Romanticism was a style that reflected ideals of freedom and began in Paris. The style spread to other areas of Europe including Spain, Britain, the German states, Russia, and North America. Romanticism flourished in music and literature until the end of the nineteenth century. The themes used by the Romantic artists emphasized social justice, freedom, and a sense of national pride (Parrott).

In 1853 Richard Wagner published the librettos to *Der Ring des Nibelungen* (*The Ring Cycle*): *Das Rheingold, Die Walküre*, Seigfried, and *Die Gotterdamerung*. *The Ring Cycle* is considered one of the most ambitious musical projects ever undertaken by a single person. In 1877 Iliac Tchaikovsky finished *Swan Lake* and Johannes Brahms completed his *First Symphony*. The symphony expanded in size from the Classical symphony, however it maintained the four sections. The size of the percussion section increased. The piano became a solo instrument, and it also became a popular instrument to be used in concerto compositions.

In contrast to those of the Romantic period, the figures in paintings of the Classical period, such as Jacque-Louis David's *The Oath of the Horatii*, seem somewhat detached. In Romantic paintings the figures are more emotional and the viewers are forced to respond. For example, *Raft of the Medusa*, by Romantic painter Theodore Gericault, features a dead man on a raft in the foreground and in the upper portion of the painting is a figure waving a flag as if to signal for help. The image emphasizes the subjects' hope of rescue. However, if one looks closely one notices that a huge wave is coming toward the raft. Some think Gericault intended his work to be a social commentary. His message may have been that until the oppressed in society are taken care of, no one will be emancipated (Stokstad 992). This painting, which is considered one of the major Romantic paintings and one of Gericault's best, reflects the characteristics of Romantic painting.

Classical Painting

Detached
Emotional restraint
Subject matter many times about Greek and Roman themes

Romantic Painting

Intimate and emotional
Subjects show feelings and ideas about humanity and despair
Subject matter about everyday or contemporary issues, horror, life against death, and violence

After the early years of the French Revolution, King Charles IV of Spain reinstituted the Inquisition. The French Revolution, which had created many reforms, had filled many people with hope; among these was court painter Francesco de Goya. King Charles IV refused to allow French books to be imported into Spain. Goya produced his own commentary through a series of prints created between 1796 and 1798. They were etchings and aquatints and are known as *Los Caprichos* (*The Caprices*). Goya's prints expressed the idea that if reason sleeps, then monsters will be produced. Another of Goya's works that reflects the time period and may help define Romanticism is the painting *Execution of the Third of May*. It portrays the victim very prominently on the left side of the canvas. He stands out in his yellow and white attire and has his hand raised. On the right side of the canvas are the French soldiers who are lined up with their weapons raised and ready for action.

"In 1808 Napoléon conquered Spain and placed on its throne his brother Joseph Bonaparte. Many Spanish citizens including Goya welcomed the French at first because of the reforms they inaugurated, including a new, more liberal constitution. On May 2, 1808, however, a rumor spread in Madrid that the French planned to kill the royal family. The populace rose up, and a day of bold street fighting ensued, followed by mass arrests. Hundreds of Spanish people were herded into a convent, and a French firing squad executed these helpless prisoners in the predawn hours of May 3rd" (Stokstad 998).

Characteristics of Classical and Romantic Music

Classical Music
Piano came about
Modern sonata form emerged
Orchestra developed four sections
  (strings, woodwinds, brass, percussion)
  and featured four movements and
  certain forms (i.e., A B A form)
Emotional restraint

Composers
Beethoven
Haydn
Mozart

Romantic Music
Piano became a solo instrument
Operas became extravagant with elaborate stage sets
Orchestra increased in size and lacked formal
  structure. Not always four movements

Emotionalism
Subjectivity
Nationalism, pride of country

Composers
Brahms
Chopin
Liszt
Mendelssohn
Schubert
Schumann
Tchaikovsky
Wagner

Accomplishments of the Art Forms of the Romantic Period

The Romantic Period drew upon the French Revolution's rejection of aristocratic and social and political norms. (Source: http://www.newworldencyclopedia.org/entry/Romanticism)

The artistic topics expressed by poets, writers and musicians were about nationalism and pride for their country. Musicians used folk tunes as inspiration for composing compositions. Folk tunes were incorporated into motifs into symphonies. Some composers used melodies and added a piano accompaniment. (Franz Schubert would be an example)

During the Romantic Period, musical compositions became less formal than they had been during the Classical Period. For example, Classical symphonies usually had four movements but during the Romantic Period that rule was broken. The piano also became a solo instrument and composers such as Frederick Chopin played concerts with just the piano by itself.

Topics (subject matter) during the Romantic Period represented the way humans behave such as inhumane behavior towards one another. (Inhumanity to man theme such as the painting by Francesco de Goya *The Execution of the Third of May*) Romantic Art differs from Classical Period art in that Romantic Period Art may represent more intense emotions such as strong forceful tense feelings of hate, anger, and even show in art or through sound, brutality and compassion. Classical art tends to be less in its intensity with more emotional restraint.

NINETEENTH CENTURY 13

The name for the painting style known as "Impressionism" came about through the exhibition of a group of paintings at a show for rejected works. In the nineteenth century, a special group of jurors were selected by the French Academy to judge the art that was to be shown each year in an official annual exhibition of paintings. That art exhibit had a long, prestigious tradition, and each year many painters were left out of the exhibit. Finally, in 1863, many of the artists who were rejected rebelled and Napoléon III responded. An exhibit, called the "Salon des Refusés," was held, but it was unsuccessful because so many artists were scorned and ridiculed. Because of its poor reception, the Salon des Refusés was not held again for many years. However, several of the artists who participated in the failed exhibit would soon change art history forever (Phipp and Wink 210). A story has been told about how the name Impressionism got started. In 1874, a small group of artists decided to have a private showing of their work. The artists who exhibited at that showing included Edouard Manet, Paul Cezanne, Auguste Renoir, Camille Pissarro, Edgar Degas, and Claude Monet. Monet's painting of a boat in the water at sunrise was written about in a newspaper and derogatorily titled *Impression Sunrise*. It has been called that ever since. Monet painted *Impression Sunrise* using pure colors and very free-flowing, fluid movements with his brush. The Impressionists, as they came to be called, were able to paint outdoors in the open air since their paint came out of tubes. Before, artists had to mix their paint in the studio. The Impressionists were fascinated with the way in which reflected light changed the look of an object at different times of day. For example, Claude Monet painted a façade of one cathedral at different times of the day just to show how the light changed the color of the building.

Monet painted *Impression Sunrise* in 1873. It was oil on canvas and measured $19\frac{3}{8} \times 25\frac{1}{2}$ inches. The painting had been at the Musee Marmottan-Claude Monet in Paris, France, until it was stolen.

Students may ask why the famous Vincent Van Gogh was not in the list above.

Vincent did not live in Paris until later on, and he did not paint *Starry Night* until 1898. His brother was an art dealer, but he was unable to sell his paintings. Van Gogh was not considered an Impressionist painter, although he was influenced by the Impressionists. Particularly important to Vincent's work were the artists Toulouse Lautrec and Georges-Pierre Seurat. Both artists lived in Paris and were known by the Impressionists. Lautrec created posters for the famous cabaret Moulin Rouge, and Seurat was considered to be a pointillist. Pointillism is similar to Impressionism, but the pointillist uses little dots, rather than brushstrokes, of opposite color to create an image.

The two best-known Russian Realist authors were Leo Tolstoy (1828–1910) and Fyodor Dostoyevsky (1821–81). Tolstoy's *War and Peace* dealt with the aftermath of Napoléon's invasion of Russia, including how that invasion left an aristocratic family in Moscow in a precarious position.

Fyodor Dostoyevsky grew up in Moscow and portrayed his characters with some of his own psychological interests. His psychological portrayals of character were imbued with themes of guilt and redemption. The hero in *The Idiot* was an epileptic, and so was Dostoyevsky. The author would write about himself through his characters.

Realism also made an impact in the theater and in music. Three major Realist playwrights of the later nineteenth century, who were credited with bringing modernism to theater, were Anton Chekhov, August Strindberg, and Henrik Ibsen. In opera, Realism was expressed through realistic characters. Some of the characters of writers such as Georges Bizet were tormented by passionate feelings of love and jealously. In Italy, the type of operatic Realism that represented subjects like vulnerable women who suffer and die for love was called verismo. Realism was preoccupied with economic hardship (Parrott 193).

The subjects of Realist art were often fantasy, sentiment, and social reality. The French Realist painter Gustave Courbet said, "Show me an angel and I'll paint one." A woman who was the first woman to receive the Legion of Honor was admired internationally for her paintings of Queen Victoria and horses. Honoré Daumier had his first solo exhibition when he was seventy years old. He observed the lower class and was well known for his depictions of their deplorable living conditions. Daumier wanted to draw attention to the injustice of society through his artwork. He was determined to do something about the suffering he saw, and was working on a method of correcting problems of inhumanity to man. (Parrott)

Edouard Manet admired the art critic Emile Zola. They both agreed that artists should have the right of free expression.

Emile Zola was of the opinion that if one wrote about the inhumane behavior towards people then there could be more attention drawn to the problems, and solutions could be obtained. Édouard Manet painted Emile Zola which is considered to be a major work of Manet's career and a master portrait. Zola's writings made an impact towards improving conditions and Manet's paintings created a new form of art for that time. They both were of the mindset that writers and painters should have the right to produce their work without restrictions and have the right to express themselves through their creations.

The Pre-Raphaelites were dedicated to artistic change and social reform. Photography was a new way of representing life. It accurately recorded a moment in time. This new technique actually enhanced the illusion of realism. Private portrait studios were set up during the late nineteenth century.

After the Revolutionary War in the United States, the new country expanded its territory as settlers moved west. Between 1804 and 1806, Meriwether Lewis and William Clark led an expedition into western territories that inspired settlers to follow. In 1830, the Indian Removal Act required all Native Americans to relocate west of the Mississippi River into what is now Oklahoma. Native Americans were pushed further and further west. White men felt threatened by the Native American Ghost Dance, and they feared that the Indians would create a problem and be violent. The United States cavalry intercepted a band of Sioux and ordered them to camp at Wounded Knee. The next day a rifle went off, which started a chaotic chain of events. At the end of the day, more than three hundred people were killed. The massacre at Wounded Knee marked the end of the Ghost Dance movement. It became a symbol for the Native Americans of their people's brutalization by the United States Cavalry and some government official (Parrott).

During the nineteenth century, abolitionists in the United States tried to end slavery. John Brown, a white man, led a massacre in Kansas in which five slave owners were killed.

He was unsuccessful in freeing the slaves, and he was captured and hanged. Abolitionists and former slaves devised a network known as the Underground Railroad. People opposed to slavery helped slaves escape and travel north to freedom along this route.

The United States fought a civil war between 1861 and 1865. On January 1, 1863, Abraham Lincoln issued the Emancipation Proclamation, which officially freed slaves in rebellious states. The Civil War ended in 1865, and from 1867 to 1877, Congress imposed a policy known as Reconstruction.

The Midwest was the home of the early American skyscraper. According to Louis Henry Sullivan and other members of the Chicago School, a building's form should reflect its purpose, function, and style.

An important American author who was influenced by listening to the voices of Americans was Samuel Langhorne Clemens. Clemens was known as Mark Twain (1835–1910). He wrote *The Adventures of Tom Sawyer* and *The Adventures of Huckleberry Finn* (Parrott).

Claude Debussy (1862–1918), sometimes labeled an Impressionist, was one of the composers who changed the way music sounded. The sound that Debussy created was influenced by his desire to reflect the way things sounded in the atmosphere. This is similar to the ways Impressionist painters found inspiration in how light changes from one moment to the next. Debussy also changed the way that he composed by emphasizing the whole tone scale.

QUESTIONS

Questions to Contemplate

What was the "Salon des Refuses"?

Which of Claude Monet's paintings gave the Impressionist movement its name?

Where did Impressionism begin?

What made Impressionism different from traditional painting?

How was Daumier's subject matter different from Monet's?

Where was one of the first skyscrapers built?

NINETEENTH-CENTURY ACCOMPLISHMENTS

The style of art called Impressionism

Claude Monet, Auguste Renoir, Mary Cassatt, Edgar Degas, Paul Cezanne, Camille Pisarro, Edouard Manet (Impressionist painters)

Auguste Rodin—a great sculptor who created *The Thinker*

Vincent Van Gogh—considered to be a post-Impressionist

Admittance of women into the Legion of Honor to show work

Lewis and Clark Expedition

Underground Railroad in an attempt to help slaves escape to freedom

Civil War 1861–1865 in the United States

Emancipation Proclamation (1863) by President Abraham Lincoln

Mark Twain (Samuel Langehorne Clemens)—wrote *The Adventures of Hucklebery Finn* and *The Adventures of Tom Sawyer*

TWENTIETH CENTURY 14

Author Philip E. Bishop described the twentieth century as turbulent. He aptly stated that the twentieth century was the first time it was possible for a series of events to be capable, through the power of communication, of affecting the entire globe almost all at once. Between 1914 and 1918, a war between the European powers expanded into a world war that killed 9 million people. Russia emerged from the war as a communist state. This development created tension between Eastern and Western Europe. That unrest is reflected in the arts. By examining developments in painting, literature, and music, one can imagine the turmoil and complexity of that period. The many artistic styles were directly related to current events, and reflected the turmoil and despair that were felt by many people. The styles that emerged from that period had major repercussions upon the art world. Twentieth-century art forms reflect the lifestyle changes of people trying to keep up with the quickening pace of life.

Advancements in the field of communications ushered in a new way of thinking about the world and one's place in it. For some people, expansive new methods of communication meant more freedom. However, for others the developments encouraged new ways of living that challenged the old, traditional values. The new, fast-paced communication developments seemed too complicated and caused some people in older generations to wonder if their traditional way of life was going to disappear forever (Bishop). That created a climate for change, and artists represented the new viewpoints in their work.

Through the use of radio and the telegraph, the world was becoming more aware of what was going on in other areas of the globe. The development of a broader global awareness among people from many different countries and cultures was beginning to take shape. Television, radio, the telegraph, and motion pictures all played a role in creating a "global community." "Some people were not able to cope with the fast moving pace whereas others thrived on the rapid advances made in technology ..." (Dixon and Fleming).

There were some individuals who were very creative and expressed society's uncertainty through their artwork. For example, in 1920 William Yeats wrote a poem that reflected the attitude of the early twentieth century. The poem is about a bird who flew over the area where he lived and, without much regard for listening to his master anymore, paid no attention to what was being said. Yeats wrote:

> Turning and turning in the widening gyre
> The falcon cannot hear the falconer;
> Things fall apart; the center cannot hold;
> Mere anarchy is loosed upon the world,

> The blood-dimmed tide is loosed, and everywhere
> The ceremony of innocence is drowned;
> The best lack all conviction, while the worst
> Are full of passionate intensity.
> (William Yeats, "The Second Coming")

There were new forces rising in the world and "Western-style democracy all sought to shape mass society through the arts of mass appeal" (Bishop 390).

In a handbook for the *Arts and Ideas* text by William Fleming, Laurinda Dixon eloquently described the twentieth century in terms of "isms" and "schisms." The following are just a few of her clear statements and concise, easy-to-understand phrases that explain the twentieth century. After reading her commentary the art, music, literature, dance, and theater of the twentieth century make more sense. The purpose of abstraction and chance music and art makes perfect sense when one realizes that it has various viewpoints, that it can be seen from many angles, and that it may not mean the same thing to each individual viewing it. The twentieth century was a time of conflict, disorder, and the questioning of values.

Laurinda Dixon, Syracuse University Professor,stated that

> It had been said that the 20th century was change and variety than the past 1,000 year all told. Technology had grown with bewildering speed, and the world's store of knowledge was now so vast that it was impossible for a singe person to understand everything. During the first half of the 20th century within the memories of many people alive today, motion pictures were born; the automobile, radio and the airplane were invented and the first skyscraper was built. Science and Technology became the new gods of the modern world, and the discipline of psychoanalysis was developed to care for the psychic wound inflicted by the intolerable stress of living in such complex times. The 20th century ushered in a age of crisis, as the disputes that were contained in the 19th century broke out into open conflict. For fifty years the world was plunged into almost continuous war, made more horrible by modern machines and chemical weapons. World War I, hopefully was christened as the 'war to end all wars,' but raged from 1913 to 1918. From 1917 on, bloody revolutions broke out in Russia, Italy, Spain and Germany. In 1939 a second World War began, more horrible than the first. As a result, the cultural scene during this time reflected the constant threat of violence and annihilation as well as the pressures of industrial society. The number of different artistic styles, each ending with an 'ism', which developed during the first half of the 20th century, may seem obscure and confusing. However, it was there where knowledge of past human motives and experiences comes to our rescue. Human beings tend to react to extreme crisis in two ways: either rationally or emotionally. Some would rather escape from unpleasant things, giving vent to strong emotions and spontaneous feelings. Others prefer to detach themselves from the turmoil, so as to analyze, reform and intellectualize the crisis. Likewise, the cultural movements of thee time fall naturally into the camps: "abstract, expressionist and cubism nonobjective etc..." (Dixon and Fleming).

World War II

The war in Europe was over by May 1945, and the war in the Pacific ended by August. The Allies liberated the countries that had been conquered by the Axis powers, and they were horrified by the results. The were especially disgusted when they saw that the Nazis had placed the Jews in concentration camps. The Allies planned to invade Japan in late 1945, but on August 6, 1945 an atomic bomb was dropped on Hiroshima. Three days later another bomb hit Nagasaki. The Japanese surrendered on August 14. There were 17 million lives lost during World War II; many of the casualties were civilians. Around 6 million Jews had been starved, tortured, or killed in the concentration camps. "After the war, the USSR controlled most of eastern Europe, Germany was divided. War criminals were tried for crimes against humanity. As reconstruction began, the United Nations was formed to try to prevent future wars" (*Encyclopedia of the World*).

Expressionism

Expressionism was a term used to describe paintings that were emotionally demonstrative and often about the dark side of human nature. The artist used distortion in order to express the intensity of the emotion.

Surrealism

Surrealism was a painting style that reflected the ideas that artists used dreams and the subconscious to express their thoughts and ideas in their art. The works seemed illogical and may have almost appeared to be like a dream or even a nightmare.

Abstract Expressionism

Abstract Expressionism was a movement that developed in the United States and was characterized by the effort to avoid using forms that looked like recognizable objects. Instead, the work was intended to reflect the stream of consciousness. The piece of art may only consist of lines, colors, and shapes; there are no recognizable objects represented in the painting.

Dadaism

Dadaism was a movement that took an object and destroyed its function. For example, an iron to be made into a sculpture would have nails driven into it so it would not work. The words "da da" were used to represent the meaninglessness of the art itself. Dadaism expressed ideas of futility.

In music, the composer who wanted to represent the idea of the twelve-tone row, or serialism, was Arnold Schoenberg. He wanted to prove that he could play the composition as if it was regular music.

Accomplishments of the Twentieth Century

1901 Wireless radio transmission

1902 First international box-office smash, Georges Melies' fantasy *A Trip to the Moon* opened a new type of entertainment for the public

1903 Orville and Wilbur Wright flew an airplane aloft for 12 seconds

1905 Einstein's theory of relativity

1906 Picasso's "Cubism" famous painting *Les Demoiselle Avignon*

1906 Air conditioning

1909 Assembly line in auto industry by Henry Ford, making ownership of the Model-T affordable

1920's Jazz—America's musical contribution to the world, born in the United States and comes from the Blues

1921 Insulin was developed

1926 Television first became available and by the end of 1950s would be in many more homes in the United States

1927 Lindbergh flies the Atlantic Ocean

1930 The Empire State Building, which took 7 million man-hours to build and was the tallest skyscraper in the world

1939 Plasma and blood typing emerged

1946 First computers

1954 Polio shots available

1964 Civil rights movement in the United States

1967 First heart transplant

1989 Fall of the Berlin Wall

1990 Disabled rights movement

1991 Internet

1997 Hong Kong returned to China

1997 First mammal cloned

Source: http://cjonline.com/stories/121299/mcc_achievements.shtml#.V6VQY1srJdg

UNIT 4

Music and Listening

About This Music Unit

In this unit about music, the listening portion is essential. The listening is found in the Music examples prepared by the professor. These examples are in chronological order. Listening to music takes a longer time than looking at paintings. These examples are in the order purposely in your book and if you listen in the same order as you read along with the text it is helpful. You will understand the progression of music from the Middle Ages until more recent times and read about the composer and the factors that influenced the work and the composition.

This music unit has been written with the hopes that you will listen as well as read about the lives of the composer who wrote the music and read about why the composer wrote it and what factors influenced the work. Each composition is explained to help you understand what instruments or voices are heard. The composition is described and the life of the composer is also in the same paragraphs for you to read while listening to the composition on the computer. The time period that the composer lived is also important to notice when you read. Throughout this unit there are also lists of characteristics of the musical periods.

Music Elements

Melody: single succession of tones

Harmony: two or more tones sounding together

Rhythm: the beat or the pulsation

Tempo: rate of speed

Dynamics: degrees of loudness or softness

Four Categories of JUDGEMENT or Ways to Evaluate a Work

Sincerity
Is the artist being honest? Is the person who created or performed or composed genuine in the endeavor? An artist who is honest and genuine produces great works, not fads.

Craftsmanship
Also referred to as the technique. The ability of the singer or instrument to produce the sounds; to be able to perform that sound consistently and accurately when under pressure. Such an artist is even tempered and disciplined in the work.

Magnitude
The impact that the work or performance has on the person or people looking at it or listening or seeing it. This has to do with how it makes someone feel and if the person or audience remember it because if it leaves an impact upon them it will have left behind something for them to think about.

Universality
Universal feelings that influence many composers and writers to write about since they feel happy or sad and respond to their deep feelings. These innate feeling include sadness, happiness, fear, elation, excitement, hope, joy, anticipation, and anger.

MUSIC: COMPOSITIONS AND COMPOSERS

Why Study Music

Studying art and music builds self-esteem and self-discipline. A school pilot program showed that in schools without Fine Arts, more students acted out their hostilities than in schools where students had Fine Arts classes. Also, certain research has shown that music can improve one's ability to concentrate.

The study completed by the Texas Music Educator found that participation in music helped students succeed in the business world. The reasons for being more successful with having music in their background was that participation in music required them to have been involved in the creative process, to use their higher level thinking and problem solving skills. Music also helped students be able to relate to their employers or employees or to their clients who may be from diverse cultures or who may have diverse backgrounds and/or ideas. The study showed that music gave students a more enriched and enhanced environment which led to their success. During the study, music continued to remain a major part of the students' educational experience; music continued to be a meaningful part of their life and remained with them into their workplace.

In Humanities classes, many times questions will have several correct answers rather than a single answer. The study of humanities helps one understand how solutions to problems can take on many forms.

LISTENING TO MUSIC IN UNIT 4

When you listen to the examples of music from this unit, listen for the sounds of the music very closely. Many students automatically listen for the words of music because words are what they notice. Listening for the words is fine, but there is much more to listening to music than just the words. A musical composition that has words is called a *song*. If the music is played by a symphony orchestra and there is no singing (vocal music), then the music can be properly called a *composition*.

The word *timbre* is pronounced differently than it appears in English. It sounds like "tam-bray." *Timbre* means that the sound of the instrument that you are listening to or playing has a certain unique sound that makes its quality sound only like that particular instrument. For example, a trombone sounds very different from a clarinet due to the timbre or quality of its sound.

When you listen to a symphony orchestra play a composition, listen for the timbre. In other words, listen for which instruments are playing. Are there many instruments playing at one time or just one or two that you really notice more than others? Are there some instruments playing a melody or catchy phrase that you hear that is repeated frequently?

Do you hear a beat or pulse? This would be the element of music called the *rhythm*. The rhythm would be felt as 1,2,3 in its pulsation or in a 1,2,3,4 or 1,2 feel. We usually refer to the Baroque, Classical, and Romantic periods of music as having pulsations of duple 1,2 or triple 1,2,3 as the rhythm. The musical styles of each one of these time periods was different since the instruments and the events and the reasons for the musicians writing the musical compositions was unique to their particular time period.

Music that has a fast and slow speed and changes rapidly can express a different type of feeling than a composition that stays the same rate of speed throughout the composition. For example, when you listen to a chant from the Middle Ages, one does not hear a pulse that is very established such as what you hear when you listen to a Johann Sebastian Bach Brandenburg concerto. Times changed, such as the way people believed and the types of instruments that were available. A chant is sometimes called unmetered (without a pulse or beat).

Listen closely as you read and listen to the musical examples in this unit to the main theme or notes that are in a pattern called the melody. Ask yourself if the melody is fancy or plain in its sound. Is it fast or slow in its rate of speed (tempo)? Does the melody sound like it is moving in a flowing or jagged form? Does the melody sound like it has many sounds of tones with the melody? (Is there an accompaniment with the melody?)

Does the melody also have another melody that comes in with it so that you can hear two overlapping melodies simultaneously? (Two melodies together is considered a texture of polyphony or polyphonic texture.)

If you hear only one line of progression of tones it is monody. Chants such as the Gregorian chants named after Pope Gregory are considered to be monophonic texture.

Is there a melody accompanied with chords? (Melody with blocks of sounds is homophonic texture.)

Is the music you are listening to loud or soft or does it go between being loud to soft and soft to loud or vice versa? (This is called dynamics.)

Listen to all of the elements of music when you listen to the examples in this unit and you will learn to distinguish between the various styles of music from the Middle Ages, Renaissance, Baroque, Classical, Romantic, Impressionism, and the twentieth century.

You will find that music has unique sounds from different time periods. The reason for this is due to the economic, religious, political, and social factors that influenced the composers when they wrote their music.

Listening to music takes time and the ability to pay very close attention to details.

Example 1: *Hodie Christus Natus Est*

Gregorian chants were sung in the Christian Church during the Middle Ages. The words, which were Latin, were themselves unmetered, being sung to the text. All rhythm came from the text (Eisman et al.).

During the Middle Ages, people sang both secular and sacred music. Secular, or everyday music, was not considered an appropriate style for church use, for pagan music was distrusted by the Church. The Church also banned the use of instruments during the services. "During the fourth century St. Jerome expressed the hope that no sound of the lute or harp would ever contaminate the chastity of any woman's ears. But in the monasteries vocal music was welcomed, for it played an important part in the growing liturgy and the school curriculum" (Politoske 62).

During the Middle Ages, when the Roman Empire was fading, life for peasants and commoners was difficult, for lands were subject to invasions by bands of barbarians who destroyed their buildings and livestock. From this chaos emerged the feudal system.

> Feudalism was a political decision of territory into units, each one small enough to be governed by one man. It encouraged warfare and bloodshed since no ultimately powerful authority controlled the individual parts. Feudal lords continually raided each other in attempts to increase their wealth and property. Feudalism was based on a system of vassalage, and in that system were kings and barons, the latter supposedly responsible to, or a vassal of[,] the former. However very rarely did enough power exist at any level above the individual landholder in order to have an influence. There were many despotic rulers who were in control and who flourished. Trapped at the bottom of this rigid social structure (and often in the middle of the bloodletting) were the common people or serfs. Serfs were little more than slaves. Which were attached to work on the land and work for the local lord and be subject to the lord's bidding. It was a life of ignorance and destitution. As Christianity spread, the terrors of "today" were endured in anticipation of a reward in a life to come (Sporre, *Creative Impulse* 186–187).

The most powerful force during this time was the Christian Church. On occasion, when songs and dances were heard by Church authorities near a churchyard, commoners were told that "ballads and dancing and evil songs [will] lure the devil" (Politoske 61).

A Gregorian chant such as *Hodie Christus Natus Est* (Today Christ Is Born) was sung in unison, in which the same tone is sounded by multiple voices. Chants were known as plainsongs and were single lines of melody sung without instrumental accompaniment. Chants were unmetered or unmeasured, and tempos were chosen to fit the text. The chants during the Middle Ages were based on Church modes. (A mode is one of the various diatonic scales that begins with one sound, such as A, B, C, D, E, F, or G.) The text was sung in Latin.

Hodie Christus natus est:	Today Christ is born;
Hodie Salvator apparuit:	Today the Savior hath appeared;
Hodie e in terra ca-nunt angeli	Today angels sing on earth,
Laetantur archangeli	And Archangels rejoice;
Hodie exsultant Jusit dicentes:	Today the just exult, saying,
Gloria in excelsis Deo, alleluia	Glory to God in the highest, alleluia.

The chants were collected and classified during the reign of Pope Gregory I (590–604), for whom they were named. From that time, the Gregorian chant has been in continuous use in the Roman Catholic Church (Eisman et al 65).

Late Middle Ages

This particular piece by composer Bernart de Ventadorn may be heard on recordings found from several sources or similar compositions. This particular one is typical. If you can find a similar one to listen to in order to substitute, then listen to that particular composition of his since at times this composition is substituted by other works by this composer. Also, for your assignment if you select this composer, it is fine to use another composition by the same composer if needed.

Example 2: *Ben m'an perdut* (Bernart de Ventadorn)

During the Middle Ages singers and instrumentalists traveled from court to court and city to city entertaining. Their music was usually about love and knightly deeds done to honor a maiden. A troubadour might feel a lady to be unattainable and sing about his feelings instead. Ventadorn's *Ben m'an perdut* typifies the songs sung by the troubadours from the south of France in the late Middle Ages (twelfth and thirteenth centuries). The melody was written down as a monophonic melody but may have been accompanied by the harp or some other instrument. Little information is known about these types of pieces; records were not kept very well for secular pieces. Sacred music, however, was written down, because monks wrote out the manuscripts and preserved them. About 2,800 troubadour poems and 280 melodies have been recovered from monasteries. A *trouvere* was a term used for a secular musician from the northern part of France. The pieces that have been passed down from generation to generation have been either passed on orally or by writing.

Voice: baritone
Form: AABAABB
Text: Original language

A Bem'ab oerdyt kau ebves Bentador tuih mei amic	Now I am exiled from all my friends of Ventadorn,
Pois ma dmna n 'ama;	Since my lady loves me not;
A et es be dreugz qye hanaus kau bi tirbm	Wisest would I be never to return,
C'ades estai vas me salvatj'e grama.	For she has treated me with scorn and bitterness.
B V us per que m fai sembllan irat emorn:	And why, when she beholds me, is her face dark with anger?
Car ens'amor me deleih e m sojorn!	Only because I delight to dwell in her love; nothing
Ni de ren als no s rancura ni s clama.	Else have I done to offend her.
A Aissi c o; peis qui s' eslaiss' el cadorn e n sap	Like the unwatchful fish that leaps to seize the bait
Mot	and finds himself hooked,
Tro que s'es pres en l'ama,	So did I plunge, unheeding, into too great a love,

A m'eslaissei eu vas trop amar um jorn.,	Knowing not, till I was in the flame, that it would burn
C'anc no m gardei, tro fui en mei la flma,	Me more cruelly than any furnace.
B que m'art plus fort. No a faire focs forn;	Yet now I cannot make a move to escape,
E ges per so n om poso partir un dorn,	So close a prisoner does love hold me.
Aissi m te pres s'amors e m'aliama.	My beautiful one, God works such marvels through you
B Mos Bells Vezers, pers vos fai Deus vertutz	That no one, seeing you, could fail to be taken captive
Tals c'om nous ve que no si'ereubutz	Beholding the unequalled beauty of your words and ways.
Dels bels plazers que sabtz dir e faire.	(Politoske 62).

The Renaissance

Example 3: *Kyrie from Missa Pange Lingua* (Josquin des Prez)

In this Kyrie, notice the melody of the Gregorian chant, which is used imitatively in all the voices. A motet such as this one has a lower voice coming in with similar phrases. Toward the end of the Renaissance, motets became more complex in style and longer in length. The motet such as a Kyrie which was used in the Mass would be an example of a more complex style. The Renaissance, which began in the fourteenth century, was a time of intense creative flowering in Italy, and its ideas spread throughout Europe. A new type of visual art and literature was developing during the Renaissance, and in music the canon and imitation, which added a new layer of melody, created a new form of musical composition known as polyphony. Imitation and the emergence of more than one melody to be added to another would become a new style (Miller 26–29).

Josquin des Prez lived from 1450 to 1521, in Italy, where he served in the Sforza court in Milan. He was a major composer in the Sforza court, for the papal choir in Rome, and for the courts of Louis XII of France. He was also a contemporary of Leonardo da Vinci and lived in the Netherlands for a time. Josquin des Prez lived as a composer who wrote for the royalty and the Church. He was in some ways quite daring in his canons, in which he was able to place some melodies together that were daring for his time. It may have been possible for Josquin des Prez to produce some of his more creative works that were ahead of his time because he was able to travel and was afforded the liberty of writing for both secular and sacred events during his career. Des Prez was able to pass one melody or voice to another and then to another (Politoske 84).

Voice: unaccompanied four-part choir

A Kyrie eleison; Kyrie eleison; Kyrie eleison. Lord, have mercy; Lord, have mercy; Lord, have mercy.

B Christe eleison; Christe eleison; Christe eleison Christ, have mercy; Christ, have mercy; Christ, have mercy.

C Kyrie eleison; Kyrie eleison; Kyrie eleison. Lord, have mercy; Lord, have mercy; Lord, have mercy.

The liturgy of the Mass is as follows:

Proper	Ordinary
Introit (processional)	Kyrie eleison ("Lord, have mercy on mercy on us")
Collect (prayer on behalf of the congregation)	Gloria in excelsis Deo ("Glory to God in the highest")
Epistle (from the Epistles of the New Testament)	Credo (in unum Deum) "I believe in one God"
Gradual (a psalm verse)	Sanctus ("Holy, holy, holy")
Alleluia (or Tract) (During a time of penitence, such as Lent, the Alleluia is replaced by a psalm, called a Tract.)	Bendictus qui venit ("Blessed is he that cometh")
Sequence (a form of hymn)	Canon (a series of prayers said by the priest in a low voice during the consecration of the bread and wine)
Gospel (from one of the New Testament Gospels)	Agnus Dei (qui tollis Peccata mundi) ("Lamb of God, who taketh away the sins of the world")
Offertory	Ite missa est ("Go") (the congregation is dismissed)
Communion	
Post-Communion (a prayer of prayers)	

(Hickock 90).

The Reformation in the 1500s

The Reformation was a turning point not only for Christianity but for human history as well. But today some people are unsure of the events that actually occurred during that period. The account in this paragraph will not do the Reformation justice, but in order to understand why music began to sound so differently in various countries and places of worship, it is important to understand the impact that the Reformation had on the belief systems of the people of that time.

According to Dr. Hugh Miller,

> The rise of Protestantism had a great effect upon music which the effects were manifest principally in Germany, and to a lesser extent in France and England, and not at all in Italy. However, not until after the 16th century did Protestant music rival the great art of Catholic Church Music of the Renaissance (Miller 40).

A central figure of the Protestant Reformation was Martin Luther, who lived from 1483 to 1546. He was against the production and sale of indulgences in order to raise funds for building projects that included such enormous cathedrals and structures as Saint Peter's. Much of Martin Luther's criticism was that money and taxation given to and levied by the Church were going toward wasteful uses. The Church was not being of service to the people. Luther believed in praying directly to God and in worshiping him in the vernacular (everyday language, rather than Latin). He modified the music of the Catholic Church, substituting German for Latin. Luther felt that music was a very important part of worship, so he encouraged congregational participation in the Protestant service, a practice that had been abandoned by the Catholic Church. The development of the chorale was important during his time as well. A chorale is a choir piece that has four sung parts. Chorales are usually sung by congregations or a choir. This sort of music became extremely important during the next period, and especially in Germany during the time of Johann Sebastian Bach, when he wrote chorales for Lutheran church services during the Baroque period.

Martin Luther wrote the very well-known choral melody *Ein' feste Burg ist unser Gott* (A Mighty Fortress Is Our God) (Miller 36–40).

The Renaissance Period

Example 4: *Now Is the Month of Maying* (Thomas Morley)

Now Is the Month of Maying is a ballet written in choral style. "Each stanza is divided into two sections, both of which are repeated with a fa-la-la-la refrain" (Politoske 91).

The vocals are accompanied with instruments typical of the Renaissance period (Politoske 91).

Thomas Morley was sometimes called the father of the English madrigal. Nadeau and Tesson wrote in *Listen: A Guide to the Pleasures of Music* that Thomas Morley also cultivated the secular music and that he wrote for the virginal and the lute.

Morley was a Renaissance composer who lived in England from 1552 to 1602. Many of his compositions were simplified versions of the Italian madrigal. They are also sometimes referred to as ballades which may be confusing in a way since they have words such as *fa-la-la* in the text.

Stanzas: ABC
Form: AABBAABBAABB

A Now is the month of maying,
  When merry lads are playing
  Fa-la-la . . . . . .

B each with his bonny lass
  Upon the greeny grass,
  Fa-la-la . . . . . .

A The spring, clad all in gladness,
  Doth laugh at winter's sadness,
  Fa-la-la . . . . . .

B And to the bagpipe's sound
  The nymphs tread out their ground.

A Fie then, why sit we musing,
  Youth's sweet delight refusing?
  Fa-la-la . . . . . .

B Say, dainty nymphs, and speak,
  Shall we play barley-break?
  Fa-la-la . . . . . .

(Politoske page #).

Baroque Period

Example 5: Four Seasons Op. 8 No. 4, First Movement, Baroque Period (Antonio Vivaldi, composer)

Antonio Vivaldi was a composer who was influenced by four sonnets about seasons, including the following sonnet about winter.

Shivering, frozen in the snow and ice,

Battered by a terrible wind's harsh blow,

Stamping your feet, to run while time seems slow;

And from such cold your chattering teeth freeze;

To spend, content by the fire, quiet days

While the rain outside soaks things through and through.

To walk over ice with pace so slow,

Afraid to fall; to go, looking for ways

To move on strongly;

To slip to the earth;

To start again on the ice;

To run headlong

Until the ice breaks up and opens a path;

To feel, from the iron gates issuing,

The southeast, north, all the wind's warring breath:

This is winter, but joys it also brings. (translated by Martin Robbins)

The winter concerto had a fast-slow and then fast portion. Its orchestra was not as large as the orchestras that you may see today in the symphony halls in New York, Vienna, or Dallas: it was the Baroque orchestra. Except for the harpsichord, it consisted entirely of stringed instruments. The technical brilliance that Vivaldi created can be heard in all of the four seasons. Anyone who takes the time to listen to *The Four Seasons* and listens to *Winter*, as well as the other seasons, will enjoy Vivaldi for a lifetime, not least by understanding how much he gave to the world of music.

While listening to *Winter*, try to identify the images while you listen to the instruments.

Movement 1. Allegro Non Molto

Measure 1: *Agghizcciato tremar tr nefi algenti*/**To shiver, frozen in the snow and ice**

The concerto begins quietly with repeated single notes first in the cellos, and then accumulating harmonic mass as violas, second violins, and first violins progressively join in:

As the chordal texture thickens, listen for the dissonant quality that results in a bleak and wintry atmosphere.

Measure 12: *Al severo spirar d'orrido vento*/**Battered by a terrible wind's harsh blow**

The virtuosic solo violin that comes in perfectly suggests the violence of the wind. You will hear this characteristic passage in the solo part three times, each time bridged by soft, repeated chords in the orchestra.

Next a crescendo begins at measure 20, leading to a charming tone painting of the following words:

Measure 22: *Corrrer battendo I piedi ogni momento*/**To run, stamping your feet every moment**

The orchestra and soloist play a sequential passage where a rush of notes makes it seem almost as if someone is pounding.

After the violin solo comes a dramatic tremolo response by the orchestra. The movement ends in a cadence with the sound of the piece's key, F minor (Nadeau and Tesson 145, 146).

Antonio Vivaldi

1678–1741

Italy (Italian)

Antonio Vivaldi was born in Venice, Italy. He was a violinist and wrote about thirty operas. He was a teacher at a girls orphanage for a short time and also worked in the

Church of St. Mark's in Venice, where his father was employed. He served as an ordained priest for a short time.

According to Nadeau and Tesson, Vivaldi modeled his concerti after Corelli and used a style that was increasingly robust (432). Another famous set of concerti grossi that is very well known today is his *Four Seasons*. Vivaldi also composed vocal music. His *Gloria in D Major* (1708) is another of his well-known works and is performed by choral groups around the world.

According to the *World Book Encyclopedia*, J. S. Bach may have used ten of Vivaldi's melodies as inspiration in arrangements for some of his own work for harpsichord and organ (*World Book Encyclopedia*).

Example 6: *Little Fugue in G Minor* (Johann Sebastian Bach)

A fugue is a type of organ piece that uses a melody that is played over and over simultaneously. It is a polyphonic (having several melodies) composition, generally for two to four voices (vocal or instrumental), in which the same themes are passed from voice to voice and combined in counterpoint, two or more melodic lines sung or played simultaneously in a single unified composition (Cunningham 194).

> Johann Sebastian Bach was born in Germany. He has often been called the "master of masters," for his compositions inspired many of the famous musicians who followed him, including Mozart, Beethoven, Mendelssohn, Schumann, Liszt, and Wagner.
>
> When Bach was only ten years old, his mother passed on, followed only a year later by his father. He went to live with his elder brother, Johann Christoph Bach, a church organist. At the age of fifteen, Bach began earning a living by singing and playing the violin in the royal orchestra at Weimar, where he finally became court organist and concertmaster. During this time he wrote most of his organ works.
>
> In 1717, upon an invitation from Prince Leopold, Johann S. Bach became concertmaster and director at Kothen. Since the prince played violin and bass viol, much of the music written during this period was of an instrumental nature, much being written for the Prince himself.
>
> From 1723 until the time of his death, Johann Sebastian Bach was in charge of music at the Saint Thomas Church in Leipzig and director of music at the University of Leipzig. During this period of time he wrote the most magnificent of all of his choral literature (Sur et al.).

Bach wrote his music daily. He was in charge of the boys choir, teaching as well as directing the choirs and playing the organ on Sunday. Johann Sebastian Bach was an extremely busy musician. Bach wrote choral works, organ works, Baroque chamber works, and compositions for the harpsichord. The symphony orchestra then was not as large as it is today. The symphony was developing during his time and included violins, cellos, and many of the woodwind instruments. The piano, however, came along after Bach, during Mozart's lifetime. Bach was known for the many works he produced for the organ, at which he was a master.

Do you know the difference between a band and an orchestra? An orchestra has stringed instruments in it, but a band does not.

Organ during the Baroque Period

During the Baroque period some of the finest organs ever built were constructed. Many modern pipe organs, such as the one at the Morton Meyerson Symphony Center, are imitations of the Baroque pipe organs. Some of the greatest organs were built in Germany during the seventeenth and eighteenth centuries. Bach (1685–1750) was known as a great organist during his own lifetime. He gave recitals and was often asked to test newly built organs. "His organ works are considered by many people to be the greatest ever written for the instrument" (Eisman et al. 59).

The organ has an interesting history. This instrument probably originated in Egypt around 250 B.C., but the Romans are said to have improved their organs, which were powered by water. During most of the Middle Ages, the organ was not used in Europe. It was not until the late Middle Ages that organs were built once more. But the organs of the time were small enough for musicians to carry around their necks. An organist pumped small bellows with one hand to force air into the pipes and played the keys with the other. In the Cathedral of Halberstadt, Germany, one of the first pipe organs to have pedal keys for use with the feet was built in the year 1361. The following century (the fifteenth century) is the period that music historians usually recognize as the beginning of written composition for the organ. The mechanics of the organ devised at that time are still used today.

Example 7: *Brandenburg Concerto No. 5* (Johann Sebastian Bach)

Bach wrote six Brandenburg concertos in 1721 for the margrave of Brandenburg, which had merged into Prussia, the fastest-rising state in Europe at that time. Musicians who analyze music in today's major universities would probably agree that the Brandenburg concertos are some of the finest examples of Baroque concertos grosso ever written. Concertos grosso are Baroque concertos in which concertinos, or small groups of soloists (commonly two violins and contnuo), play against a small orchestra, the tutti or ripieno. The concerto grosso is considered the forerunner of the modern concerto (Politoske 469). A concerto is a solo work for a solo instrument or instruments accompanied by orchestra and usually has three movements, the first of which often contains a condenza.

A concerto grosso usually begins with the ritornello, and Bach used the ritornello in the first movement. The ritornello is a Baroque form with alternating tutti and solo passages in which the tutti returns to modified forms of the opening theme, as the soloist elaborates on it or contrasts with it in virtuoso fashion (Politoske 475). Bach is said to have had an encyclopedic mind. He decided to write each concerto for a different combination of instruments, some of them never used before or afterwards. He also wanted to be able to say that he had written a concerto in every key. Listen for the flute, violin, and harpsichord as you listen to the *Brandenburg Concerto No. 5*.

Johann Sebastian Bach

1685–1750
Germany (German)
Johann Sebastian Bach was born into a family of professional musicians. His father, a musician, died when Bach was ten years old and he had to go live with his oldest brother. His mother had previously died.

Bach was able to make a living from his musical ability even as a youth. During his teenage years he began his career as a singer in a choir at St. Michael's Church School in Luneburg, Germany. He was greatly influenced at an early age by the organists Georg Bohm and Johnnes-Kirche, and he walked to Hamburg to hear the organist Johann Reinken. This period was very influential for Bach's musical career.

During the next phase of Bach's career, he wrote some of his most renowned organ music. In 1708, he was reprimanded for his organ compositions on the grounds that they had too many notes and were overly ornate. He was ordered to return to his earlier, simpler style and was evaluated badly. He was also called before the board of consistory members of the church over his handling of his teaching of the boys in his music classes.

In 1707, Bach married Maria Barbara. Together, they had seven children. Bach was expected to handwrite every part for each church service held on Sundays and Wednesdays, and all the choirs needed original music. He also had to play the organ and conduct the boys' choir, as well as teach the boys Latin each day in school. In 1718, his wife died. In 1722, he remarried and become a director at St. Thomas Church, trying to forget his first wife's death. When he lost his new position, he applied at Leipzig and was given the position after two other possible hires turned down the job.

In fact, Bach was the hiring committee's last resort. He turned out to be a controversial employee. He was written up for not keeping good discipline and was expected to compose music for every church service. He was very busy, and his employers did not consider him as talented as the other possibilities who refused the job. Bach's employers overworked him so much that it is no wonder he went blind. The young boys in his choir played pranks on him and badmouthed him to his employers when they wanted to cause him trouble. Nevertheless, Bach is remembered down through history for his sublime music.

Despite losing his eyesight, Bach was able to write and continue his work, which he dictated to his daughter. Strangely, ten days before he died, his sight returned, and he wrote a fugue that used the four German letters of his surname (the German letters sound B flat A C B) (Nadeau and Tesson).

Characteristics of Baroque Music

Melody: a continuous spinning out of a single melodic idea
Rhythm: forward rhythmic drive
Texture: balance of homophonic and polyphonic texture
Timbre: string winds and harpsichord, with conspicuous lack of percussion
Contrasting dynamic levels were achieved by

- Increasing and decreasing instrumentation
- Abrupt shifts in dynamics, resulting in terraces of tonal intensity (Eisman et al.)

Example 8: *Hallelujah Chorus* from *The Messiah* (George Frederic Handel)

The Messiah is considered by many to be George Frederic Handel's most famous work. *The Messiah* was written in twenty-four days in the year 1741 in London and was performed in Dublin the following year. It is divided into three major sections dealing with the life of Jesus: how he was born, how he died, and how he was raised to life (Politoske 139).

The beginning of *The Messiah* has the Baroque orchestra performing an overview of the compositions of the entire sound of the oratorio. The music which is performed consists of recitative, arias, and choruses.

The *Hallelujah Chorus* is only a small portion of the entire lengthy production, but it is the most familiar part, since it was the piece during which King George II stood in reverence. Even today, audiences stand during the *Hallelujah Chorus* in reverence to the composition, just as the audience of Handel's day stood in the presence of the king when he leapt to his feet in amazement at Handel's music.

Handel is one of the foremost composers of the Baroque period. He and Bach were born in the same year, 1685, and their lives represent a time when music flowered. Both were extremely important Baroque composers whose music is still performed and studied today, and both went blind at the end of their lives.

Handel was born in a province in Germany known as Saxony. He was always intrigued with opera and studied in Italy as a young man, where he developed a style of opera that helped him when he moved to London. He suffered a stroke at fifty-two but recovered and was able to produce oratorios and brass music, including some music designed to be played on river barges in what was called water music.

Handel fought his way out of debt and conducted and performed concerts for the middle-class English. Even when he was blind and aged, he continued to perform, and at the age of seventy-four, he collapsed while performing *The Messiah* and died a few days later.

Example 9: *Fireworks Music* (George Frederic Handel)

The best known of Handel's instrumental works are his *Water Music* and *Royal Fireworks Music*. The *Royal Fireworks Music* was composed to celebrate the end of the Austrian Succession (sometimes known as King George's War) in 1749.

> These works and these occasions remind us of the role Handel took for himself as musical spokesman for the eighteenth-century England expressing its satisfaction, its value, and its aspirations. The popular tone which he achieved on such occasions, and for which he had to bend his normal style only slightly, still has very strong appeal today (Kerman 117).

The *Fireworks Music* was written for a large band. It had a total of sixty trumpets, French horns, drums, and bassoons. Handel later added the string parts. There are several parts to the *Fireworks Music*. The *La Rejouissance* means rejoice. According to Kerman, "it sounds like a military rejoicing rather than a peaceful rejoicing." She also stated that "this would have made a perfect quick march for the redcoats, whose baroque military pomp fared so poorly thirty years later in the America colonies" (Kerman 119).

When the rehearsal for the *Fireworks Music* was held at Vauxhall Gardens, 12,000 people attended the event. "At the celebration itself, which was led off by a hundred brass cannon, everything went wrong: The great set piece caught fire, the crowd stampede, two spectators died, and the man in charge of the fireworks had a mad fit. Music should stay indoors" (Kerman 119).

George Frederic Handel
1685–1759
Germany (German)
George Frederic Handel was born in Germany but was buried with great pomp and ceremony in Westminster Abbey, in London. One of the greatest German composers of the Baroque period, he wrote music for George I and George II. Two of his most famous works are still performed today: *The Messiah*, which was an oratorio, and *Water Music*, which he wrote for a Baroque orchestra to play on barges at royal aquatic events on the Thames River. The king was quite amazed that Handel had the ability to write music for both types of occasions. According to Doris Van de

Bogart, Handel may have been a somewhat progressive composer for his day and time. "There are many foreshadowings of the new classic style in his music" (178). Handel's operas were successful in the courts of the king, but he was not able to please the English public of the time. He also had some difficulty with his business during that part of his career, caused by his handling of the payment of his musicians while he tried to simultaneously compose music and run the other aspects of his business. When Handel went bankrupt, he decided to write oratorios in order to stay out of jail. After raising himself out of his financial plight, he found that oratorios were less difficult than operas to create, since they did not need expensive costumes and set designs. He also liked writing oratorios because the words were taken directly from biblical texts, making them quicker to write. Handel also created certain pieces he hoped would please the king, and he succeeded—fortunately for him. According to Van de Bogart, if Handel had not pleased the king, he would have been in trouble professionally. The king, who thought Handel had decided to only write oratorios, was very surprised when he heard Handel perform his *Water Music* as the king and his friends rode on their barges up and down the Thames. Handel's compositions were written for brass instruments and had a rapid tempo with an upbeat, friendly, free-flowing sound. Handel's *Water Music* is still performed frequently today.

Handel was born in 1685 in Halle, Saxony. His father was a barber-surgeon who was not happy with his son's career as a musician. A friend of his gave George Frederic a clavier to practice in the attic. When Handel was seven years old, his father refused to take him along on a short trip, and young George Frederic ran after the coach on foot until his father finally gave in to his son's wishes and allowed him to go. This same persistence drove Handel to study music by listening to the organists in church. Melodies lingered in his mind, and he was seen singing them over and over, making new melodies fit over old ones. Even though Handel had such interest in music and had such talent for it, his father continued to "look down upon music as an idle pursuit, [wishing] his son to be a lawyer" (*The American People's Encyclopedia*). After Handel's father passed away, Handel did pursue law, and he studied hard. He missed his father greatly. But he found that he was able to make his living through the Church—and he needed to, in order to support his mother, who had no income.

One of Handel's most famous works is his oratorio *The Messiah*, which takes several hours to perform. It includes a choir and an orchestra; sometimes the choir is accompanied by an organ if a Baroque orchestra is not available.

Even though King George was unhappy with some of Handel's early work—and for a short time was unhappy with Handel—in time Handel changed the king's mind. It has been said that the *Water Music* is what convinced King George that Handel was a musician worth retaining; certainly it was a turning point in Handel's career, and in the king's attitude toward Handel. After the king changed his mind about Handel and his music, Handel remained in England for the rest of his life. Toward the end of his life Handel's eyesight failed and his secretary took down much of the notation for his work as he went totally blind. When Handel died, he was buried in Westminster Abbey, a famous church where usually only the English-born are buried.

Classical Period

Example 10: *Surprise Symphony (Symphony No. 94)* (Franz Joseph Haydn)

It is useful to understand the Classical period as a certain period of music, not merely as a popular term used to describe a certain genre of music. Classical music, most strictly, is a style of music written during the period when music's form and structure made use of a body of instrumentalists playing in an orchestra. It was during the Classical period that the orchestra began, and it was led by a conductor. Classical music was written from 1750 to about 1820 or 1827 (depending on whether Beethoven's death is taken as the end of the period). In studying the purpose of Classical music and taking time to listen to it, we can approach listening as a way to enjoy taking time to think about what we hear.

The Classical period was marked politically by the rise of the lower and middle classes in the French Revolution in a tumultuous time in European history. Before the French Revolution, the Seven Years' War (1756–1763), in which Prussia had allied with England against Austria and France, spread through Europe, India, and America (in the latter as the French and Indian War). The American Revolution and the writing of the Declaration of Independence were events that occurred in the Americas at that time.

The symphonies written by Haydn were usually written for orchestras with four sections: woodwind, brass, strings, and percussion. This arrangement was the basis of the modern orchestra. Composers began paying attention to instruments' *color*, or how they sounded together, and *timbre*, or quality of sound. Instruments began to be created that could be played both loudly and softly, allowing composers to make use of different *dynamics*. Haydn was a composer who worked for the royalty, and he had to please them by his writing style and performances, but it has been told how Haydn became tired of performing, and especially of having some of the older women fall asleep during his concerts. Because of this, during his *Symphony No. 94* he placed the loud percussion of cymbals with a sudden dynamic shift to wake them up. Dynamics were being used differently in the Classical period. During the previous period of Handel and Bach, instruments did not have the capability of playing dynamically. Classical music was introducing new techniques to the concert hall.

One of these instruments was the piano. During the Baroque period, the harpsichord had been used, which always played at the same volume. The piano, which could be played both loudly and softly, completely changed the way that composers created their compositions. At the beginning of Classical music, Haydn influenced both Ludwig van Beethoven and Wolfgang Amadeus Mozart. The entire sound of music was to change forever.

The Classical Piano and the Baroque Harpsichord

In the second half of the eighteenth century, the piano (invented earlier that century) began to make progress as a musical medium.

Not until the nineteenth century, however, did it completely replace the older keyboard instruments (harpsichord, clavichord) from which it differed mainly in the way in which is was struck.

The piano has felt hammers, whereas the harpsichord, for example, has a quill that is struck across a string. The piano has a greater sonority than the Baroque keyboard instruments, because its hammers can strike the keys with different levels of force.

Haydn wrote the *Surprise Symphony*, which is actually called *Symphony No. 94*. The first performance was in London on March 23, 1772. It was immediately successful, probably because of the second movement, which included the "surprise" portion that gave it its name with its sudden contrast from *andante* (slow) to *vivace assai* (very fast). It startled audiences, but they enjoyed the sound, which might seem somewhat surprising to us today. Changes from C major to G major also offered listeners a tonal contrast. Haydn is also credited with creating the four-movement symphony by introducing the minuet as a third movement. Although new sounds and performances are not always accepted when they are first performed, Haydn's *Surprise Symphony* was immediately considered a masterpiece of Classical music and is still considered so today. It is one of the best symphonies written during that period.

The strings were the heart of the Classical orchestra. In the *Surprise Symphony*, the brass instruments are situated behind the string players so that the strings can be heard more clearly. The conductor makes sure that the orchestra's different sections are balanced; if any instrument is too overbearing or too loud, the conductor gives it a hand signal to change its volume.

The identifying characteristics of Classical music are helpful in distinguishing between it from other periods, such as the earlier Baroque and later Romantic. Eighteenth-century Classicism was a rejection of the highly complex texture and elaborate ornamentation of the Baroque period. Classicism, inspired in part by interest in the literature and ideas of Greece and Rome, was

- Refined
- Balanced
- Ordered
- Structured

During the Classical period, three great revolutions took place: the Industrial Revolution, the American Revolution, and the French Revolution. The downfall of kings and rise of the middle class soon affected musicians' ability to get work. At the beginning of the Classical period, musicians had been mainly working for the kings and queens or for the Church. The change was beginning to shift.

Haydn remained a servant to a prince during his entire career, unlike Mozart, who found himself unable to deal with aristocrats. Haydn was expected to behave as a self-respecting officer of a princely court. He presented himself to the court each day and had his orchestra ready to perform whenever the royalty demanded it. He wore a uniform at all times and was responsible for his orchestral players. It is no wonder that the music had four movements and it was of the sonata allegro form. The music reflected the time.

Characteristics of Classical Music

Melody: short, clearly defined phrases

Rhythm: regular, clearly defined beat or pulse

Texture: usually homophonic or composed of melodic chords

Timbre: interplay between all four orchestral sections

Franz Joseph Haydn

1732–1809
Austria (Austrian)
Franz Joseph Haydn was born on March 31, 1732, in Rohrau, Austria.

He was educated in a school in Hamburg and studied in a school in Stephen's Cathedra, in Vienna. He wrote his first set of string quartets for his patron, Karl Joseph Furnberg, in 1755.

From 1761 to 1790, Haydn served as Kapellmeister to the Prince Esterhazy. He became acquainted with Mozart during that time. In 1795, at the age of sixty-three, he moved to Vienna, where he produced two oratorios, *The Creation* and *The Seasons*. He died in Vienna on May 31, 1809.

Example 11: *Don Giovanni* (Wolfgang Amadeus Mozart)

In the late eighteenth century, the importance of comic opera grew to equal that of the serious operas of the Baroque era. A new style emerged that appealed to the middle class because of its casual nature. "Mozart wrote some German comic operas; he also composed Italian comic operas for the Vienna, just as Handel, another German, had once written Italian operas for London" (Wold and Cykler, *Introduction* 187). Italian comic opera was called opera buffa, but most of the time it seems difficult to consider *Don Giovanni* as only a comic opera or only a tragic opera, because it is an opera that has elements of both. Mozart developed a masterpiece when he wrote his story and created the music to display the character of the Don Juan in his opera. The character of Don Juan was a semi-legendary Spanish lover who had been written about in poetry and literature. Mozart took a legendary character and created music to go along with the story that stunned his audience. He created such suspense that the personalities that he wanted to portray through the story are audible in his music. The hero in the opera is Don Giovanni, who has been pursuing several women. He has no conscience and no fear. He wants instant gratification and chases one woman after another. His assistant, Leporello, has a singing role in the opera that only serves to add to the humor of the story. But the story also includes murder, intrigue, guilt, and remorse in its entangled plot. Mozart's music is absolutely riveting when his unrepentant main character is seen in a graveyard, unable to come to terms with his life. The audience cannot help but realize that Mozart has written an opera whose music reveals both the bravery of the main character and his inner flaw. Mozart's deeply meaningful composition reveals Don Giovanni as a character refusing to live by standards that Mozart felt were illogical and at times even absurd.

Example 12: *Symphony in C* (Jupiter) K. 551 (Wolfgang Amadeus Mozart)

1757–1791

Salzburg, Austria (Austrian)

Wolfgang Amadeus Mozart lived for thirty-five years, from 1757 to 1791. He is one of the most important composers of the Classical period, for his music influenced many other composers. Mozart's father was a musician and a teacher. The year that Mozart was born, his father published a method book for teaching the violin, a book that was used for many years in Salzburg. As a small boy, Mozart was exposed to many musical styles. He was from a family with two children, and his parents took a special interest in their children's lives, since they wanted them to perform with Leopold, their father, traveling to aristocratic palaces and giving concerts. They traveled together with Mozart's mother.

The Mozart family had two children, and Wolfgang was very fond of his sister Nannerl, who was five years older than Mozart. The two were very close and performed together until she was fifteen, when their father decided that she should stop performing, since it was not proper for a girl her age to travel and perform.

The trips that the Mozart family took were sometimes very long, and the children caught illnesses frequently. But they were taught to perform no matter what and acquired tremendous discipline. In 1766, Wolfgang wrote his first oratorio, at the age of ten. It was a success, and at fourteen he wrote a successful opera.

Mozart became a successful composer and learned many techniques when he met Franz Joseph Haydn, from whom he learned the form of the sonata allegro. Mozart grew up in Salzburg and traveled around Europe. In his early twenties, he decided to move to Vienna.

Mozart wanted to be a freelance writer, for he refused to work for a single aristocrat alone. Because of this, he had trouble supporting his family. Although Mozart did make money from some of his operas, he had financial problems, struggling to pay his musicians even as some of his operas turned out not to be financially successful.

One of the last works that Mozart wrote, which was left unfinished with his death, was a piece called the *Requiem*. A mysterious visitor, now known to have been the steward of one Count Walsegg, commissioned the work under an oath of secrecy. The count, unbeknownst to Mozart, intended the *Requiem* to be performed as his own work, stealing the credit due Mozart.

After Mozart died, his wife was able to piece the manuscript of the *Requiem* together and have the last parts of the "Requiem" written so that it could be published. Later, she let a reputable musician see it who paid a small fee for the work. But Mozart's wife was never able to obtain much for her husband's work.

Mozart's children were not very physically strong, and his son died before he became knowledgeable in his father's line of work. Several of Mozart and his wife's children suffered from illnesses; their son did not live into adulthood.

Mozart died at thirty-five, leaving no one directly in his family to inherit his harpsichord, violin, or piano. He had been one of the first musicians in Salzburg to own a piano. A cousin of Mozart inherited his piano. The instrument is now in the Mozart museum in Salzburg, Austria, located on the floor of the building where his father Leopold's family lived when he was growing up.

About the *Jupiter Symphony*

This symphony by Mozart was nicknamed the *Jupiter Symphony* by an unknown admirer, and it is still called that name today. The actual name of the symphony is *Symphony No. 41* (K. 551 in C Major). The K represents the numbering system established by an Austrian nobleman named Kochel, who published and numbered Mozart's works in a system known as the Kochel index.

This symphony was one of the last symphonies Mozart wrote, along with two other symphonies and seven other compositions, during the summer of 1788. But there is no sign of haste in his symphonies, even though they were written in such a short period of time. An explanation from Homer Ulrich's *Music: A Design for Listening* was helpful in explaining the *Jupiter Symphony*. It was the last of three symphonies written by Mozart during that summer of 1788 and featured strong contrast in its dynamics. It incorporated strong mood changes and was more optimistic than *Symphony No. 39*, which Mozart wrote earlier that summer. Mozart's melodies followed one right after the other; he made use of the sonata allegro form that he had been using in previous symphonies. He started out with a simple melody and after a few measures blended together into something intricate and magical. The unusual use of a portion of polyphony near the end of the *Jupiter* was rare in Classical symphonies. Mozart was an artist who never stopped amazing audiences in his own lifetime, and his music can still be listened to over and over again without becoming tiresome. There is more to hear in Mozart's music upon each listening.

Example 13: *Sonata 4 in F Major* (Ludwig van Beethoven)

During the Classical period, symphonies and piano sonatas were written in the sonata allegro form, which had emerged in the 1700s. It was considered to be logical, because it went from its theme to another sound and then back to the theme again. It featured both repetition and variation. In the Classical period, the form would be expressed as AABA. The exposition was always repeated in the symphonies of Haydn and Mozart and was considered essential in impressing the main themes on listeners. It was not omitted until Beethoven wrote his last symphony in a form other than AABA, at the same time omitting one movement; this led to the next musical period, the Romantic period, in which changes were made to more traditional forms. Emotional reactions began to be considered appropriate for composers to express and were soon heard in the way that chords were put together.

A Classical sonata is usually played on the piano and written in the sonata allegro form:

A Exposition	Main theme	Tonic key
B Development	One or both theme	One or both of the themes developed or varied, often by modulating to new keys; new thematic material sometimes introduced and developed
A Recapitulation	Principal theme	Principal theme, subordinate theme, and closing section and coda

Example 14: *Prometheus* (Ludwig van Beethoven)

Prometheus, also titled *The Creatures of Prometheus*, was a ballet first performed in Vienna on March 28, 1801, at the Burg Theatre. The ballet was commissioned to be written by Beethoven to honor Empress Maria Theresa and was based on a book supplied by Vigano. The book has been lost, but a summary from a theater-bill is in a museum in Vienna.

The ballet was so successful that it was repeated more than twenty times. "Only a sketch of the scenario survives" (Thompson 132). The ballet continued to be produced after Beethoven's death. In 1910, the ballet was produced by Andrias Pavley, and again in 1929 by Serge Lifar, by Aurel Milloss in 1933, and by Elsa Marianne von Rosen in 1958.

This ballet was Beethoven's first venture in writing music tied to a literary model. According to Homer Ulrich, Beethoven was influenced by Mozart, something audible in the themes whose moods contrast from weak sections to strong sections, influenced by Mozart's *Figaro*. These contrasting themes represent the triumph of human intelligence and freedom over tyranny of the gods. The main theme in *Prometheus* is referred by Homer Ulrich as the "Prometheus melody," for it reveals the triumph of one element over another. For his finale, Beethoven used some contredanses (No. Opus 14. Nos. 7 and 11) he had written previously. These themes reflect determination and heroism in battling against difficulties and were used again in different variations in a piano work in 1802, and again in the finale of the *Eroica Symphony (Heroic Symphony)* in 1803.

Ballet dancers have danced to Beethoven's piano music and continue to find it very intriguing. Choreography has been inspired by it long after his death, in the works of Anna Pavlova, David Holmes, and Jerome Robbins.

Ludwig van Beethoven
1770–1827
Germany (German)
Ludwig van Beethoven was born in Bonn, Germany, on December 16, 1770. His grandfather was a court musician (Kapellmeister) in the town of Bonn. His father,

Johann van Beethoven, was a competent musician who was employed by the prince elector to teach violin and clavier and to sing in the chapel. Ludwig was somewhat clumsy as a boy and seemed to many to be quite unsociable. He began to learn to play the harpsichord when he was four, but his father, an alcoholic, was not a very patient teacher. At six Beethoven was given lessons at a Franciscan monastery in Bonn. He learned to play the organ very rapidly and started to substitute as an organist upon occasion. Beethoven was only nine years old when he played a concert on a clavier along with a student of his father's in a concert hall at a music academy. Around that same time, Ludwig's father took his son to meet some of the more senior officials in hopes of introducing his son to give him exposure to musicians in the court. That experience, however, was not very fruitful. He was given neither a salary nor any work. But he did accidentally meet a conductor named Christian Gottlob Neefe; it turned out that Ludwig was playing a very difficult composition composed by Neefe himself for the organ. Neefe was impressed to hear someone playing his difficult organ piece, and when he saw the disheveled boy playing the composition, he asked Beethoven to play for him during a short absence. The two struck up a friendship. When Neefe returned, he began to teach Beethoven several instruments which Ludwig quickly learned. Beethoven learned to play the piano, the viola, the violin, and all the percussion instruments. He found out how to arrange brass instruments, and he learned orchestration.

In 1784, Prince Elector Maximilian Franz gave Ludwig an allowance and officially made him a court musician. In the spring of 1787, Beethoven went to Vienna to call on Wolfgang Amadeus Mozart, who is said to have remarked that the improvisation that Beethoven played was not actually improvised. Mozart warned that people should watch Beethoven, for he would give the world something to talk about. During the two weeks that Beethoven was in Vienna, Mozart and Beethoven saw each other frequently, and Beethoven took some lessons from Mozart. But Beethoven's time in Vienna was cut short when his mother fell ill, and he returned to Bonn. He left Vienna and took care of his brothers for a time until he was able to return to Vienna a few years later to get back into his musical career.

One of the main problems in Beethoven's life was his increasing deafness, which worsened throughout his career. But even after he became completely deaf, he was still able to conduct the *Ninth Symphony*, the last one he wrote, by watching his players and feeling the vibrations and pulsations of the music he had written.

Beethoven wrote nine symphonies as well as hundreds of other compositions, including many for the piano. He wrote works for stringed instruments, ensembles, string quartets, quintets, and chamber music.

Beethoven's last seven years were marked by his fame as a composer, absorption in his work, and increased isolation, to hide his deafness, which made normal social contacts difficult and frustrating for him. But his health deteriorated steadily from 1818 to 1828, and he sought cures for his hearing problem but to no avail. He avoided many events, but he did perform for the public, and he continued to give concerts. It was in Beethoven's day that for the first time the average person in his area of the world was able to freely listen to his sort of music. Beethoven wished to break barriers of class and wealth to allow everyone to hear music. When he died, over 20,000 people marched through the streets hoping to attend his funeral, all mourning his death. Beethoven was loved by the common man.

Beethoven was successful with virtually every new type of composition that he composed. His music is still performed and enjoyed today. Although the bulk of his music is Classical, his last compositions were Romantic, embodying intense emotion, passion, and drive.

Prometheus

Prometheus was a mortal who defied the gods, seriously offending Jupiter by stealing fire from Mount Olympus and giving it to mankind. He also tricked Jupiter by disguising roasted entrails. Prometheus was chained by Jupiter to a rock on the top of the Caucasus Mountains for his behavior. A vulture ate his liver each day, which regenerated nightly only to be re-eaten the following day.

Romantic Period

Example 15: *Erlkonig (The Elfking)* **(Franz Schubert)**

Franz Schubert was so impressed and excited by a poem written by Johann Wolfgang von Goethe that he decided to set it to music. In doing so, he produced the famous work named the *Erl-King (Elfking)*. The *Erl-King* is a form of composition known as an art song. Generally speaking, an art song is a musical work inspired by a poem. The *Erl-King* has a solo voice accompanied by the piano. Schubert believed a song should express a deep-felt emotion through the perfect unity of words, melody, and piano accompaniment. He composed more than 600 art songs during his short life and is considered by many to be the greatest master of this form of music (Machlis).

When listening to the piano accompaniment, it is important to understand that the piece is Romantic and that it expresses the feelings of the loss of a child. Its sound is supposed to be fearful, a sound of impending doom.

The *Erlkonig*, or *Elfking*, as it is also spelled, was written as a musical setting for a Romantic poem that dealt with a dark, tense, and moody subject. The story is about a father on a horse who sees the demonic Elfking, who takes away children when they are near death. The piano accompaniment is fast, pulsating, and furious, evoking the father's attempts to prevent the monster from capturing his child. Then it worsens, and by the time the child arrives at home in his father's arms, he has passed away. The piano hammers away repeatedly, suggestive of the horse's hooves pounding down the road as the father tries desperately to save his son. These types themes were much in vogue in Romantic music.

Johann Wolfgang von Goethe

>Who rides so late through the night and wind?
>
>It is the father with his child.
>
>He holds the youngster tight in his arm,
>
>Grasps him securely, keeps him warm.
>
>"Son, what makes you afraid to look?"
>
>"Don't you see, father, the Elfking there?
>
>The King of the elves with his crown and tail?"

"Son, it's only a streak of mist.

"Daring child, come away with me!"

I will play the finest of games with you;

Many gay flowers grow by the shore;

My mother has many golden robes."

"Father, father, do you not hear

What the Elfking is softly promising me?"

"Calm yourself, be calm, my son:

The dry leaves are rustling in the wind."

"Well, you fine boy, won't you come with me?

My daughter will wait upon you.

My daughters lead the nightly round,

They will rock you, dance for you, sing you to sleep!"

"Father, father, do you not see

The Elfking's daughters there in the dark?"

"Son, my son, I see only too well: It is the grey gleam in the old willow trees."

"I love you, your beauty allures me,

And if you're not willing, then I shall use force."

"Father, father, now he is seizing me!

The Elfking is hurting me!"

Fear grips the father, he rides like the wind

He holds in his arms the moaning child;

With effort and toil he reaches the house;

The child in his arms was dead. (Kerman 253–254).

Characteristics of the Romantic Music Period

- The size of the symphony orchestra became larger than it was during the Classical Period.

- Orchestral instruments were improved and new ones were developed.

- The types of tone color and timbre were very important for orchestral composers.

- The piano became an instrument to be performed upon by itself alone instead of with an orchestra.

- The art song developed which was a solo for a vocalist and a piano player (accompanist).

- Major themes used by composers were based on themes about national pride, love of country, love between individuals, painful love, loss, death and dying, fear, hope, happiness, and extreme emotional expressions.

Franz Schubert

1797–1828

Austria (Austrian)

It has been said that Franz Schubert went to see Beethoven several days before he died. Schubert was a torchbearer at Beethoven's funeral and died a few months later of typhoid fever.

Schubert was a son of a lower–middle-class schoolmaster from Vienna. He sang in the Vienna boys' choir and studied music during his schooling. Schubert was trained in composition and was an excellent pianist and vocalist. He particularly searched for gloomy texts and poems, being a writer who wrote music that went along with words. Schubert wrote choral works—it is said that he may have written over 600 pieces to be sung and played. Some accounts say that he met the court composer, Antonio Salieri, who knew Mozart. If this was the case, then he might have been about eleven or twelve years old.

Schubert was only thirty-one years old when he died, but he left behind many marvelous works, including the *Trout* quintet, *Fifth Mass in A Flat Major*, the *Wanderer Fantasy*, and the *Eighth Symphony*, to name only a few.

Example 16: *Prelude No. 4 in E Minor* (Frederic Chopin)

Prelude No. 4 in E Minor was written with a melody for the right hand and then repeated with chords played by the left. The texture, or combination of the sound, is homophonic. Chopin's preludes were composed while he stayed with a woman named Madame Aurore Dudevant, who used a man's name, George Sand, so that her literary works would be published. The island where Chopin composed his prelude, Majorca, was off the coast of Spain.

Although political and social unrest continued throughout the nineteenth century, Europe in 1820 was remarkably different from what it had been a hundred years earlier. For a long time dreams of freedom and equality had been just that, but now they looked as if they might some day come true. No longer did a man have to be a servant unless he chose to be one. He was free to raise himself as high as his own abilities and initiative allowed.

The Romantic spirit spread over most of Europe, influencing all the fine arts. In contrast to the Classicists' ideals of logic, refinement, and controlled emotion, the Romantics placed great emphasis on personal feelings and emotions. They were interested in the unusual and fantastic, particularly in folklore.

The music of the Romantic period was filled with sounds that made people feel deep emotions. Literature and writing were used to intensify personal expression. Romantic composers felt that the Classical forms had been too binding by their structure. They wanted more freedom to express themselves, and Romanticism found expression in a variety of musical forms. One was the art song, which featured words and used a symphony in the background, playing along with the singer. The use of additional percussion instruments added a wider range of dynamics and increased the depth of compositions' sound. More and more sound effects were being created by the symphony orchestra, and audiences greeted with delight the new sounds that were being developed.

The piano became a very popular instrument with the Romantics. Although it had been played along with orchestras and used in concertos, the piano's position as a solo instrument now solidified (Nadeau and Tesson 222). Frederic Chopin was a composer and performer who made the instrument really sing, responding to extremely expressive chords and new registers. His compositions in his concerts were improvised, but enough of them were written down for them to be played and performed today, although some of them are extremely difficult to master. The combinations of notes and the patterns represent some of the most luscious music of the Romantic period.

Frederic Chopin

1810–1849

near Warsaw, Poland (Polish)

Frederic Chopin lived in France and on the island of Majorca, off the coast of France. His famous *Revolutionary Etude* has been said to express his anguish over the Russian capture of Warsaw in 1831. It does exemplify Romantic music; certainly anyone listening to it will remember Frederic Chopin's music from then on.

Chopin's mother was from Poland, and his father was from Paris. When Frederic was twenty years old, he settled in Paris. He played some concerts in public, but health problems caused him major difficulties. After the end of his affair with a very close female friend, George Sand, he became very ill. She did not even attend his funeral, and she then wrote a novel containing some unkind comments about him.

Chopin wrote "night pieces," or nocturnes, which are slow, beautiful piano pieces. He also wrote fast, triple-metered dances called mazurkas. He was a brilliant composer despite suffering from intense pain because of his illness. Eventually, however, he had to stop performing publicly, and he died very young, at thirty-nine (Nadeau and Tesson 160; Kerman).

Example 17: *Symphony No. 6 Third Movement Allegro Molto Vivace* (Peter Ilich Tchaikovsky)

The first public performance of *Symphony No. 6* was given in St. Petersburg, on October 16, 1893. Tchaikovsky conducted his own symphony that evening, and the press was largely favorable, but Tchaikovsky did not think his performance had gone well at all.

Tchakovsky's brother, Modeste, revealed the origin of the title of *Symphony No. 6* in a biography about his brother. Peter, he said, did not want simply to number the piece but wanted to call it something with a tragic meaning. Modeste was in a quandary over this, and when he began exclaiming *pathetique!*, Peter took a pen and wrote that as the name on his score: *pathetique*. Eight days after the premiere of the performance, Tchaikovsky died suddenly of cholera after drinking contaminated water that had not been boiled as had been thought. The *Sixth Symphony* turned out to have been *pathetique* after all. It was performed at a memorial concert for Tchaikovsky under the direction of Napravnik, and it was well received by the public. Experts have said that the four movements of the symphony sound as if they depict youth, love, disappointment, and death. The ending died away as noticed on recordings and noted by professor David Lloyd-Jones. That sound was also noticed on a disc in the Richland College Music Lab.

In the third movement, the violins and the violas can be heard at the beginning of the allegro molto vivace, or the very fast part. In the tenth through twelfth measures, listen carefully to the tempo of the full orchestra to hear how rapidly the string players are playing. Tchaikovsky's music can be called Romantic, for it includes many changes in tempo and dynamics and even in the number of instruments being played at once—from only a few to very many. The music can be extremely bold, with the entire orchestra playing, but it can also be very soft. The Romantic orchestra of Tchaikovsky's day could create scary, loud, crashing sounds or beautiful, lovely, calm tones. Because "allegro" means fast, "molto" means much, and "vivace" means very fast, the entire movement was written to be conducted at a fast tempo.

Peter Ilich Tchaikovsky
1840–1893
Russia (Russian)
Peter Tchaikovsky was born in the Russian countryside. He is still famous today for his ballets *The Nutcracker, Sleeping Beauty,* and *Swan Lake*.

Tchaikovsky was a hypersensitive child who married a woman who later died in an asylum. He had a troubled adulthood and ultimately died after drinking contaminated water. But he created some of the most outstanding musical ballets ever written, as well as some of the best Romantic music ever heard and still performed today.

Interestingly enough, a wealthy, reclusive widow, named Madame Nadezhda von Meck, gave Tchaikovsky an allowance to enable him to create his music, but she herself did not desire to meet him. Without her assistance, he would not always have been able to support himself, and he certainly would not have been free to write as much as he did. He was extremely capable, which allowed him to be very creative in the outpouring of music that resulted. His work reflected sensitivity, moodiness, expressiveness, introspectiveness, and a deep and personal sense of sadness.

Impressionistic Period

Example 18: *Prélude à l'après-midi d'un faune* (Claude Debussy) French 1862–1918

I remember listening to this piece in my college music appreciation class. At the time, I thought that Debussy's music sounded pretty strange, but the more I listened to it, the more I enjoyed it. I was taking an art appreciation class at the same time, in which we were studying Claude Monet's *Water Lilies*. Monet's painting did not have clear or distinct edges, because Monet was trying to express an idea that was a fleeting moment. It occurred to me that sound can help with visualization.

Both Debussy and Monet were Impressionists. In Debussy's *Prelude to the Afternoon of the Faun*, he wrote about a mythological creature, half man and half goat, in a forest—a very passionate being, according to mythology. Upon awaking from a wonderful dream, he tries to remember whether he was actually just visited by three lovely nymphs. Was it a dream, or not? Just what had happened to him?

Debussy's *Prelude* was inspired by a poem written by Stephane Mallarme, describing a day that might have occurred in a story derived from pagan themes, with a mythological, almost improbable storyline. This supported Debussy in his desire to explore the tonality of the whole musical scale, leaving listeners with an ever deeper sense of wonder combined with only a vague understanding of what was actually going on in the story. This was exactly Debussy's intent. The first two measures open with the flute playing a tri-tone interval from C sharp to G natural, setting a mood of vagueness and instability at once.

> In the traditional tonal sense this interval could suggest a resolution in the key of D. However, in measure 3 the G *natural* is canceled and Debussy makes the first reference to E, which is the tonal center of the work. When the chromatic figure of the opening measures is stated throughout the work, one can begin to listen for new harmonizations (Nadeau and Tesson 284).

Example 19: *Bolero* (Maurice Ravel)

Maurice Ravel's *Bolero* has been labeled Impressionistic but also sometimes Romantic. It is an enjoyable piece in which the instruments of the orchestra play the beautiful, catchy melody in a very memorable way. The repetition created by Ravel can be almost hypnotic.

Ravel composed *Bolero* in 1928 as an orchestral experiment in exchanging a melody from instrument to instrument, ultimately building to a crescendo (loud climax). His piece is based on a Spanish dance rhythm. The first instrument to play the melody is the flute. Then comes the clarinet, the bassoon, the contrabassoon, the E flat clarinet, the oboe d'amore, the trumpet, the oboe, the English horn, the trombone, the soprano saxophone, the tenor saxophone, the celeste, the piccolo, the first and second violins, the viola, and finally the strings.

The piece itself has an interesting background. When Ravel was out to dinner on one occasion, he got into an intense discussion about music and wagered that he could write a composition whose melody repeated itself at least fifteen times without becoming monotonous. He won the bet. Bolero repeats its melody even more times than that, and even today it is considered a great orchestral arrangement.

Maurice Ravel

1875–1937
Spain (Spanish); he lived in Paris where he grew up
Maurice Ravel was working on a tribute to a Baroque composer of the early 1900s named Couperin when he was called to military duty. Later, he completed part of the work, which was produced as *Le Tombeau de Couperin*.

But Ravel was very emotionally scarred from the effects of World War I, an experience that deeply affected his musical career. His music is vibrant, with a new color and a spark of something that brings excitement. It fused French and Spanish folk elements, seeming at the same time to fuse the past with the present. His melodies and rhythms were intriguing, for he had developed something not only original but unique.

When Ravel was sixty-two, he died from a rare disease that caused him to lose his motor coordination and his ability to speak (Hickok 344).

Music of the Twentieth Century

Example 20: *Rite of Spring (Le Sacre du printemps Sacrificia)* (Igor Stravinsky)

Characteristics of Twentieth-Century Music

Atonal music has no root position and thus does not telegraph where it is going. It features complex rhythms and dissonant harmonies, with sounds that do not always sound like traditional ones. Even electrical or mechanical sounds added within pitches can be music (Eisman et al. 84).

Stravinsky's original idea for his *Rite of Spring* came through what he called a dream or vision, in which he saw a young girl dance herself to death in front of wise elders who sat in a circle watching her. He persuaded Diaghilev to cast it in the form of a ballet. The first performance, which was in 1913, was not accepted by the audience, because the ballet did not have a story. A fistfight broke out in the concert hall, and the performance had to be stopped. Reviews were appalling. But a year later Stravinsky decided to give the *Rite of Spring* another try, and this second performance was spoken of highly and garnered rave reviews. The new audience raved about the performance, and Stravinsky had revitalized his career (Sporre, *Reality*).

Igor Stravinsky

1882–1971

Russia (Russian)

Igor Stravinsky was born in Russia. He was exposed to music as a child and was given lessons on the piano, but because he was expected to study law, his parents did not take his music lessons seriously. For a time Igor tried to study both law and music, but his parents did not support him even in this.

Stravinsky studied under Nikolai Rimsky-Korsakov, a nationalist composer who was well known at the time, and he learned to compose for the Russian Ballet. In 1910, at the age of twenty-eight, Stravinsky composed his *Firebird*. At twenty-nine, he produced *Petruska*. The great dancers Vaslav Nijinsky and Tamara Karavina were the leading dancers in his ballet, and the coupling of their dancing his writing skill made Stravinsky a leader in twentieth-century music.

During World War I, Stravinsky spent time in Switzerland, where he began to use folkloric themes in his compositions. In 1925, he visited the United States, where he guest-conducted the New York Philharmonic Orchestra and played piano for the Boston Symphony.

In 1927, Stravinsky performed *Oedipus Rex* in Paris, France. He applied for citizenship in both France and the United States. He composed his *Ebony Concerto* for Woody Herman's jazz band, and his late music showed tendencies toward jazz forms, even to the point of featuring jazz in his work.

Example 21: *Pulcinella* (Igor Stravinsky)

After World War I and the Russian Revolution, Stravinsky lived in Paris for fifteen years. "Still associated with Ballet Ruse, he was called upon to orchestrate some eighteenth-century music by Pergolesi for a ballet... entitled 'Pulcinella'" (Politoske 375). Stravinsky stated, "Pulcinella was my discovery of the past, the epiphany through which the whole of my late work became possible. It was a backward look, of course—the first of many love affairs in the direction—but it was a look in the mirror too" (from Expositions and Developments in 1962). After *Pulcinella*, he entered his neoclassical phase.

> The orchestra for both "Pulcinella" and the suite derived from it is much smaller than that for "The Rite of Spring". Stravinsky specified a number of solo string players, a small group of orchestral strings, and a small wind section, and stipulated that the entire orchestra should consist of thirty-three players (Politoske 375).

Example 22: *Pierrot Lunaire, Op. 21* (Arnold Schoenberg)

Atonality literally means "without tonality," and implies that all twelve tones of the chromatic scale are treated equally, without emphasizing any note more than any other (Politoske 375–377).

Schoenberg was pioneer in the development of atonal music, which was a result of much study, and which transformed nineteenth-century harmony. Schoenberg was influenced by Brahms and Wagner.

> [From Brahms he] learned the technique of using a motive for continuous development, with each new theme evolving almost imperceptibly from the previous one. From Wagner he derived an increasingly dissonant, chromatic harmony as in his string sextet the "Transfigured Night" (1899).

Shoenberg's early works were atonal but sounded more Romantic in their styles. He was not satisfied with chromaticism, with its tonal feel, so he gradually moved into his twelve-tone style, which was closely related to that of the Expressionists in Germany. Schoenberg has also been said to have been influenced by Emile Nolde, and he himself painted some paintings in the Expressionist style.

Arnold Schoenberg

1874–1951

Austria (Austrian); moved to the United States

Arnold Schoenberg is known today as the twentieth-century composer who invented the twelve-tone technique. He is known as the composer who wrote atonal music. Atonal music is music that does not have a feeling or sound of a key. His use of atonality led him to develop his twelve tones which he used to create music with a series of randomly selected twelve notes. The sound of these tones in order created a sound that was quite unusual compared to traditional types of compositions. The first work that he created using the twelve-tone row was done between 1921 and 1923 named the "Suite for Piano."

Schoenberg changed the way in which harmonic relationships were accepted in the twentieth century. His music was very innovative and had a dramatic and significant influence on the musical world. He opened the door for new methods of composing, according to author Robert Hickok (in *Music Appreciation*). Schoenberg began his musical career in Berlin as a theater conductor after working in a bank for several years in Vienna. He became acquainted with the great musician Richard Strauss who helped him obtain a teaching position. During World War I, Schoenberg served in the Austrian army and then began teaching again. His first wife died and he remarried and moved to Berlin. With the Nazi party becoming powerful, he lost his job and went to live in France and then moved to the United States. He died at the age of seventy-seven in Los Angeles.

Example 23: *Violin Concerto* (Alban Berg)

Alban Berg was one of Schoenberg's most successful students. His *Violin Concerto* was analogous to the increasing decorative design in the architecture of the middle of the twentieth century, according to Politoske. Berg wrote his *Violin Concerto* in 1935; it was his last completed work. The American violinist Louis Krasner commissioned it in memory of Manon Gropius, the eighteen-year-old daughter of Alma Mahler, the widow of Gustav Mahler and the wife of architect Walter Gropius. The young girl had died from infantile paralysis, and this concerto's form and expression were products of the affection Alban Berg felt for her (Nadau and Tesson 467).

The *Concerto* makes use of both the modern dissonance of twelve-tone music and traditional harmony. The notes in the twelve-tone row start with the G below middle C and proceed up to F natural.

Alban Berg
1885–1935
Austria (Austrian)
Alban Berg was born February 9, 1885, in Vienna, Austria. He was a close associate and friend of Arnold Schoenberg, with whom he worked from 1904 to 1911, when he married singer Helene Nahowski. The majority of Berg's career, during which he composed most of his chief works, featured his serial style. Some of his major works were *Four Pieces for Clarinet and Piano* and *Three Orchestral Pieces*. His early works were free of atonality, but his later works blended the twelve-tone technique and slight amounts of more traditional tonality.

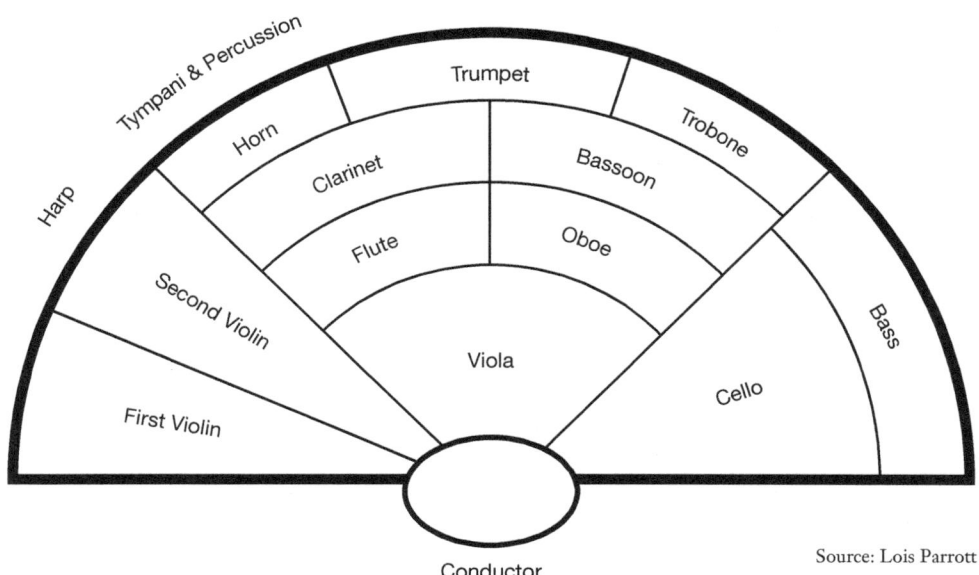

Source: Lois Parrott

Igor Stravinsky
Russian (1882–1971)

J. S. Bach
(1685–1750)

STRING INSTRUMENTS

BRASS INSTRUMENTS

Images © Shutterstock, Inc.

Music: Compositions and Composers 211

WOODWIND INSTRUMENTS

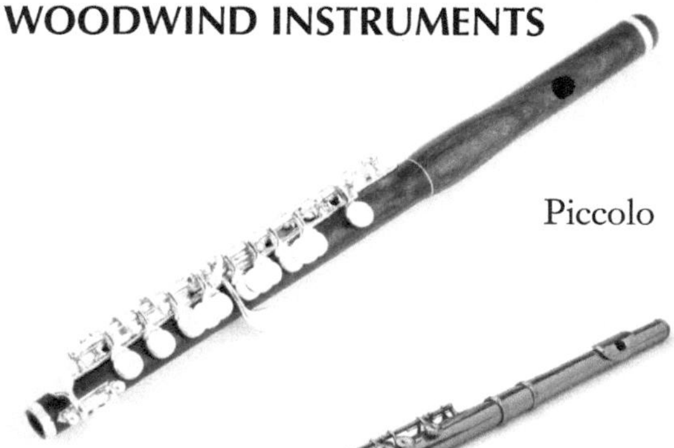

Piccolo

Flute

Bass clarinet

Clarinet 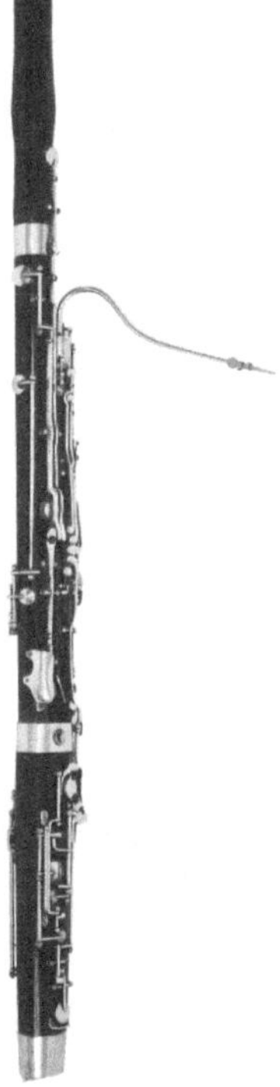 Bassoon 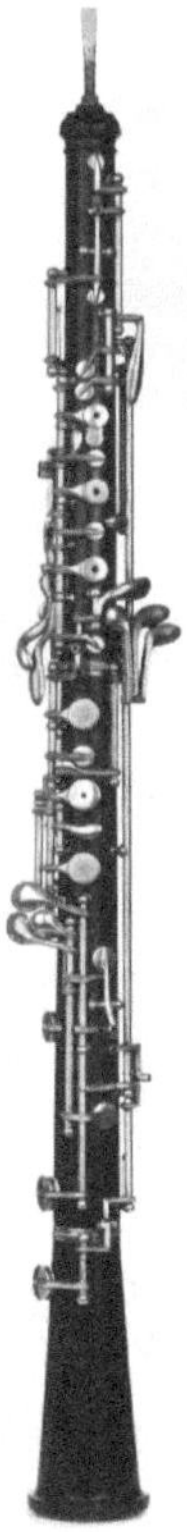 Oboe

PERCUSSION INSTRUMENTS

Timpani

Triangle

Cymbal and drumsticks

Images © Shutterstock, Inc.

Example 24: *Rhapsody in Blue* (George Gershwin)

Rhapsody in Blue showed that George Gershwin not only possessed the talent to produce musical comedies but that he was also a composer capable of writing for the concert hall and the orchestra. He would soon be producing large forms of music developing his style. His early success as a composer of popular songs and show tunes was phenomenal, but that was only the beginning of his career.

Rhapsody in Blue was first written for the Paul Whitman Band in 1924. Gershwin originally wrote it for the piano and a jazz band, but he later composed an arrangement for an entire orchestra. His *Concerto in F* for piano and orchestra was a composition that used jazz and blues effects together with an orchestra, something very unusual for that time. Gershwin himself played the solo piano when he performed *Rhapsody in Blue* and *Concerto in F*.

Theme 1 of *Rhapsody in Blue* features the clarinet trill and glissando that it has made so well known. Theme 2 is introduced by a dissonant trumpet trill accompanied by light decorative figures on the piano (Nadeau and Tesson 338).

Gershwin's music combined the classical discipline of orchestra with popular jazz and its improvised variations of riffs and blue notes. The combination is as stunning today as it was then.

Twentieth-Century Music

Popular music was almost entirely a non-notated music until the nineteenth century. Its record is fragmentary, for it depends almost entirely on the art and music of recognized composers. Illustrations and accounts of folk songs and folk dances give evidence of the existence of popular music from the earliest times, but it was not until the nineteenth century that any real attempt was made to collect and notate such music.

George Gershwin

1898–1937
United States (American)
In 1919 George Gershwin wrote *Swanee*, his first successful popular song. It was a tremendous hit and was sung by Al Jolson. In 1924, Gershwin wrote the musical comedy *Tip-Toes*, and in 1930 he wrote the Broadway musical *Girl Crazy*. He was also a success in the concert hall. His *Rhapsody in Blue* (1924) was a piece written for a jazz band with a lead piano, and he later added parts for an entire orchestra. His other major works, which demonstrate the breadth of his talent, are his *An American in Paris* (1928) and the famous "folk opera" *Porgy and Bess*.

> The record of popular music is sparse, indeed, until the end of the nineteenth century, by which not only popular folk music was being collected and published, but songs and dances were being written and published for the general public. While unnamed composers continued to invent folk music such as the black and white spirituals, as well as early ragtime dances, protection of composers through copyright laws, along with enlarged production of sheet music, began to flood the market with quantities of popular tunes. The twentieth century ushered in the real widespread dissemination of popular music when mass printing was superseded by electronic communication and reproductive media.

The social and political upheavals resulting from World Wars I and II and the technological developments spread popular culture in all its forms, including music, to all corners of the globe. A tremendous increase in the role of popular music in the post 1950's can be attributed to the following: (1) dissemination of popular music by means of the electronic media, (2) the attractive possibility of business profit generated by the laws of copyright and patent of published music, (3) recorded tapes and records, (4) television, radio and motion pictures, and (5) the enormous audience supplied by revolting youth with their antagonism toward the music of their elders. All of this resulted in an outburst of popular music production such as the world had never seen before. This inundation of the airways, and the recording media have had their influence on all phases of musical life (Wols and Cyckler).

Musical Genres Developed during the Twentieth Century

New Orleans Jazz
Early New Orleans jazz was characterized by a type of free counterpoint improvisation played by the clarinet, trumpet, and trombone. New Orleans jazz combines two basic styles, ragtime and the blues.

Ragtime: strong syncopation, with weak beats and strong beats
Blues: an outgrowth of the sorrowful slave songs of the American South, using a regular twelve-bar pattern with free interpolation of both words and music

Dixieland
As African Americans, blacks, and Creoles created new sounds and new music, whites were creating a similar sound called Dixieland. It was through this movement that jazz spread north to Chicago and New York. Dixieland hit it big about the time of World War I.

Swing Jazz
Swing jazz came about with the big band era. Benny Goodman, Count Basie, and Louis Armstrong were some of the most prominent swing musicians. "The orchestra and soloists combined to make an impression of big sounds merged with a lighter texture of solo against an orchestral background" (Wold and Cykler, *Outline* 311).

Bebop
Bebop came from Kansas City and spread to New York City. It was a sound that used a fifth that was lowered in pitch, called the flatted fifth. This interval, also called a "blue note," prevailed in the melodic line.

Cool Jazz
During the 1950s the term "cool jazz" came into use to describe relaxed, mellow, dreamy jazz melodies. It remained jazz, although dotted eighth and sixteenth note passages were replaced by smooth passages instead.

Free Jazz

In the 1960s, free jazz included music from other cultures (especially non-Western cultures) such as those of the Far East and India. Steel drums were added, and new instruments were also used to create a new type of jazz.

Rock

A strong sense of beat is evident in rock. Amplifiers make the sound of electric guitars extremely audible above the beat of the music.

Country-Western

Since the 1950s, country-western music has been popular with the many people who relate to the words of its songs, which deal with love, sorrow, and everyday. The chords support the vocal line, and the violin, string bass, and guitar are commonly used.

Nonmetric Rhythm

Much non-Western music is not metric in organization: the accents do not group themselves into a single regular pattern. The rhythmic organization of African drum music, for example, can be extremely complex and irregular. In recent Western music there has also been a tendency on the part of some composers to move toward non-metric rhythm. Not surprisingly, the earliest efforts in this direction occurred about 1910, just at the time that the first atonal pieces appeared. Example 13, part of the "Sacrificial Dance" from Stravinsky's *Sacre du Printemps*, was composed in 1913. Although the sixteenth note functions as a pulse, the larger groupings of the pulse are quite irregular, as can be seen by the various time signatures, which frequently change from measure to measure.

Musical Theater of the 21st Century

Hip-Hop Music
Hamilton, the Hip-hop Musical by Lin-Manuel Miranda

Lin-Manuel Miranda's new musical *Hamilton*, is about the Founding Father Alexander Hamilton. Hamilton was born in the Caribbean and came to America as a young man. He became an assistant to George Washington, went to law school, and founded the Bank of New York. A book written by Ron Chernow about Hamilton's life is what Miranda based his story on when he wrote his hip-hop music and the rap type arrangements heard in this award-winning Broadway musical. Hamilton believed in strong central government and led the Federalist Party against Thomas Jefferson and James Madison. They thought that Hamilton's views would weaken their Republicanism.

Source: http://stageagent.com/shows/musical/4417/ham https://en.wikipedia.org/wiki/Alexander_Hamiltonilton

The musical covers the life of Hamilton as he helps create a Department of the Treasury and create trust in the economy in the newly formed nation. The characters in the musical along with Hamilton are Eliza Hamilton, Thomas Jefferson, and of course, Aaron Burr who is the one who brings Hamilton's life to a dramatic end.

Source: http://www.broadway.com/shows/hamilton-broadway/story/

One reason Aaron Burr was upset with Hamilton was over the presidential election of 1801. Hamilton helped to defeat Burr who was tied for the presidency in the Electoral College, and then helped to elect Jefferson. In 1804, Burr ran for governor of New York State and Hamilton campaigned against him as an unfit candidate. Due to some of Hamilton's comments during the campaign, Burr challenged him to a duel. Hamilton was mortally wounded and succumbed to death the very next day.

Spencer Kornhaber, in his article, "The Case for Hamilton as Album of the Year," 2015, wrote, "Each and every line has been carefully sculpted so that you can hear new bits of cleverness in them each time you listen" to "Hamilton." The actors are extremely talented and good musically with ranges and timbre fitting to their rapping of cadences. Spencer said that most importantly, the emotional machinery "just works" and that this musical was emotional and moved very quickly. At the conclusion the audience sensed a deep feeling of sadness at the death of Hamilton.

Source: "The Case for Hamilton as Album of the Year" by Spencer Kornhaber, December 17, 2015 article http://www.theatlantic.com/entertainment/archive/2015/12/hamilton-cast-album-best-album-of-2015/420975/

UNIT 5

Acting, Theater, Film, and Dance

FILM

Elements of Film

Script
Organization of the shots as well as the words and phrases spoken by the actors.

Sound and Audio
Actual sound captured by the filming and sounds added by editing them in.

Camera Angles and Camera Movements
The way in which the camera moves in order to capture images to portray mood and show actors' expressions and emotions.

Acting
The actresses and actors portraying characters, making situations believable.

Lighting
Use of light, to capture mood, draw attention, and create suspense if needed. This is noticeable especially in black-and-white films' use of values and shadows.

Costumes and Makeup
These add details and information to the story and characterization. The costumes must be authentic in historic films. Makeup can also help in creating believable characters in film.

Editing
Placing pieces of film together in a fashion to create a story. This may also be the arrangement of scenes to create mood. Editing also helps explain who the characters are and their location in varying scenes. Editing can help create suspense by using intercutting. Editing is also done to add sound and special effects. Before highly technical computerized film editing software, an optical printer was used. For example, special effects in the scene of the parting of the Red Sea in the film, *The Ten Commandments*, created believable events in film.

Elements of Music

Melody: single succession of tones

Harmony: two or more tones sounding together

Rhythm: the beat or pulsation rhythm

Tempo: rate of speed

Dynamics: loudness or softness

Timbre: quality of sound used to distinguish between one instrument or voice and another

Texture: one line of melody by itself which is monophonic, or two or more melodies together which is polyphonic, or the sameness of sound like a chord with melody which is homophonic

Film is considered the newest art form. An outgrowth of film is video. Video and film are probably the most accessible and widely experienced art forms for many people. Film is a work of art that communicates through form within a time frame. It is seen in three-dimensional space compressed into a two-dimensional image.

Film is also highly technical. It evolved from the principles of photography and developed into projected images. Many early filmmakers composed their works by adding single photographs to each other, frame by frame. The eye's physiological limitations cause the movement in motion pictures. It cannot perceive the black line between frames when the filmstrip is moved. Your eye sees the succession of frames minus the lines that divide them. The image in each frame does not actually move but seems to move. This phenomenon is called *persistence of vision*.

The theory of persistence of vision means that it takes the eye a fraction of a second to record the image's impression and then send it to the brain. The eye retains the image for about one-tenth of a second after the actual image has disappeared. Motion picture film is usually projected at a speed of twenty-four frames per second. Images are merged through the theory called *persistence of image*.

Filmmakers are also designers, and they attempt to create each individual frame as carefully as they would a still photograph or a painting. A student of film will soon notice that the greatest films make use of detail, individual frame design, and composition. Excellent examples of this artistry are Ingmar Bergman's *Seventh Seal*, Jean Renoir's *Grand Illusion*, David Lean's *Lawrence of Arabia*, and Orson Welles' *Citizen Kane*.

Film as Art

Film consists of many elements. A worthwhile, remarkable film is considered a work of art when the elements all work well together. The film needs to be technically well done, and the camera shots, movements, and angles need to be visually exciting. The film also needs to be presented in an original and imaginative manner.

In watching films be sure to be observant. Narrative films have actors in them and usually there is a plot and a story, which is memorable.

A narrative can be analyzed by taking time to really examine the way that the director, the director of photography, the musical director and composer, and the editor put the entire film together.

You may want to view a list of great films by using the website of the American Film Institute and look at the list of the top ten films of all time. Classic films are studied by the great directors piece by piece and dissected when they are in film school. Directors learn from each other and as time goes on more technological advancements help make films seem even more believable.

When you watch a film, try not to just watch it for entertainment purposes. Try to watch it as an individual who is observing the use the film elements such as the use of the sound, lighting, acting, script, camera angles and movements. Ask yourself questions as you watch a film scene and be sure you pay close attention to the details. You must watch the scene several times in order to fully see that the elements were used by the director.

Be sure to pay attention to the camera angles, sound, soundtrack (the music used), and camera movements. Pay attention to the script and the sound as well as the set design, costumes, makeup, any use of special effects, and the acting. You may want to watch the film more than once or even twice. Ask yourself questions about the film such as:

- Did the camera move towards the subject or did the actor (subject) walk towards the camera? (**Zoom in** is going towards theobject; **zoom out** is going away from the object.)
- Did the sound used by the editor sound natural or were sounds added? Did they use scary music or soft friendly music? What type of music was it? Was it an orchestra or piano or vocal that was heard in the sound track?
- Was the setting in a city? In a house? On a street? In the rain? Inside or outside? Was it natural light? Low or brightly lit?

Be very observant and watch a scene paying close attention to detail. This helps to understand the way films are made and how much attention goes into lighting, camera movements and camera angles, costumes, makeup, set design, musical sound track, actual sounds, acting, and script—the film elements.

Film Elements

The elements of film are direction, script, sound and audio, camera angles and movements, acting, photography, lighting, sets, costumes, makeup, music, special effects, and editing, to list a few.

The individuals involved in making a film are many. They are the producer, director, actors, scriptwriters, musicians, audio and camera operators, grips, gaffers, continuity person, and makeup artists, among others. These individuals and the film elements are interesting to observe when analyzing films.

Three Types of Film

There are basically three types of films that encompass most works: narrative, documentary, and absolute.

Narrative Film

A narrative film is a very popular type of film—it tells a story. Popular novels and stories are often transformed into narrative films. Can you think of any narrative films that you have seen recently? Narrative films are usually similar to literary construction. As in the theater, the people or characters in the story are portrayed by professional actors under the guidance of a director. Many narrative films are written in styles called genre films. Popular genres are detective, horror, western, mystery, and love stories.

Documentary Film

A documentary film is similar to watching a news program that does not use actors. It is shot on location, and many times a reporter will narrate the findings. Events are not staged or reenacted by professional actors. Documentary films record actual events in a journalistic approach. They convey a sense of reality and record the time and place of the camera person.

Absolute Film

An absolute film is sometimes called an experimental film. It exists for its own sake. It tells no story, but exists for the purpose of the movement, or the colors and shapes, or the combinations of sound and light. Absolute films may use innovative techniques or special effects and try new ideas. They are considered an artistic expression. Museums sometimes show experimental films, and some are used in the educational market.

Theatrical vs. Cinematic Style

In the first films, the directors thought in terms of theatrical productions they had seen before. The camera sat in front, like the audience, and never moved. The unit of action, as in the theater, was the scene. Gradually, however, filmmakers began to realize the special possibilities of filming. They began to move the camera about as the action seemed to indicate, and the scene was broken down into shots. Thus the film freed itself of the limitations of the theatrical approach. D. W. Griffith, more than any other individual, was responsible for this.

The Lumiere Brothers

In 1895, two Frenchmen named Lumiere shot their first film. They titled it *Workers Leaving the Lumiere Factory*. Their invention, which was both camera and projector, was called the cinematographe. They opened the first movie theater in the basement of a Paris cafe on December 28, 1895. Their films were all composed of single scenes such as a train arriving at a station or the feeding of a baby.

Thomas Edison

As early as 1891, Thomas Edison patented a movie camera, the KINETOGRAPH, and a peephole viewer, the KINETOSCOPE, through which his single-scene pictures, such as Fred Ott's *Sneeze*, could be viewed. Edison did not have confidence in the future of motion pictures, so he refused to spend $150 to extend his patent rights to England and Europe. His biggest contribution to film was the sprocket holes that permit the film to move through the camera and projector.

George Melies

Melies, a French magician, added interest to films through his skills in camera trickery. Disappearances and transformations play a part in many of his films. The showmanship and humor of his films, such as *The Terrible Turkish Executioner* and *A Trip to the Moon*, make them enjoyable even today. Melies contributed the superimposure (one image overlapping another), the lap dissolve (one scene fades out as another fades in), and the cut (the film is cut apart and spliced together to produce some effect).

Edwin S. Porter

As the director of production for Edison's studio, Edwin S. Porter made several contributions to the development of film. In *The Life of an American Fireman*, he invented film editing, putting together a series of scenes to tell a story. This film is also the first to present a narrative on location. In *The Great Train Robbery*, the first western, Porter continued to improve his editing techniques. He also introduced the pan and the elliptical jump forward in time, which is now a common feature of film.

D. W. Griffith

David Wark Griffith, who got into films more or less accidentally, turned out to be the most important director of the silent era. He was the first filmmaker to move the camera about freely, combining a variety of angles and positions to produce a truly cinematic effect. In his films, such as *The Lonedale Operator*, *Birth of a Nation*, and *Intolerance*, Griffith introduced some of the first great stars of film: Mary Pickford, Blanch Sweet, Lionel Barrymore, and Lillian and Dorothy Gish.

In the early 1920s, the sound pictures began and the first sound film was entitled *The Jazz Singer*. Al Jolson was the main star in that film. He sang, "You ain't seen nothin' yet." Films such as *Thirty Nine Steps* by Alfred Hitchcock were considered to be a very scary and suspenseful film. Hitchcock became known as the master of suspense. Some films made around the time of World War II composed in Italy are now referred to as the Neo-realists which were films featuring bold and realistic situations dealing with the oppression of people.

Genre (Films)	Themes (of Films)
Mystery	Battle of the Sexes
Western	Love
Science Fiction	Man and Society
Animation	
Documentary	

When artists, writers, lighting directors, choreographers, and musicians work together on a production they may produce an opera which is a combined art or it may be a musical. The types of music used in musicals can vary. Music theater has been around for many years.

"It took many years for the American musical theatre to acquire its own identity. The first musical production in the Colonies was *Flora*, a performance that took place in a court room in Charleston, South Carolina, on February 8, 1735. *Flora* was a ballad opera imported from England. The English ballad opera remained popular in the Colonies for several decades." (Source: http://www.theatrehistory.com/american/musical030.html)

Special Information / Key Terms

Animation

Animation consists of a series of individual pictures that are drawn and painted before they are photographed. The animation is done on cels (individual pieces of acetate) and then photographed one by one. When they are run through a projector, they appear to move. *Steamboat Willie* was the original Mickey Mouse cartoon.

Documentary

The documentary is to dramatic film as nonfiction is to fiction. The documentary draws upon fact, presenting actual people, places, and events rather than imaginary ones. The term *direct cinema* has also been used for this form. *Gray Gardens* was a television program by David and Albert Maysles, documentary filmmakers who did documentaries on public television as well as for Jeanne-Claude and Christo documenting their art projects over the years.

Shots

A *shot* is a single unit of filming; what the camera records from the time it is turned on until it is turned off is one shot. There are many types of shots, and new ones are being invented constantly. A master shot is one that records all of the action in a scene from beginning to end. Using the master shot as a cutaway, a shorter shot may be used that records some detail of the scene. This is sometimes done to cover a mistake in the master shot or simply to add variety and interest.

Shots are also described in terms of the distance between the camera and the subject: a long shot gives a panoramic effect, recording the action at a distance; a medium shot gives a midrange view, as if the camera were a few feet from the subject; a close-up moves in tight to exclude all background distractions. Of course, there are many gradations in between: medium close-up, extreme close-up, medium long shot, and so on.

Camera Movements

There are several terms that describe camera movements. One is the *zoom in*. If the camera retreats from the subject, it is a *zoom out*. If the camera eye moves horizontally without changing its base (as if the viewer's head is turning), it is called a *pan*. If the camera moves vertically (as if the viewer is looking up or down), it is called a *tilt*.

Storyboard

The storyboard, which is made as a part of preproduction, resembles a large comic strip. It pictures each of the important shots in the film in the sequence in which they will occur. It is used by the director, the director of photography, and the editor.

Stripping the Script

The scenes in a film are never shot in the sequence in which they finally appear. To save time and money, the director may want to shoot all the scenes in one location on a certain day or all the scenes involving a particular actor. The process of deciding in what order the scenes are to be shot is called *stripping the script*.

Rushes

The rushes are the selected "takes" or shots from which the editor and director choose and arrange the portions to be included in the finished film.

Special Effects

A special effect is any alteration or combination of film images in a film. These effects are produced with a machine called an optical printer, and they may be as simple as a freeze-frame or as complicated as the parting of the Red Sea in *The Ten Commandments*. Other films that are heavy with special effects are *Alien, Star Trek, I Am Legend,* and *Harry Potter and the Order of the Phoenix*.

Three Phases of Production

Preproduction

The idea for a film may come from many sources. It begins to become a film with the writing of the script. After the scriptwriter's job is done, the director carefully plans the production. The producer is in charge of selecting locations, casting actors, assembling a crew, and renting equipment. Anything that occurs before filming starts is preproduction.

Production

The director controls all aspects of the actual production of the film. With the actors, the director works to create the characterizations. With the director of photography, the director plans and executes the visual aspects of the film. With the sound crew, the director arranges the recording of sound for the film. The director of photography communicates ideas to the camera operator who sets up the shots and runs the cameras. The sound crew is assisted by the mike crew, or boom crew, who position the sound equipment. Usually, there is a script or continuity person, who keeps a careful record of the shots and makes sure that the visual details match. There are also grips who do the physical labor on the set. A makeup person is also usually present to keep the actors looking good. The grip carries equipment. A gaffer carries equipment that is connected to an electrical outlet.

Postproduction

The editor may be present during production to make sure that the shots will cut together, but his or her job really begins after filming is over. The editor works closely with the director to put the individual shots of the film together into their final form.

Amadeus

The film *Amadeus* is about the life of the composer Wolfgang Amadeus Mozart. Throughout the film, the musical sound track utilized music composed by Mozart. As you know, Mozart was the Classical composer who died at age thirty-five.

The film opens when two helpers go to the door of another composer named Salieri, a court composer to the archbishop. They are delivering food to Salieri but he is not answering the door.

However, the film takes the viewer through many series of flashbacks which are explained to the viewer with Salieri's conversation as he talks to the young priest. The young priest has come to seek a confession from Salieri who has been placed in an asylum for the mentally impaired.

Salieri is talking to the priest who is interviewing him because Salieri is being accused of poisoning Mozart who has just died.

The musical soundtrack was recorded in Prague, Czechoslovakia. The main characters in *Amadeus* were played by Tom Hulce as Mozart and Murry Abraham as Salieri. Hulce was convincing when at the piano because he played the piano in the film and practiced for four hours a day in preparation.

In a scene when his father visits him and he and his wife go to a party Hulce actually plays the piano on his back in a scene. Source: http://www.imdb.com/title/tt0086879/trivia

At the end of *Amadeus*, Mozart's coffin is carried out of the church and thrown into a pauper's grave while the powerful music of the sound track offers a portion of the *Requiem* titled "Lacrimosa." The song is sung in Latin and adds to the emotional drama of the scene. The text's meaning as translated is about asking God to be merciful and spare the guilty man and give them rest.

Another theme of Amadeus that strikes a universal chord is the sad spectacle of a towering genius poorly rewarded by society. No more shocking or dramatic example in all of history can be found than Mozart.

Source: http://www.angelfire.com/film/theamadeus/music/process.html

The cast in Amadeus

F. Murray Abraham	Antonio Salieri
Tom Hulce	Wolfgang Amadeus Mozart
Elizabeth Berridge	Constanze Mozart
Roy Dotrice	Leopold Mozart
Simon Callow	Emanuel Schikaneder
Christine Ebersole	Katerina Cavalieri
Jeffrey Jones	Emperor Joseph II

Study Guide

1. a. What are three phases in the production of a film?
   b. Who are the principle participants in each of these phases? Explain in detail what each one is responsible for and what they do.
2. What are the major problems that can occur in producing a film and marketing it?
3. What is a "shot"? What terms are used to differentiate between shots?

4. What terms are used to describe camera movements?
5. Describe the roles of the following people:
   a. director
   b. producer
   c. continuity person
   d. editor
   e. sound crew
   f. director of photography
   g. grip
   h. gaffer
6. Define the following terms:
   a. cutaway
   b. rushes
   c. tilt
   d. pan
   e. storyboard
   f. zoom
   g. master shot
   h. stripping the script

Film Title	Director
Lawrence of Arabia	David Lean
Annie Hall	Woody Allen
Citizen Kane	Orson Welles
Amadeus	Milos Foreman

William Shakespeare

Hamlet

Except for the Bible, Shakespeare's *Hamlet* is perhaps the West's most famous literary work. Hardly a day passes without this play being acted, either on a commercial stage or in a school or college; and many versions of the play, on film and on tape, ensure its universal visibility. Hamlet's role is usually defined as the most difficult in the theater, and many actors, and a few actresses, often choose to play Hamlet as a crown to their careers. It is so well known that the world uses the term *Hamletlike* to describe people unable to make up their minds.

The hectic world in which *Hamlet* appeared gave no forecast of the play's future greatness. First staged in 1600, the play was one of a series that William Shakespeare (1564–1616) was turning out for the nearly insatiable demands of the commercial stage. He was fresh to London in 1590 from a middle-class youth in Stratford-upon-Avon. When Shakespeare retired to gentlemanly leisure in Stratford in 1610, he had written thirty-seven dramas—almost two plays a year.

The London audiences did not want masterpieces; instead, they craved violence, ghosts, and murders galore. They wanted revenge tragedies, the most popular dramatic form in the Age of Elizabeth (1558–1603), England's golden age. This taste for blood is not surprising, for Elizabethan England made national heroes of pirate patriots like Francis Drake and accepted as normal that Protestants and Catholics should burn heretics alive. It was for this violence-filled age that Shakespeare wrote *Hamlet*, based on a bloody revenge tale that had already inspired one play during the 1580s.

Reading the Selection

Shakespeare's *Hamlet* is set at the royal Danish court. Its revenge theme is activated by the murder of old King Hamlet. Prince Hamlet, depressed by his father's death, is plunged into a court seething with intrigue, carousing, ghosts, and spies. There are also wandering actors, an oath sworn on swords, a secret letter, a deadly duel, and a hasty funeral. Lest these devices be insufficiently entertaining, Hamlet himself veers from madman to scholar to prince to swordsman before he gets his revenge. At the end, the stage is littered with corpses and the major characters are all dead.

What rescues *Hamlet* from mere melodrama and pushes it into the stratosphere of great art are Shakespeare's majestic language and complete mastery of psychology. The theater, reborn in medieval productions like *Everyman*, with its simple morals and even simpler psychology, now came to maturity in Shakespeare's hands.

Dramatis Personae
CLAUDIUS *King of Denmark*
HAMLET *Son to the late, and nephew to the present king*
POLONIUS *Lord Chamberlain*
HORATIO *Friend to Hamlet*
LAERTES *Son to Polonius*
VOLTIMAND   *Courtiers*
CORNELIUS
ROSENCRANTZ
GUILDENSTERN
OSRIC
A GENTLEMAN
A PRIEST
MARCELLUS   *Officers*
BERNARDO
FRANCISCO *A soldier*
REYNALDO *Servant to Polonius*
PLAYERS
TWO CLOWNS *Grave-diggers*
FORTINBRAS *Prince of Norway*
A CAPTAIN
ENGLISH AMBASSADORS
GERTRUDE *Queen of Denmark, and mother to Hamlet*
OPHELIA *Daughter to Polonius*
LORDS, LADIES, OFFICERS, SOLDIERS, SAILORS, MESSENGERS, and OTHER ATTENDANTS
GHOST *of Hamlet's father*

SCENE—DENMARK

ACT IV
SCENE I. A room in the castle.
Enter KING CLAUDIUS, QUEEN GERTRUDE, ROSENCRANTZ, and GUILDENSTERN

KING CLAUDIUS
There's matter in these sighs, these profound heaves:
You must translate: 'tis fit we understand them.
Where is your son?

QUEEN GERTRUDE
Bestow this place on us a little while.
Exeunt ROSENCRANTZ and GUILDENSTERN
Ah, my good lord, what have I seen to-night!

KING CLAUDIUS
What, Gertrude? How does Hamlet?

QUEEN GERTRUDE
Mad as the sea and wind, when both contend
Which is the mightier: in his lawless fit,
Behind the arras hearing something stir,

Whips out his rapier, cries, 'A rat, a rat!'
And, in this brainish apprehension, kills
The unseen good old man.

KING CLAUDIUS
O heavy deed!
It had been so with us, had we been there:
His liberty is full of threats to all;
To you yourself, to us, to every one.
Alas, how shall this bloody deed be answer'd?
It will be laid to us, whose providence
Should have kept short, restrain'd and out of haunt,
This mad young man: but so much was our love,
We would not understand what was most fit;
But, like the owner of a foul disease,
To keep it from divulging, let it feed
Even on the pith of Life. Where is he gone?

QUEEN GERTRUDE
To draw apart the body he hath kill'd:
O'er whom his very madness, like some ore
Among a mineral of metals base,
Shows itself pure; he weeps for what is done.

KING CLAUDIUS
O Gertrude, come away!
The sun no sooner shall the mountains touch,
But we will ship him hence: and this vile deed
We must, with all our majesty and skill,
Both countenance and excuse. Ho, Guildenstern!
Re-enter ROSENCRANTZ and GUILDENSTERN
Friends both, go join you with some further aid:
Hamlet in madness hath Polonius slain,
And from his mother's closet hath he dragg'd him:
Go seek him out; speak fair, and bring the body
Into the chapel. I pray you, haste in this.
Exeunt ROSENCRANTZ and GUILDENSTERN
Come, Gertrude, we'll call up our wisest friends;
And let them know, both what we mean to do,
And what's untimely done. O, come away!
My soul is full of discord and dismay.
Exeunt

SCENE II. Another room in the castle.
Enter HAMLET

HAMLET
Safely stowed.

ROSENCRANTZ: GUILDENSTERN:
[Within] Hamlet! Lord Hamlet!

HAMLET
What noise? who calls on Hamlet?
O, here they come.

Enter ROSENCRANTZ and GUILDENSTERN

ROSENCRANTZ
What have you done, my lord, with the dead body?

HAMLET
Compounded it with dust, whereto 'tis kin.

ROSENCRANTZ
Tell us where 'tis, that we may take it thence
And bear it to the chapel.

HAMLET
Do not believe it.

ROSENCRANTZ
Believe what?

HAMLET
That I can keep your counsel and not mine own.
Besides, to be demanded of a sponge! what
replication should be made by the son of a king?

ROSENCRANTZ
Take you me for a sponge, my lord?

HAMLET
Ay, sir, that soaks up the king's countenance, his
rewards, his authorities. But such officers do the
king best service in the end: he keeps them, like
an ape, in the corner of his jaw; first mouthed, to
be last swallowed: when he needs what you have
gleaned, it is but squeezing you, and, sponge, you
shall be dry again.

ROSENCRANTZ
I understand you not, my lord.

HAMLET
I am glad of it: a knavish speech sleeps in a foolish ear.

ROSENCRANTZ
My lord, you must tell us where the body is, and go
with us to the king.

HAMLET
The body is with the king, but the king is not with
the body. The king is a thing--

GUILDENSTERN
A thing, my lord!

HAMLET
Of nothing: bring me to him. Hide fox, and all after.
Exeunt

SCENE III. Another room in the castle.
Enter KING CLAUDIUS, attended

KING CLAUDIUS
I have sent to seek him, and to find the body.
How dangerous is it that this man goes loose!
Yet must not we put the strong law on him:
He's loved of the distracted multitude,
Who like not in their judgment, but their eyes;
And where tis so, the offender's scourge is weigh'd,
But never the offence. To bear all smooth and even,
This sudden sending him away must seem
Deliberate pause: diseases desperate grown
By desperate appliance are relieved,
Or not at all.
Enter ROSENCRANTZ
How now! what hath befall'n?

ROSENCRANTZ
Where the dead body is bestow'd, my lord,
We cannot get from him.

KING CLAUDIUS
But where is he?

ROSENCRANTZ
Without, my lord; guarded, to know your pleasure.

KING CLAUDIUS
Bring him before us.

ROSENCRANTZ
Ho, Guildenstern! bring in my lord.
Enter HAMLET and GUILDENSTERN

KING CLAUDIUS
Now, Hamlet, where's Polonius?

HAMLET
At supper.

KING CLAUDIUS
At supper! where?

HAMLET
Not where he eats, but where he is eaten: a certain convocation of politic worms are e'en at him. Your worm is your only emperor for diet: we fat all creatures else to fat us, and we fat ourselves for maggots: your fat king and your lean beggar is but variable service, two dishes, but to one table: that's the end.

KING CLAUDIUS
Alas, alas!

HAMLET
A man may fish with the worm that hath eat of a king, and cat of the fish that hath fed of that worm.

KING CLAUDIUS
What dost you mean by this?

HAMLET
Nothing but to show you how a king may go a progress through the guts of a beggar.

KING CLAUDIUS
Where is Polonius?

HAMLET
In heaven; send hither to see: if your messenger find him not there, seek him i' the other place yourself. But indeed, if you find him not within this month, you shall nose him as you go up the stairs into the lobby.

KING CLAUDIUS
Go seek him there.
To some Attendants

HAMLET
He will stay till ye come.
Exeunt Attendants

KING CLAUDIUS
Hamlet, this deed, for thine especial safety,--
Which we do tender, as we dearly grieve
For that which thou hast done,--must send thee hence
With fiery quickness: therefore prepare thyself;
The bark is ready, and the wind at help,
The associates tend, and every thing is bent
For England.

HAMLET
For England!

KING CLAUDIUS
Ay, Hamlet.

HAMLET
Good.

KING CLAUDIUS
So is it, if thou knew'st our purposes.

HAMLET
I see a cherub that sees them. But, come; for
England! Farewell, dear mother.

KING CLAUDIUS
Thy loving father, Hamlet.

HAMLET
My mother: father and mother is man and wife; man
and wife is one flesh; and so, my mother. Come, for
England!
Exit

KING CLAUDIUS
Follow him at foot; tempt him with speed aboard;
Delay it not; I'll have him hence to-night:
Away! for every thing is seal'd and done
That else leans on the affair: pray you, make haste.
Exeunt ROSENCRANTZ and GUILDENSTERN
And, England, if my love thou hold'st at aught--
As my great power thereof may give thee sense,
Since yet thy cicatrice looks raw and red
After the Danish sword, and thy free awe
Pays homage to us--thou mayst not coldly set
Our sovereign process; which imports at full,
By letters congruing to that effect,
The present death of Hamlet. Do it, England;
For like the hectic in my blood he rages,
And thou must cure me: till I know 'tis done,
Howe'er my haps, my joys were ne'er begun.
Exit

SCENE IV. A plain in Denmark.
Enter FORTINBRAS, a Captain, and Soldiers, marching

PRINCE FORTINBRAS
Go, captain, from me greet the Danish king;
Tell him that, by his licence, Fortinbras
Craves the conveyance of a promised march
Over his kingdom. You know the rendezvous.
If that his majesty would aught with us,
We shall express our duty in his eye;
And let him know so.

Captain
I will do't, my lord.

PRINCE FORTINBRAS
Go softly on.
Exeunt FORTINBRAS and Soldiers
Enter HAMLET, ROSENCRANTZ, GUILDENSTERN, and others

HAMLET
Good sir, whose powers are these?

Captain
They are of Norway, sir.

HAMLET
How purposed, sir, I pray you?

Captain
Against some part of Poland.

HAMLET
Who commands them, sir?

Captain
The nephews to old Norway, Fortinbras.

HAMLET
Goes it against the main of Poland, sir,
Or for some frontier?

Captain
Truly to speak, and with no addition,
We go to gain a little patch of ground
That hath in it no profit but the name.
To pay five ducats, five, I would not farm it;
Nor will it yield to Norway or the Pole
A ranker rate, should it be sold in fee.

HAMLET
Why, then the Polack never will defend it.

Captain
Yes, it is already garrison'd.

HAMLET
Two thousand souls and twenty thousand ducats
Will not debate the question of this straw:
This is the imposthume of much wealth and peace,
That inward breaks, and shows no cause without
Why the man dies. I humbly thank you, sir.

Captain
God be wi' you, sir.
Exit

ROSENCRANTZ
Wilt please you go, my lord?

HAMLET
I'll be with you straight go a little before.
Exeunt all except HAMLET
How all occasions do inform against me,
And spur my dull revenge! What is a man,
If his chief good and market of his time
Be but to sleep and feed? a beast, no more.
Sure, he that made us with such large discourse,
Looking before and after, gave us not
That capability and god-like reason
To fust in us unused. Now, whether it be
Bestial oblivion, or some craven scruple
Of thinking too precisely on the event,
A thought which, quarter'd, hath but one part wisdom
And ever three parts coward, I do not know
Why yet I live to say 'This thing's to do;'
Sith I have cause and will and strength and means
To do't. Examples gross as earth exhort me:
Witness this army of such mass and charge
Led by a delicate and tender prince,
Whose spirit with divine ambition puff'd
Makes mouths at the invisible event,
Exposing what is mortal and unsure
To all that fortune, death and danger dare,
Even for an egg-shell. Rightly to be great
Is not to stir without great argument,
But greatly to find quarrel in a straw
When honour's at the stake. How stand I then,
That have a father kill'd, a mother stain'd,
Excitements of my reason and my blood,
And let all sleep? while, to my shame, I see
The imminent death of twenty thousand men,
That, for a fantasy and trick of fame,
Go to their graves like beds, fight for a plot
Whereon the numbers cannot try the cause,
Which is not tomb enough and continent
To hide the slain? O, from this time forth,
My thoughts be bloody, or be nothing worth!
Exit

SCENE V. Elsinore. A room in the castle.
Enter QUEEN GERTRUDE, HORATIO, and a Gentleman

QUEEN GERTRUDE
I will not speak with her.

Gentleman
She is importunate, indeed distract:
Her mood will needs be pitied.

QUEEN GERTRUDE
What would she have?

Gentleman
She speaks much of her father; says she hears
There's tricks i' the world; and hems, and beats her heart;
Spurns enviously at straws; speaks things in doubt,
That carry but half sense: her speech is nothing,
Yet the unshaped use of it doth move
The hearers to collection; they aim at it,
And botch the words up fit to their own thoughts;
Which, as her winks, and nods, and gestures yield them,
Indeed would make one think there might be thought,
Though nothing sure, yet much unhappily.

HORATIO
'Twere good she were spoken with; for she may strew
Dangerous conjectures in ill-breeding minds.

QUEEN GERTRUDE
Let her come in.
Exit HORATIO
To my sick soul, as sin's true nature is,
Each toy seems prologue to some great amiss:
So full of artless jealousy is guilt,
It spills itself in fearing to be spilt.
Re-enter HORATIO, with OPHELIA

OPHELIA
Where is the beauteous majesty of Denmark?

QUEEN GERTRUDE
How now, Ophelia!

OPHELIA
[Sings]
How should I your true love know
From another one?
By his cockle hat and staff,
And his sandal shoon.

QUEEN GERTRUDE
Alas, sweet lady, what imports this song?

OPHELIA
Say you? nay, pray you, mark.

Sings
He is dead and gone, lady,
He is dead and gone;
At his head a grass-green turf,
At his heels a stone.

QUEEN GERTRUDE
Nay, but, Ophelia,--

OPHELIA
Pray you, mark.
Sings
White his shroud as the mountain snow,--
Enter KING CLAUDIUS

QUEEN GERTRUDE
Alas, look here, my lord.

OPHELIA
[Sings]
Larded with sweet flowers
Which bewept to the grave did go
With true-love showers.

KING CLAUDIUS
How do you, pretty lady?

OPHELIA
Well, God 'ild you! They say the owl was a baker's daughter. Lord, we know what we are, but know not what we may be. God be at your table!

KING CLAUDIUS
Conceit upon her father.

OPHELIA
Pray you, let's have no words of this; but when they ask you what it means, say you this:
Sings
To-morrow is Saint Valentine's day,
All in the morning betime,
And I a maid at your window,
To be your Valentine.
Then up he rose, and donn'd his clothes,
And dupp'd the chamber-door;
Let in the maid, that out a maid
Never departed more.

KING CLAUDIUS
Pretty Ophelia!

OPHELIA
Indeed, la, without an oath, I'll make an end on't:
Sings
By Gis and by Saint Charity,
Alack, and fie for shame!
Young men will do't, if they come to't;
By cock, they are to blame.
Quoth she, before you tumbled me,
You promised me to wed.
So would I ha' done, by yonder sun,
An thou hadst not come to my bed.

KING CLAUDIUS
How long hath she been thus?

OPHELIA
I hope all will be well. We must be patient: but I cannot choose but weep, to think they should lay him i' the cold ground. My brother shall know of it: and so I thank you for your good counsel. Come, my coach! Good night, ladies; good night, sweet ladies; good night, good night.
Exit

KING CLAUDIUS
Follow her close; give her good watch,
I pray you.
Exit HORATIO
O, this is the poison of deep grief; it springs
All from her father's death. O Gertrude, Gertrude,
When sorrows come, they come not single spies
But in battalions. First, her father slain:
Next, your son gone; and he most violent author
Of his own just remove: the people muddied,
Thick and unwholesome in their thoughts and whispers,
For good Polonius' death; and we have done but greenly,
In hugger-mugger to inter him: poor Ophelia
Divided from herself and her fair judgment,
Without the which we are pictures, or mere beasts:
Last, and as much containing as all these,
Her brother is in secret come from France;
Feeds on his wonder, keeps himself in clouds,
And wants not buzzers to infect his ear
With pestilent speeches of his father's death;
Wherein necessity, of matter beggar'd,
Will nothing stick our person to arraign
In ear and ear. O my dear Gertrude, this,
Like to a murdering-piece, in many places
Gives me superfluous death.
A noise within

QUEEN GERTRUDE
Alack, what noise is this?

KING CLAUDIUS
Where are my Switzers? Let them guard the door.
Enter another Gentleman
What is the matter?

Gentleman
Save yourself, my lord:
The ocean, overpeering of his list,
Eats not the flats with more impetuous haste
Than young Laertes, in a riotous head,
O'erbears your officers. The rabble call him lord;
And, as the world were now but to begin,
Antiquity forgot, custom not known,
The ratifiers and props of every word,
They cry 'Choose we: Laertes shall be king:'
Caps, hands, and tongues, applaud it to the clouds:
'Laertes shall be king, Laertes king!'

QUEEN GERTRUDE
How cheerfully on the false trail they cry!
O, this is counter, you false Danish dogs!

KING CLAUDIUS
The doors are broke.
Noise within
Enter LAERTES, armed; Danes following

LAERTES
Where is this king? Sirs, stand you all without.

Danes
No, let's come in.

LAERTES
I pray you, give me leave.

Danes
We will, we will.
They retire without the door

LAERTES
I thank you: keep the door. O thou vile king,
Give me my father!

QUEEN GERTRUDE
Calmly, good Laertes.

LAERTES
That drop of blood that's calm proclaims me bastard,
Cries cuckold to my father, brands the harlot
Even here, between the chaste unsmirched brow
Of my true mother.

KING CLAUDIUS
What is the cause, Laertes,
That thy rebellion looks so giant-like?
Let him go, Gertrude; do not fear our person:
There's such divinity doth hedge a king,
That treason can but peep to what it would,
Acts little of his will. Tell me, Laertes,
Why thou art thus incensed. Let him go, Gertrude.
Speak, man.

LAERTES
Where is my father?

KING CLAUDIUS
Dead.

QUEEN GERTRUDE
But not by him.

KING CLAUDIUS
Let him demand his fill.

LAERTES
How came he dead? I'll not be juggled with:
To hell, allegiance! vows, to the blackest devil!
Conscience and grace, to the profoundest pit!
I dare damnation. To this point I stand,
That both the worlds I give to negligence,
Let come what comes; only I'll be revenged
Most thoroughly for my father.

KING CLAUDIUS
Who shall stay you?

LAERTES
My will, not all the world:
And for my means, I'll husband them so well,
They shall go far with little.

KING CLAUDIUS
Good Laertes,
If you desire to know the certainty
Of your dear father's death, is't writ in your revenge,
That, swoopstake, you will draw both friend and foe,
Winner and loser?

LAERTES
None but his enemies.

KING CLAUDIUS
Will you know them then?

LAERTES
To his good friends thus wide I'll ope my arms;
And like the kind life-rendering pelican,
Repast them with my blood.

KING CLAUDIUS
Why, now you speak
Like a good child and a true gentleman.
That I am guiltless of your father's death,
And am most sensible in grief for it,
It shall as level to your judgment pierce
As day does to your eye.

Danes
[Within] Let her come in.

LAERTES
How now! what noise is that?
Re-enter OPHELIA
O heat, dry up my brains! tears seven times salt,
Burn out the sense and virtue of mine eye!
By heaven, thy madness shall be paid by weight,
Till our scale turn the beam. O rose of May!
Dear maid, kind sister, sweet Ophelia!
O heavens! is't possible, a young maid's wits
Should be as moral as an old man's life?
Nature is fine in love, and where 'tis fine,
It sends some precious instance of itself
After the thing it loves.

OPHELIA
[Sings]
They bore him barefaced on the bier;
Hey non nonny, nonny, hey nonny;
And in his grave rain'd many a tear:--
Fare you well, my dove!

LAERTES
Hadst thou thy wits, and didst persuade revenge,
It could not move thus.

OPHELIA
[Sings]
You must sing a-down a-down,
An you call him a-down-a.
O, how the wheel becomes it! It is the false
steward, that stole his master's daughter.

LAERTES
This nothing's more than matter.

OPHELIA
There's rosemary, that's for remembrance; pray,
love, remember: and there is pansies. that's for
thoughts.

LAERTES
A document in madness, thoughts and remembrance
fitted.

OPHELIA
There's fennel for you, and columbines: there's rue
for you; and here's some for me: we may call it
herb-grace o' Sundays: O you must wear your rue with
a difference. There's a daisy: I would give you
some violets, but they withered all when my father
died: they say he made a good end,--
[Sings]
For bonny sweet Robin is all my joy.

LAERTES
Thought and affliction, passion, hell itself,
She turns to favour and to prettiness.

OPHELIA
[Sings]
And will he not come again?
And will he not come again?
No, no, he is dead:
Go to thy death-bed:
He never will come again.
His beard was as white as snow,
All flaxen was his poll:
He is gone, he is gone,
And we cast away moan:
God ha' mercy on his soul!
And of all Christian souls, I pray God. God be wi' ye.
Exit

LAERTES
Do you see this, O God?

KING CLAUDIUS
Laertes, I must commune with your grief,
Or you deny me right. Go but apart,
Make choice of whom your wisest friends you will.
And they shall hear and judge 'twixt you and me:
If by direct or by collateral hand
They find us touch'd, we will our kingdom give,
Our crown, our life, and all that we can ours,

To you in satisfaction; but if not,
Be you content to lend your patience to us,
And we shall jointly labour with your soul
To give it due content.

LAERTES
Let this be so;
His means of death, his obscure funeral--
No trophy, sword, nor hatchment o'er his bones,
No noble rite nor formal ostentation--
Cry to be heard, as 'twere from heaven to earth,
That I must call't in question.

KING CLAUDIUS
So you shall;
And where the offence is let the great axe fall.
I pray you, go with me.
Exeunt

SCENE VI. Another room in the castle.
Enter HORATIO and a Servant

HORATIO
What are they that would speak with me?

Servant
Sailors, sir: they say they have letters for you.

HORATIO
Let them come in.
Exit Servant
I do not know from what part of the world
I should be greeted, if not from Lord Hamlet.
Enter Sailors

First Sailor
God bless you, sir.

HORATIO
Let him bless thee too.

First Sailor
He shall, sir, an't please him. There's a letter for
you, sir; it comes from the ambassador that was
bound for England; if your name be Horatio, as I am
let to know it is.

HORATIO
[Reads] 'Horatio, when thou shalt have overlooked
this, give these fellows some means to the king:
they have letters for him. Ere we were two days old
at sea, a pirate of very warlike appointment gave us
chase. Finding ourselves too slow of sail, we put on
a compelled valour, and in the grapple I boarded
them: on the instant they got clear of our ship; so
I alone became their prisoner. They have dealt with
me like thieves of mercy: but they knew what they
did; I am to do a good turn for them. Let the king
have the letters I have sent; and repair thou to me
with as much speed as thou wouldst fly death. I
have words to speak in thine ear will make thee
dumb; yet are they much too light for the bore of
the matter. These good fellows will bring thee
where I am. Rosencrantz and Guildenstern hold their
course for England: of them I have much to tell
thee. Farewell.
'He that thou knowest thine, HAMLET.'
Come, I will make you way for these your letters;
And do't the speedier, that you may direct me
To him from whom you brought them.
Exeunt

SCENE VII. Another room in the castle.
Enter KING CLAUDIUS and LAERTES

KING CLAUDIUS
Now must your conscience my acquaintance seal,
And you must put me in your heart for friend,
Sith you have heard, and with a knowing ear,
That he which hath your noble father slain
Pursued my life.

LAERTES
It well appears: but tell me
Why you proceeded not against these feats,
So crimeful and so capital in nature,
As by your safety, wisdom, all things else,
You mainly were stirr'd up.

KING CLAUDIUS
O, for two special reasons;
Which may to you, perhaps, seem much unsinew'd,
But yet to me they are strong. The queen his mother
Lives almost by his looks; and for myself--
My virtue or my plague, be it either which--
She's so conjunctive to my life and soul,
That, as the star moves not but in his sphere,
I could not but by her. The other motive,
Why to a public count I might not go,
Is the great love the general gender bear him;
Who, dipping all his faults in their affection,
Would, like the spring that turneth wood to stone,
Convert his gyves to graces; so that my arrows,
Too slightly timber'd for so loud a wind,

Would have reverted to my bow again,
And not where I had aim'd them.

LAERTES
And so have I a noble father lost;
A sister driven into desperate terms,
Whose worth, if praises may go back again,
Stood challenger on mount of all the age
For her perfections: but my revenge will come.

KING CLAUDIUS
Break not your sleeps for that: you must not think
That we are made of stuff so flat and dull
That we can let our beard be shook with danger
And think it pastime. You shortly shall hear more:
I loved your father, and we love ourself;
And that, I hope, will teach you to imagine--
Enter a Messenger
How now! what news?

Messenger
Letters, my lord, from Hamlet:
This to your majesty; this to the queen.

KING CLAUDIUS
From Hamlet! who brought them?

Messenger
Sailors, my lord, they say; I saw them not:
They were given me by Claudio; he received them
Of him that brought them.

KING CLAUDIUS
Laertes, you shall hear them. Leave us.
Exit Messenger
[Reads]
'High and mighty, You shall know I am set naked on
your kingdom. To-morrow shall I beg leave to see
your kingly eyes: when I shall, first asking your
pardon thereunto, recount the occasion of my sudden
and more strange return. 'HAMLET.'
What should this mean? Are all the rest come back?
Or is it some abuse, and no such thing?

LAERTES
Know you the hand?

KING CLAUDIUS
'Tis Hamlets character. 'Naked!
And in a postscript here, he says 'alone.'
Can you advise me?

LAERTES
I'm lost in it, my lord. But let him come;
It warms the very sickness in my heart,
That I shall live and tell him to his teeth,
'Thus didest thou.'

KING CLAUDIUS
If it be so, Laertes--
As how should it be so? how otherwise?--
Will you be ruled by me?

LAERTES
Ay, my lord;
So you will not o'errule me to a peace.

KING CLAUDIUS
To thine own peace. If he be now return'd,
As checking at his voyage, and that he means
No more to undertake it, I will work him
To an exploit, now ripe in my device,
Under the which he shall not choose but fall:
And for his death no wind of blame shall breathe,
But even his mother shall uncharge the practise
And call it accident.

LAERTES
My lord, I will be ruled;
The rather, if you could devise it so
That I might be the organ.

KING CLAUDIUS
It falls right.
You have been talk'd of since your travel much,
And that in Hamlet's hearing, for a quality
Wherein, they say, you shine: your sum of parts
Did not together pluck such envy from him
As did that one, and that, in my regard,
Of the unworthiest siege.

LAERTES
What part is that, my lord?

KING CLAUDIUS
A very riband in the cap of youth,
Yet needful too; for youth no less becomes
The light and careless livery that it wears
Than settled age his sables and his weeds,
Importing health and graveness. Two months since,
Here was a gentleman of Normandy:--
I've seen myself, and served against, the French,
And they can well on horseback: but this gallant
Had witchcraft in't; he grew unto his seat;

And to such wondrous doing brought his horse,
As he had been incorpsed and demi-natured
With the brave beast: so far he topp'd my thought,
That I, in forgery of shapes and tricks,
Come short of what he did.

LAERTES
A Norman was't?

KING CLAUDIUS
A Norman.

LAERTES
Upon my life, Lamond.

KING CLAUDIUS
The very same.

LAERTES
I know him well: he is the brooch indeed
And gem of all the nation.

KING CLAUDIUS
He made confession of you,
And gave you such a masterly report
For art and exercise in your defence
And for your rapier most especially,
That he cried out, 'twould be a sight indeed,
If one could match you: the scrimers of their nation,
He swore, had had neither motion, guard, nor eye,
If you opposed them. Sir, this report of his
Did Hamlet so envenom with his envy
That he could nothing do but wish and beg
Your sudden coming o'er, to play with him.
Now, out of this,--

LAERTES
What out of this, my lord?

KING CLAUDIUS
Laertes, was your father dear to you?
Or are you like the painting of a sorrow,
A face without a heart?

LAERTES
Why ask you this?

KING CLAUDIUS
Not that I think you did not love your father;
But that I know love is begun by time;
And that I see, in passages of proof,
Time qualifies the spark and fire of it.
There lives within the very flame of love
A kind of wick or snuff that will abate it;
And nothing is at a like goodness still;
For goodness, growing to a plurisy,
Dies in his own too much: that we would do
We should do when we would; for this 'would' changes
And hath abatements and delays as many
As there are tongues, are hands, are accidents;
And then this 'should' is like a spendthrift sigh,
That hurts by easing. But, to the quick o' the ulcer:--
Hamlet comes back: what would you undertake,
To show yourself your father's son in deed
More than in words?

LAERTES
To cut his throat i' the church.

KING CLAUDIUS
No place, indeed, should murder sanctuarize;
Revenge should have no bounds. But, good Laertes,
Will you do this, keep close within your chamber.
Hamlet return'd shall know you are come home:
We'll put on those shall praise your excellence
And set a double varnish on the fame
The Frenchman gave you, bring you in fine together
And wager on your heads: he, being remiss,
Most generous and free from all contriving,
Will not peruse the foils; so that, with ease,
Or with a little shuffling, you may choose
A sword unbated, and in a pass of practise
Requite him for your father.

LAERTES
I will do't:
And, for that purpose, I'll anoint my sword.
I bought an unction of a mountebank,
So mortal that, but dip a knife in it,
Where it draws blood no cataplasm so rare,
Collected from all simples that have virtue
Under the moon, can save the thing from death
That is but scratch'd withal: I'll touch my point
With this contagion, that, if I gall him slightly,
It may be death.

KING CLAUDIUS
Let's further think of this;
Weigh what convenience both of time and means
May fit us to our shape: if this should fail,
And that our drift look through our bad performance,
'Twere better not assay'd: therefore this project
Should have a back or second, that might hold,
If this should blast in proof. Soft! let me see:

We'll make a solemn wager on your cunnings: I ha't.
When in your motion you are hot and dry--
As make your bouts more violent to that end--
And that he calls for drink, I'll have prepared him
A chalice for the nonce, whereon but sipping,
If he by chance escape your venom'd stuck,
Our purpose may hold there.
Enter QUEEN GERTRUDE
How now, sweet queen!

QUEEN GERTRUDE
One woe doth tread upon another's heel,
So fast they follow; your sister's drown'd, Laertes.

LAERTES
Drown'd! O, where?

QUEEN GERTRUDE
There is a willow grows aslant a brook,
That shows his hoar leaves in the glassy stream;
There with fantastic garlands did she come
Of crow-flowers, nettles, daisies, and long purples
That liberal shepherds give a grosser name,
But our cold maids do dead men's fingers call them:
There, on the pendent boughs her coronet weeds
Clambering to hang, an envious sliver broke;
When down her weedy trophies and herself
Fell in the weeping brook. Her clothes spread wide;
And, mermaid-like, awhile they bore her up:
Which time she chanted snatches of old tunes;
As one incapable of her own distress,
Or like a creature native and indued
Unto that element: but long it could not be
Till that her garments, heavy with their drink,
Pull'd the poor wretch from her melodious lay
To muddy death.

LAERTES
Alas, then, she is drown'd?

QUEEN GERTRUDE
Drown'd, drown'd.

LAERTES
Too much of water hast thou, poor Ophelia,
And therefore I forbid my tears: but yet
It is our trick; nature her custom holds,
Let shame say what it will: when these are gone,
The woman will be out. Adieu, my lord:
I have a speech of fire, that fain would blaze,
But that this folly douts it.
Exit

KING CLAUDIUS
Let's follow, Gertrude:
How much I had to do to calm his rage!
Now fear I this will give it start again;
Therefore let's follow.
Exeunt

ACT V
SCENE I. A churchyard.
Enter two Clowns, with spades, &c

First Clown
Is she to be buried in Christian burial that
wilfully seeks her own salvation?

Second Clown
I tell thee she is: and therefore make her grave
straight: the crowner hath sat on her, and finds it
Christian burial.

First Clown
How can that be, unless she drowned herself in her
own defence?

Second Clown
Why, 'tis found so.

First Clown
It must be 'se offendendo;' it cannot be else. For
here lies the point: if I drown myself wittingly,
it argues an act: and an act hath three branches: it
is, to act, to do, to perform: argal, she drowned
herself wittingly.

Second Clown
Nay, but hear you, goodman delver,--

First Clown
Give me leave. Here lies the water; good: here
stands the man; good; if the man go to this water,
and drown himself, it is, will he, nill he, he
goes,--mark you that; but if the water come to him
and drown him, he drowns not himself: argal, he
that is not guilty of his own death shortens not his own
life.

Second Clown
But is this law?

First Clown
Ay, marry, is't; crowner's quest law.

Second Clown
Will you ha' the truth on't? If this had not been a gentlewoman, she should have been buried out o' Christian burial.

First Clown
Why, there thou say'st: and the more pity that great folk should have countenance in this world to drown or hang themselves, more than their even Christian. Come, my spade. There is no ancient gentleman but gardeners, ditchers, and grave-makers: they hold up Adam's profession.

Second Clown
Was he a gentleman?

First Clown
He was the first that ever bore arms.

Second Clown
Why, he had none.

First Clown
What, art a heathen? How dost thou understand the Scripture? The Scripture says 'Adam digged:' could he dig without arms? I'll put another question to thee: if thou answerest me not to the purpose, confess thyself--

Second Clown
Go to.

First Clown
What is he that builds stronger than either the mason, the shipwright, or the carpenter?

Second Clown
The gallows-maker; for that frame outlives a thousand tenants.

First Clown
I like thy wit well, in good faith: the gallows does well; but how does it well? it does well to those that do in: now thou dost ill to say the gallows is built stronger than the church: argal, the gallows may do well to thee. To't again, come.

Second Clown
'Who builds stronger than a mason, a shipwright, or a carpenter?'

First Clown
Ay, tell me that, and unyoke.

Second Clown
Marry, now I can tell.

First Clown
To't.

Second Clown
Mass, I cannot tell.
Enter HAMLET and HORATIO, at a distance

First Clown
Cudgel thy brains no more about it, for your dull ass will not mend his pace with beating; and, when you are asked this question next, say 'a grave-maker: 'the houses that he makes last till doomsday. Go, get thee to Yaughan: fetch me a stoup of liquor.
Exit Second Clown
He digs and sings
In youth, when I did love, did love,
Methought it was very sweet,
To contract, O, the time, for, ah, my behove,
O, methought, there was nothing meet.

HAMLET
Has this fellow no feeling of his business, that he sings at grave-making?

HORATIO
Custom hath made it in him a property of easiness.

HAMLET
'Tis e'en so: the hand of little employment hath the daintier sense.

First Clown
[Sings]
But age, with his stealing steps,
Hath claw'd me in his clutch,
And hath shipped me intil the land,
As if I had never been such.
Throws up a skull

HAMLET
That skull had a tongue in it, and could sing once: how the knave jowls it to the ground, as if it were Cain's jaw-bone, that did the first murder! It might be the pate of a politician, which this ass now o'er-reaches; one that would circumvent God, might it not?

HORATIO
It might, my lord.

HAMLET
Or of a courtier; which could say 'Good morrow, sweet lord! How dost thou, good lord?' This might be my lord such-a-one, that praised my lord such-a-one's horse, when he meant to beg it; might it not?

HORATIO
Ay, my lord.

HAMLET
Why, e'en so: and now my Lady Worm's; chapless, and knocked about the mazzard with a sexton's spade: here's fine revolution, an we had the trick to see't. Did these bones cost no more the breeding, but to play at loggats with 'em? mine ache to think on't.

First Clown
[Sings]
A pick-axe, and a spade, a spade,
For and a shrouding sheet:
O, a pit of clay for to be made
For such a guest is meet.
Throws up another skull

HAMLET
There's another: why may not that be the skull of a lawyer? Where be his quiddities now, his quillets, his cases, his tenures, and his tricks? why does he suffer this rude knave now to knock him about the sconce with a dirty shovel, and will not tell him of his action of battery? Hum! This fellow might be in's time a great buyer of land, with his statutes, his recognizances, his fines, his double vouchers, his recoveries: is this the fine of his fines, and the recovery of his recoveries, to have his fine pate full of fine dirt? will his vouchers vouch him no more of his purchases, and double ones too, than the length and breadth of a pair of indentures? The very conveyances of his lands will hardly lie in this box; and must the inheritor himself have no more, ha?

HORATIO
Not a jot more, my lord.

HAMLET
Is not parchment made of sheepskins?

HORATIO
Ay, my lord, and of calf-skins too.

HAMLET
They are sheep and calves which seek out assurance in that. I will speak to this fellow. Whose grave's this, sirrah?

First Clown
Mine, sir.
[Sings]
O, a pit of clay for to be made
For such a guest is meet.

HAMLET
I think it be thine, indeed; for thou liest in't.

First Clown
You lie out on't, sir, and therefore it is not yours: for my part, I do not lie in't, and yet it is mine.

HAMLET
'Thou dost lie in't, to be in't and say it is thine: 'tis for the dead, not for the quick; therefore thou liest.

First Clown
'Tis a quick lie, sir; 'twill away gain, from me to you.

HAMLET
What man dost thou dig it for?

First Clown
For no man, sir.

HAMLET
What woman, then?

First Clown
For none, neither.

HAMLET
Who is to be buried in't?

First Clown
One that was a woman, sir; but, rest her soul, she's dead.

HAMLET
How absolute the knave is! we must speak by the card, or equivocation will undo us. By the Lord, Horatio, these three years I have taken a note of

it; the age is grown so picked that the toe of the peasant comes so near the heel of the courtier, he gaffs his kibe. How long hast thou been a grave-maker?

First Clown
Of all the days i' the year, I came to't that day that our last king Hamlet overcame Fortinbras.

HAMLET
How long is that since?

First Clown
Cannot you tell that? every fool can tell that: it was the very day that young Hamlet was born; he that is mad, and sent into England.

HAMLET
Ay, marry, why was he sent into England?

First Clown
Why, because he was mad: he shall recover his wits there; or, if he do not, it's no great matter there.

HAMLET
Why?

First Clown
'Twill, a not be seen in him there; there the men are as mad as he.

HAMLET
How came he mad?

First Clown
Very strangely, they say.

HAMLET
How strangely?

First Clown
Faith, e'en with losing his wits.

HAMLET
Upon what ground?

First Clown
Why, here in Denmark: I have been sexton here, man and boy, thirty years.

HAMLET
How long will a man lie i' the earth ere he rot?

First Clown
I' faith, if he be not rotten before he die--as we have many pocky corses now-a-days, that will scarce hold the laying in--he will last you some eight year or nine year: a tanner will last you nine year.

HAMLET
Why he more than another?

First Clown
Why, sir, his hide is so tanned with his trade, that he will keep out water a great while; and your water is a sore decayer of your whoreson dead body. Here's a skull now; this skull has lain in the earth three and twenty years.

HAMLET
Whose was it?

First Clown
A whoreson mad fellow's it was: whose do you think it was?

HAMLET
Nay, I know not.

First Clown
A pestilence on him for a mad rogue! a' poured a flagon of Rhenish on my head once. This same skull, sir, was Yorick's skull, the king's jester.

HAMLET
This?

First Clown
E'en that.

HAMLET
Let me see.
Takes the skull
Alas, poor Yorick! I knew him, Horatio: a fellow of infinite jest, of most excellent fancy: he hath borne me on his back a thousand times; and now, how abhorred in my imagination it is! my gorge rims at it. Here hung those lips that I have kissed I know not how oft. Where be your gibes now? your gambols? your songs? your flashes of merriment, that were wont to set the table on a roar? Not one now, to mock your own grinning? quite chap-fallen? Now get you to my lady's chamber, and tell her, let her paint an inch thick, to this favour she must come; make her laugh at that. Prithee, Horatio, tell me one thing.

HORATIO
What's that, my lord?

HAMLET
Dost thou think Alexander looked o' this fashion i' the earth?

HORATIO
E'en so.

HAMLET
And smelt so? pah!
Puts down the skull

HORATIO
E'en so, my lord.

HAMLET
To what base uses we may return, Horatio! Why may not imagination trace the noble dust of Alexander, till he find it stopping a bung-hole?

HORATIO
'Twere to consider too curiously, to consider so.

HAMLET
No, faith, not a jot; but to follow him thither with modesty enough, and likelihood to lead it: as thus: Alexander died, Alexander was buried, Alexander returneth into dust; the dust is earth; of earth we make loam; and why of that loam, whereto he was converted, might they not stop a beer-barrel? Imperious Caesar, dead and turn'd to clay, Might stop a hole to keep the wind away: O, that that earth, which kept the world in awe, Should patch a wall to expel the winter flaw! But soft! but soft! aside: here comes the king.
Enter Priest, &c. in procession; the Corpse of OPHELIA, LAERTES and Mourners following; KING CLAUDIUS, QUEEN GERTRUDE, their trains, & The queen, the courtiers: Who is this they follow?
And with such maimed rites? This doth betoken
The corse they follow did with desperate hand
Fordo its own life: 'twas of some estate.
Couch we awhile, and mark. *Retiring with HORATIO*

LAERTES
What ceremony else?

HAMLET
That is Laertes,
A very noble youth: mark.

LAERTES
What ceremony else?

First Priest
Her obsequies have been as far enlarged
As we have warrantise: her death was doubtful;
And, but that great command o'ersways the order,
She should in ground unsanctified have lodged
Till the last trumpet: for charitable prayers,
Shards, flints and pebbles should be thrown on her;
Yet here she is allow'd her virgin crants,
Her maiden strewments and the bringing home
Of bell and burial.

LAERTES
Must there no more be done?

First Priest
No more be done:
We should profane the service of the dead
To sing a requiem and such rest to her
As to peace-parted souls.

LAERTES
Lay her i' the earth:
And from her fair and unpolluted flesh
May violets spring! I tell thee, churlish priest,
A ministering angel shall my sister be,
When thou liest howling.

HAMLET
What, the fair Ophelia!

QUEEN GERTRUDE
Sweets to the sweet: farewell!
Scattering flowers
I hoped thou shouldst have been my Hamlet's wife;
I thought thy bride-bed to have deck'd, sweet maid,
And not have strew'd thy grave.

LAERTES
O, treble woe
Fall ten times treble on that cursed head,
Whose wicked deed thy most ingenious sense
Deprived thee of! Hold off the earth awhile,
Till I have caught her once more in mine arms:
Leaps into the grave
Now pile your dust upon the quick and dead,
Till of this flat a mountain you have made,
To o'ertop old Pelion, or the skyish head
Of blue Olympus.

HAMLET
[Advancing] What is he whose grief
Bears such an emphasis? whose phrase of sorrow
Conjures the wandering stars, and makes them stand
Like wonder-wounded hearers? This is I,
Hamlet the Dane.
Leaps into the grave

LAERTES
The devil take thy soul!
Grappling with him

HAMLET
Thou pray'st not well.
I prithee, take thy fingers from my throat;
For, though I am not splenitive and rash,
Yet have I something in me dangerous,
Which let thy wiseness fear: hold off thy hand.

KING CLAUDIUS
Pluck them asunder.

QUEEN GERTRUDE
Hamlet, Hamlet!

All
Gentlemen,--

HORATIO
Good my lord, be quiet.
The Attendants part them, and they come out of the grave

HAMLET
Why I will fight with him upon this theme
Until my eyelids will no longer wag.

QUEEN GERTRUDE
O my son, what theme?

HAMLET
I loved Ophelia: forty thousand brothers
Could not, with all their quantity of love,
Make up my sum. What wilt thou do for her?

KING CLAUDIUS
O, he is mad, Laertes.

QUEEN GERTRUDE
For love of God, forbear him.

HAMLET
'Swounds, show me what thou'lt do:
Woo't weep? woo't fight? woo't fast? woo't tear thyself?
Woo't drink up eisel? eat a crocodile?
I'll do't. Dost thou come here to whine?
To outface me with leaping in her grave?
Be buried quick with her, and so will I:
And, if thou prate of mountains, let them throw
Millions of acres on us, till our ground,
Singeing his pate against the burning zone,
Make Ossa like a wart! Nay, an thou'lt mouth,
I'll rant as well as thou.

QUEEN GERTRUDE
This is mere madness:
And thus awhile the fit will work on him;
Anon, as patient as the female dove,
When that her golden couplets are disclosed,
His silence will sit drooping.

HAMLET
Hear you, sir;
What is the reason that you use me thus?
I loved you ever: but it is no matter;
Let Hercules himself do what he may,
The cat will mew and dog will have his day.
Exit

KING CLAUDIUS
I pray you, good Horatio, wait upon him.
Exit HORATIO
To LAERTES
Strengthen your patience in our last night's speech;
We'll put the matter to the present push.
Good Gertrude, set some watch over your son.
This grave shall have a living monument:
An hour of quiet shortly shall we see;
Till then, in patience our proceeding be.
Exeunt

SCENE II. A hall in the castle.
Enter HAMLET and HORATIO

HAMLET
So much for this, sir: now shall you see the other;
You do remember all the circumstance?

HORATIO
Remember it, my lord?

HAMLET
Sir, in my heart there was a kind of fighting,

That would not let me sleep: methought I lay
Worse than the mutines in the bilboes. Rashly,
And praised be rashness for it, let us know,
Our indiscretion sometimes serves us well,
When our deep plots do pall: and that should teach us
There's a divinity that shapes our ends,
Rough-hew them how we will,--

HORATIO
That is most certain.

HAMLET
Up from my cabin,
My sea-gown scarf'd about me, in the dark
Groped I to find out them; had my desire.
Finger'd their packet, and in fine withdrew
To mine own room again; making so bold,
My fears forgetting manners, to unseal
Their grand commission; where I found, Horatio,--
O royal knavery!--an exact command,
Larded with many several sorts of reasons
Importing Denmark's health and England's too,
With, ho! such bugs and goblins in my life,
That, on the supervise, no leisure bated,
No, not to stay the grinding of the axe,
My head should be struck off.

HORATIO
Is't possible?

HAMLET
Here's the commission: read it at more leisure.
But wilt thou hear me how I did proceed?

HORATIO
I beseech you.

HAMLET
Being thus be-netted round with villanies,--
Ere I could make a prologue to my brains,
They had begun the play--I sat me down,
Devised a new commission, wrote it fair:
I once did hold it, as our statists do,
A baseness to write fair and labour'd much
How to forget that learning, but, sir, now
It did me yeoman's service: wilt thou know
The effect of what I wrote?

HORATIO
Ay, good my lord.

HAMLET
An earnest conjuration from the king,
As England was his faithful tributary,
As love between them like the palm might flourish,
As peace should stiff her wheaten garland wear
And stand a comma 'tween their amities,
And many such-like 'As'es of great charge,
That, on the view and knowing of these contents,
Without debatement further, more or less,
He should the bearers put to sudden death,
Not shriving-time allow'd.

HORATIO
How was this seal'd?

HAMLET
Why, even in that was heaven ordinant.
I had my father's signet in my purse,
Which was the model of that Danish seal;
Folded the writ up in form of the other,
Subscribed it, gave't the impression, placed it safely,
The changeling never known. Now, the next day
Was our sea-fight; and what to this was sequent
Thou know'st already.

HORATIO
So Guildenstern and Rosencrantz go to't.

HAMLET
Why, man, they did make love to this employment;
They are not near my conscience; their defeat
Does by their own insinuation grow:
'Tis dangerous when the baser nature comes
Between the pass and fell incensed points
Of mighty opposites.

HORATIO
Why, what a king is this!

HAMLET
Does it not, think'st thee, stand me now upon--
He that hath kill'd my king and whored my mother,
Popp'd in between the election and my hopes,
Thrown out his angle for my proper life,
And with such cozenage--is't not perfect conscience,
To quit him with this arm? and is't not to be damn'd,
To let this canker of our nature come
In further evil?

HORATIO
It must be shortly known to him from England
What is the issue of the business there.

HAMLET
It will be short: the interim is mine;
And a man's life's no more than to say 'One.'
But I am very sorry, good Horatio,
That to Laertes I forgot myself;
For, by the image of my cause, I see
The portraiture of his: I'll court his favours.
But, sure, the bravery of his grief did put me
Into a towering passion.

HORATIO
Peace! who comes here?
Enter OSRIC

OSRIC
Your lordship is right welcome back to Denmark.

HAMLET
I humbly thank you, sir. Dost know this water-fly?

HORATIO
No, my good lord.

HAMLET
Thy state is the more gracious; for 'tis a vice to know him. He hath much land, and fertile: let a beast be lord of beasts, and his crib shall stand at the king's mess: 'tis a chough; but, as I say, spacious in the possession of dirt.

OSRIC
Sweet lord, if your lordship were at leisure, I should impart a thing to you from his majesty.

HAMLET
I will receive it, sir, with all diligence of spirit. Put your bonnet to his right use; 'tis for the head.

OSRIC
I thank your lordship, it is very hot.

HAMLET
No, believe me, 'tis very cold; the wind is northerly.

OSRIC
It is indifferent cold, my lord, indeed.

HAMLET
But yet methinks it is very sultry and hot for my complexion.

OSRIC
Exceedingly, my lord; it is very sultry,--as 'twere,--I cannot tell how. But, my lord, his majesty bade me signify to you that he has laid a great wager on your head: sir, this is the matter,--

HAMLET
I beseech you, remember--
HAMLET moves him to put on his hat

OSRIC
Nay, good my lord; for mine ease, in good faith. Sir, here is newly come to court Laertes; believe me, an absolute gentleman, full of most excellent differences, of very soft society and great showing: indeed, to speak feelingly of him, he is the card or calendar of gentry, for you shall find in him the continent of what part a gentleman would see.

HAMLET
Sir, his definement suffers no perdition in you; though, I know, to divide him inventorially would dizzy the arithmetic of memory, and yet but yaw neither, in respect of his quick sail. But, in the verity of extolment, I take him to be a soul of great article; and his infusion of such dearth and rareness, as, to make true diction of him, his semblable is his mirror; and who else would trace him, his umbrage, nothing more.

OSRIC
Your lordship speaks most infallibly of him.

HAMLET
The concernancy, sir? why do we wrap the gentleman in our more rawer breath?

OSRIC
Sir?

HORATIO
Is't not possible to understand in another tongue? You will do't, sir, really.

HAMLET
What imports the nomination of this gentleman?

OSRIC
Of Laertes?

HORATIO
His purse is empty already; all's golden words are spent.

HAMLET
Of him, sir.

OSRIC
I know you are not ignorant--

HAMLET
I would you did, sir; yet, in faith, if you did, it would not much approve me. Well, sir?

OSRIC
You are not ignorant of what excellence Laertes is--

HAMLET
I dare not confess that, lest I should compare with him in excellence; but, to know a man well, were to know himself.

OSRIC
I mean, sir, for his weapon; but in the imputation laid on him by them, in his meed he's unfellowed.

HAMLET
What's his weapon?

OSRIC
Rapier and dagger.

HAMLET
That's two of his weapons: but, well.

OSRIC
The king, sir, hath wagered with him six Barbary horses: against the which he has imponed, as I take it, six French rapiers and poniards, with their assigns, as girdle, hangers, and so: three of the carriages, in faith, are very dear to fancy, very responsive to the hilts, most delicate carriages, and of very liberal conceit.

HAMLET
What call you the carriages?

HORATIO
I knew you must be edified by the margent ere you had done.

OSRIC
The carriages, sir, are the hangers.

HAMLET
The phrase would be more german to the matter, if we could carry cannon by our sides: I would it might be hangers till then. But, on: six Barbary horses against six French swords, their assigns, and three liberal-conceited carriages; that's the French bet against the Danish. Why is this 'imponed,' as you call it?

OSRIC
The king, sir, hath laid, that in a dozen passes between yourself and him, he shall not exceed you three hits: he hath laid on twelve for nine; and it would come to immediate trial, if your lordship would vouchsafe the answer.

HAMLET
How if I answer 'no'?

OSRIC
I mean, my lord, the opposition of your person in trial.

HAMLET
Sir, I will walk here in the hall: if it please his majesty, 'tis the breathing time of day with me; let the foils be brought, the gentleman willing, and the king hold his purpose, I will win for him an I can; if not, I will gain nothing but my shame and the odd hits.

OSRIC
Shall I re-deliver you e'en so?

HAMLET
To this effect, sir; after what flourish your nature will.

OSRIC
I commend my duty to your lordship.

HAMLET
Yours, yours.
Exit OSRIC
He does well to commend it himself; there are no tongues else for's turn.

HORATIO
This lapwing runs away with the shell on his head.

HAMLET
He did comply with his dug, before he sucked it. Thus has he--and many more of the same bevy that I know the dressy age dotes on--only got the tune of the time and outward habit of encounter; a kind of yesty collection, which carries them through and

through the most fond and winnowed opinions; and do but blow them to their trial, the bubbles are out.
Enter a Lord

Lord
My lord, his majesty commended him to you by young Osric, who brings back to him that you attend him in the hall: he sends to know if your pleasure hold to play with Laertes, or that you will take longer time.

HAMLET
I am constant to my purpose; they follow the king's pleasure: if his fitness speaks, mine is ready; now or whensoever, provided I be so able as now.

Lord
The king and queen and all are coming down.

HAMLET
In happy time.

Lord
The queen desires you to use some gentle entertainment to Laertes before you fall to play.

HAMLET
She well instructs me.
Exit Lord

HORATIO
You will lose this wager, my lord.

HAMLET
I do not think so: since he went into France, I have been in continual practise: I shall win at the odds. But thou wouldst not think how ill all's here about my heart: but it is no matter.

HORATIO
Nay, good my lord,--

HAMLET
It is but foolery; but it is such a kind of gain-giving, as would perhaps trouble a woman.

HORATIO
If your mind dislike any thing, obey it: I will forestall their repair hither, and say you are not fit.

HAMLET
Not a whit, we defy augury: there's a special providence in the fall of a sparrow. If it be now, 'tis not to come; if it be not to come, it will be now; if it be not now, yet it will come: the readiness is all: since no man has aught of what he leaves, what is't to leave betimes?
Enter KING CLAUDIUS, QUEEN GERTRUDE, LAERTES, Lords, OSRIC, and Attendants with foils, &c

KING CLAUDIUS
Come, Hamlet, come, and take this hand from me.
KING CLAUDIUS puts LAERTES' hand into HAMLET's

HAMLET
Give me your pardon, sir: I've done you wrong;
But pardon't, as you are a gentleman.
This presence knows,
And you must needs have heard, how I am punish'd
With sore distraction. What I have done,
That might your nature, honour and exception
Roughly awake, I here proclaim was madness.
Was't Hamlet wrong'd Laertes? Never Hamlet:
If Hamlet from himself be ta'en away,
And when he's not himself does wrong Laertes,
Then Hamlet does it not, Hamlet denies it.
Who does it, then? His madness: if't be so,
Hamlet is of the faction that is wrong'd;
His madness is poor Hamlet's enemy.
Sir, in this audience,
Let my disclaiming from a purposed evil
Free me so far in your most generous thoughts,
That I have shot mine arrow o'er the house,
And hurt my brother.

LAERTES
I am satisfied in nature,
Whose motive, in this case, should stir me most
To my revenge: but in my terms of honour
I stand aloof; and will no reconcilement,
Till by some elder masters, of known honour,
I have a voice and precedent of peace,
To keep my name ungored. But till that time,
I do receive your offer'd love like love,
And will not wrong it.

HAMLET
I embrace it freely;
And will this brother's wager frankly play.
Give us the foils. Come on.

LAERTES
Come, one for me.

HAMLET
I'll be your foil, Laertes: in mine ignorance
Your skill shall, like a star i' the darkest night,
Stick fiery off indeed.

LAERTES
You mock me, sir.

HAMLET
No, by this hand.

KING CLAUDIUS
Give them the foils, young Osric. Cousin Hamlet,
You know the wager?

HAMLET
Very well, my lord
Your grace hath laid the odds o' the weaker side.

KING CLAUDIUS
I do not fear it; I have seen you both:
But since he is better'd, we have therefore odds.

LAERTES
This is too heavy, let me see another.

HAMLET
This likes me well. These foils have all a length?
They prepare to play

OSRIC
Ay, my good lord.

KING CLAUDIUS
Set me the stoops of wine upon that table.
If Hamlet give the first or second hit,
Or quit in answer of the third exchange,
Let all the battlements their ordnance fire:
The king shall drink to Hamlet's better breath;
And in the cup an union shall he throw,
Richer than that which four successive kings
In Denmark's crown have worn. Give me the cups;
And let the kettle to the trumpet speak,
The trumpet to the cannoneer without,
The cannons to the heavens, the heavens to earth,
'Now the king dunks to Hamlet.' Come, begin:
And you, the judges, bear a wary eye.

HAMLET
Come on, sir.

LAERTES
Come, my lord.
They play

HAMLET
One.

LAERTES
No.

HAMLET
Judgment.

OSRIC
A hit, a very palpable hit.

LAERTES
Well; again.

KING CLAUDIUS
Stay; give me drink. Hamlet, this pearl is thine;
Here's to thy health.
Trumpets sound, and cannon shot off within
Give him the cup.

HAMLET
I'll play this bout first; set it by awhile. Come.
They play
Another hit; what say you?

LAERTES
A touch, a touch, I do confess.

KING CLAUDIUS
Our son shall win.

QUEEN GERTRUDE
He's fat, and scant of breath.
Here, Hamlet, take my napkin, rub thy brows;
The queen carouses to thy fortune, Hamlet.

HAMLET
Good madam!

KING CLAUDIUS
Gertrude, do not drink.

QUEEN GERTRUDE
I will, my lord; I pray you, pardon me.

KING CLAUDIUS
[Aside] It is the poison'd cup: it is too late.

HAMLET
I dare not drink yet, madam; by and by.

QUEEN GERTRUDE
Come, let me wipe thy face.

LAERTES
My lord, I'll hit him now.

KING CLAUDIUS
I do not think't.

LAERTES
[Aside] And yet 'tis almost 'gainst my conscience.

HAMLET
Come, for the third, Laertes: you but dally;
I pray you, pass with your best violence;
I am afeard you make a wanton of me.

LAERTES
Say you so? come on.
They play

OSRIC
Nothing, neither way.

LAERTES
Have at you now!
LAERTES wounds HAMLET; then in scuffling, they change rapiers, and HAMLET wounds LAERTES

KING CLAUDIUS
Part them; they are incensed.

HAMLET
Nay, come, again.
QUEEN GERTRUDE falls

OSRIC
Look to the queen there, ho!

HORATIO
They bleed on both sides. How is it, my lord?

OSRIC
How is't, Laertes?

LAERTES
Why, as a woodcock to mine own springe, Osric;
I am justly kill'd with mine own treachery.

HAMLET
How does the queen?

KING CLAUDIUS
She swounds to see them bleed.

QUEEN GERTRUDE
No, no, the drink, the drink,--O my dear Hamlet,--
The drink, the drink! I am poison'd.
[Dies]

HAMLET
O villany! Ho! let the door be lock'd:
Treachery! Seek it out.

LAERTES
It is here, Hamlet: Hamlet, thou art slain;
No medicine in the world can do thee good;
In thee there is not half an hour of life;
The treacherous instrument is in thy hand,
Unbated and envenom'd: the foul practise
Hath turn'd itself on me lo, here I lie,
Never to rise again: thy mother's poison'd:
I can no more: the king, the king's to blame.

HAMLET
The point!--envenom'd too!
Then, venom, to thy work.
Stabs KING CLAUDIUS

All
Treason! treason!

KING CLAUDIUS
O, yet defend me, friends; I am but hurt.

HAMLET
Here, thou incestuous, murderous, damned Dane,
Drink off this potion. Is thy union here?
Follow my mother.
KING CLAUDIUS dies

LAERTES
He is justly served;
It is a poison temper'd by himself.
Exchange forgiveness with me, noble Hamlet:
Mine and my father's death come not upon thee,
Nor thine on me.
[Dies]

HAMLET
Heaven make thee free of it! I follow thee.

I am dead, Horatio. Wretched queen, adieu!
You that look pale and tremble at this chance,
That are but mutes or audience to this act,
Had I but time--as this fell sergeant, death,
Is strict in his arrest--O, I could tell you--
But let it be. Horatio, I am dead;
Thou livest; report me and my cause aright
To the unsatisfied.

HORATIO
Never believe it:
I am more an antique Roman than a Dane:
Here's yet some liquor left.

HAMLET
As thou'rt a man,
Give me the cup: let go; by heaven, I'll have't.
O good Horatio, what a wounded name,
Things standing thus unknown, shall live behind me!
If thou didst ever hold me in thy heart
Absent thee from felicity awhile,
And in this harsh world draw thy breath in pain,
To tell my story.
March afar off, and shot within
What warlike noise is this?

OSRIC
Young Fortinbras, with conquest come from Poland,
To the ambassadors of England gives
This warlike volley.

HAMLET
O, I die, Horatio;
The potent poison quite o'er-crows my spirit:
I cannot live to hear the news from England;
But I do prophesy the election lights
On Fortinbras: he has my dying voice;
So tell him, with the occurrents, more and less,
Which have solicited. The rest is silence.
[Dies]

HORATIO
Now cracks a noble heart. Good night sweet prince:
And flights of angels sing thee to thy rest!
Why does the drum come hither?
March within
Enter FORTINBRAS, the English Ambassadors, and others

PRINCE FORTINBRAS
Where is this sight?

HORATIO
What is it ye would see?
If aught of woe or wonder, cease your search.

PRINCE FORTINBRAS
This quarry cries on havoc. O proud death,
What feast is toward in thine eternal cell,
That thou so many princes at a shot
So bloodily hast struck?

First Ambassador
The sight is dismal;
And our affairs from England come too late:
The ears are senseless that should give us hearing,
To tell him his commandment is fulfill'd,
That Rosencrantz and Guildenstern are dead:
Where should we have our thanks?

HORATIO
Not from his mouth,
Had it the ability of life to thank you:
He never gave commandment for their death.
But since, so jump upon this bloody question,
You from the Polack wars, and you from England,
Are here arrived give order that these bodies
High on a stage be placed to the view;
And let me speak to the yet unknowing world
How these things came about: so shall you hear
Of carnal, bloody, and unnatural acts,
Of accidental judgments, casual slaughters,
Of deaths put on by cunning and forced cause,
And, in this upshot, purposes mistook
Fall'n on the inventors' reads: all this can I
Truly deliver.

PRINCE FORTINBRAS
Let us haste to hear it,
And call the noblest to the audience.
For me, with sorrow I embrace my fortune:
I have some rights of memory in this kingdom,
Which now to claim my vantage doth invite me.

HORATIO
Of that I shall have also cause to speak,
And from his mouth whose voice will draw on more;
But let this same be presently perform'd,
Even while men's minds are wild; lest more mischance
On plots and errors, happen.

PRINCE FORTINBRAS
Let four captains
Bear Hamlet, like a soldier, to the stage;

For he was likely, had he been put on,
To have proved most royally: and, for his passage,
The soldiers' music and the rites of war
Speak loudly for him.
Take up the bodies: such a sight as this
Becomes the field, but here shows much amiss.
Go, bid the soldiers shoot.
A dead march. Exeunt, bearing off the dead bodies;
after which a peal of ordnance is shot off

Dance

For dancers in the mid-twentieth century, it was eventful. Names such as Jerome Robbins and Merce Cunningham and Agnes De Mille, dancer and choreographer, became well known.

"**Agnes de Mille**, in full **Agnes George de Mille**, de Mille also spelled **DeMille** (born Sept. 18, 1905, New York, N.Y., U.S.—died Oct. 7, 1993, New York City) American dancer and choreographer who further developed the narrative aspect of dance and made innovative use of American themes, folk dances, and physical idioms in her choreography of musical plays and ballets."
Source: https://www.britannica.com/biography/Agnes-de-Mille

"**Jerome Robbins**, original surname **Rabinowitz** (born Oct. 11, 1918, New York, N.Y., U.S.—died July 29, 1998, New York City) one of the most popular and imaginative American choreographers of the 20th century. Robbins was first known for his skillful use of contemporary American themes in ballets and Broadway and Hollywood musicals. He won acclaim for highly innovative ballets structured within the traditional framework of classical dance movements."
Source: https://www.britannica.com/biography/Jerome-Robbins

"**Merce Cunningham** was born on April 16, 1919 in Centralia, Washington. He later joined Martha Graham's dance company and choreographed his own works using music from composer John Cage, who became his partner. In 1953, Cunningham formed his own company and garnered wide acclaim over the decades for his innovations while also collaborating with other artistic visionaries. He died on July 26, 2009."
Source: http://www.biography.com/people/merce-cunningham-9263457#early-life

Agnes De Mille began her career with the America Ballet Theater in 1939. At that time, the ballet company was called the Ballet Theatre. Her most significant works in her early career were *Rodeo* (music of Aaron Copland) and her choreography of the musical, *Oklahoma*. Her choreography added the emotional feelings in addition to their technical skills. The ballet dancers' movements, done with emotional charm and appeal, made her choreography an innovation. George Ballenchine was in great demand as a choreographer, creating over 450 works. Some of the familiar names are *Nutcracker* by Tchaikovsky and Stravinsky's *Firebird*. In 1957, Jerome Robbins choreographed Leonard Bernstein's *West Side Story*. Robbins was a great dancer and choreographer. He was

known for his Broadway musicals such as *Cats*, *Funny Girl*, and *Phantom of the Opera*.
Source: Janetta Rebold Benton and Rober DiYanni, *Handbook for the Humanities* (Boston and Upper Saddle River, NJ: Prentice Hall, 2014), 300-301. ISBN 100-205-16161-8

TWENTY-FIRST CENTURY

According to authors Janetta Rebold Benton and Robet DiYanni, professors from New York, in their recent text they stated, "the signature events of the early twenty-first century so far have been a combination of positive developments and catastrophes, natural and man-made" (311).
Source: Janetta Rebold Benton and Rober DiYanni, *Handbook for the Humanities* (Boston and Upper Saddle River, NJ: Prentice Hall, 2014), 300-301. ISBN 100-205-16161-8

Rapid developments occurred in technology and the majority of the populace found the necessity for phones. Many competing products such as the iPad created a competitive market. A number of women became appointed to the Supreme Court and President Barack Obama became the first African-American to be elected as a President of the United States.

China became an economic power and the Olympic Games in 2004 returned to its birthplace, Athens, Greece. Miraculously, the Chilean miners buried underground for days were safely rescued. The hurricane Katrina devastated portions of New Orleans and many people lost their lives in that catastrophe. Another devastating event occurred on September 11, 2001, when nearly 3,000 people were killed in the World Trade Center by terrorists.

The future trend since the late 1990s is globalization, "the unprecedented movement of information, technology, and goods and services across national borders." The agreements between countries to trade is a critical component to it success. Communication is a key necessity to globalization. Many corporations have become global corporations: "The integration of world trade and the globalization of companies have been augmented by the rise of Asian economies, including those of India, Singapore, and South Korea, as well as that of China."
Source: Janetta Rebold Benton and Rober DiYanni, *Handbook for the Humanities* (Boston and Upper Saddle River, NJ: Prentice Hall, 2014), 311. ISBN 100-205-16161-8

Another development in the first part of the twenty-first century is that of cross-cultural exchanges in ideas and new invention. The twenty-first century has had growth in the development of the fine arts, new forms of architecture, and a broader availability to the internet and methods of communication.

Presently, with so many electronic devices available, countless people can access the internet and have the ability to find out in seconds information simultaneously with others in all parts of the world. With access to the internet, the use of email, Facebook, Twitter, Google and the use of smartphones, mores changes will continue.
Source: Janetta Rebold Benton and Rober DiYanni, *Handbook for the Humanities* (Boston and Upper Saddle River, NJ: Prentice Hall, 2014), 311. ISBN 100-205-16161-8

In our own time, as our civilization continues to progress and move forward, think about our discussion in unit 1, where people began to organize, congregate around rivers, develop trade and commerce, and communicate. They formed communities and became "civilizations." We discussed various groups of people and how they were at that time and what they needed to do in order to survive or thrive and establish community living. Just as those early writers and artists tried to make sense of their world and create forms of art, artists still represent their time and place and create emotional images and representations expressing universal feelings such as happiness, sadness, despair, and elation. The Fine Arts reach the soul and have helped to mold the minds of many.

Remember how we mentioned that trade and commerce and communication were major achievements of early civilizations? For them to flourish as people living together in communities and among each other, they eventually developed methods of communication and trade and commerce. How have we as humans changed and how have we not changed? Even today, knowing how to communicate and trade with other areas of the world are important challenges for us. What have we learned from studying history? Why do we take the time to study history and read about the journey of people who have gone before us? We study those individuals with the hope that they will inspire us to live our lives with the will to go on and do something great. We study those individuals to learn to overcome our barriers and become resilient. We study so we can understand someone else who may not look like us. We study our past in order to improve our future. We study in order to know what we can do to help make our communities stronger. We study so that we know how to communicate better when we are speaking. We study so we understand the progression of how humankind has developed. We want to understand what they had to do and what they went through in order to create their art. We study in order to understand why artists create and why artists make our world a better place.

First sentence source: Janetta Rebold Benton and Rober DiYanni, *Handbook for the Humanities* (Boston and Upper Saddle River, NJ: Prentice Hall, 2014). ISBN 100-205-16161-8

APPENDIX

Prehistoric Period
1. Falling Bison, Altamira Cave, Spain
2. Venus – figure of the woman prehistoric style

1.
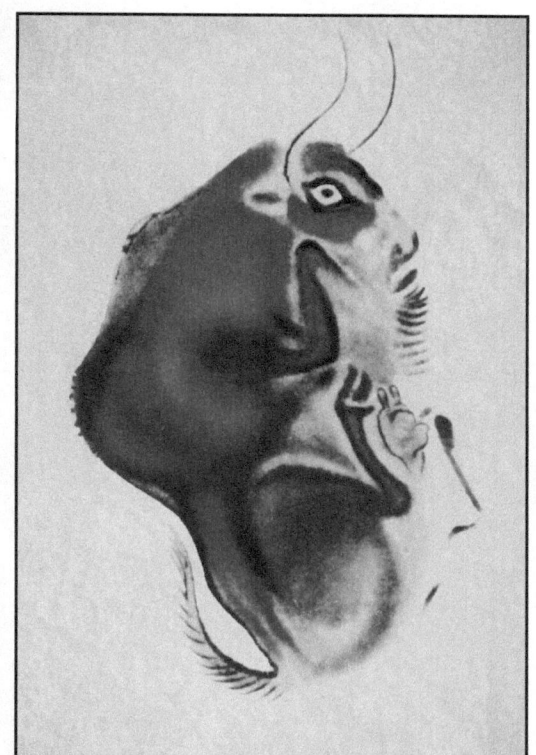

2.

Image 1 courtesy of Corel.
Image 2 © Shutterstock, Inc.

Ancient Mesopotamian Period
1. Baghdad surroundings along Tigris River
2. Babylonian stone with cuneiform writing and religious images
3. Stencil of ziggurat

1.

2.

3.

Images © Shutterstock, Inc.

Ancient Egyptian Period

1. Pyramids of Egypt
2. Abu Simbel Temple of King Ramses I
3. Abu Simbel Temple of King Ramses II, and temple of Queen Nefertari
4. Egypt, girl musicians playing and dancing at a banquet
5. Egypt, barge of the sun on its night course, Tomb of Anhurkhawi
6. Egypt, King Mycerinus and wife, Egyptian sculpture
7. Egypt, Golden Effigy of King Tutankhamen

1.
2.
3.
5.
4.
6.
7.

Images 1-3 © Shutterstock, Inc. Images 4-7 courtesy of Corel.

Ancient Greek Period

1. Ancient Greek marble statue of a maiden kore (550–540 B.C.)
2. Statue of a kouros (male youth)
3. Ancient Greek temple in the Valley of the Temples in Sicily, Italy, near Agrigento
4. Sunset light over Parthenon, Greece
5. Artistic view ancient Greek sculpture
6. Ancient Greek vase with two lions
7. Ancient Greek vase
8. Ancient Greek vase
9. Minoan large storage jar from Knossos palace (1450–1400 B.C.)
10. Greece, draped female statue
11. Greece, Zeus

1.
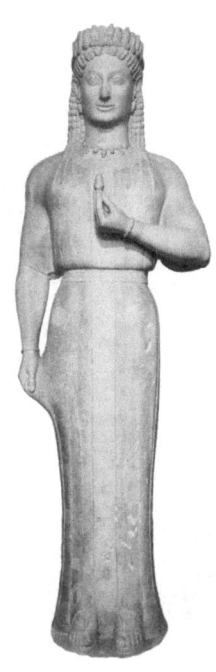

2.
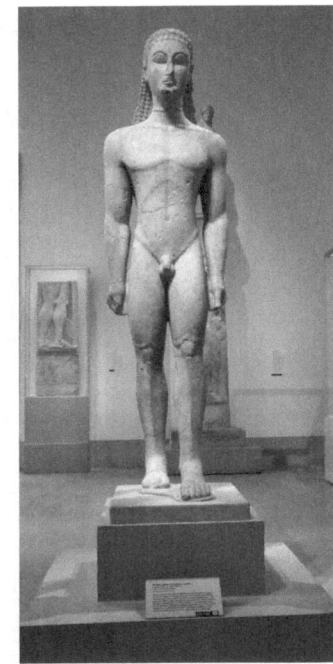

3.

4.

5.

7.

8.

6.

9.

10.

11.

Images 1-9 © Shutterstock, Inc. Images 10-11 courtesy of Corel.

Ancient Roman Period

1. The famous Roman Colosseum built around 80 A.D., seated 50,000 people. Its original Latin name was *Amphitheatrum Flavium*.
2. The Pantheon: temple of Roman gods, Rome, Italy. The Pantheon is a building in Rome, by Marcus Agrippa as a temple to all the gods of ancient Rome.
3. Ancient marble bust of the Roman emperor Hadrian
4. Roman emperor Augustus Caesar statue

1.

2.

3.

4.

Images © Shutterstock, Inc.

Middle Ages Period

1. Notre Dame la Grande, Poitiers, France. Romanesque church, 11th and 12th centuries
2. Nave of Romanesque church San Lorenzo built in the 12th century. Main altar was created by Domenico Brusarzio in 1562 in Verona, Italy.
3. Notre Dame (Paris) along the Seine River
4. Cathedral of Saint Eulalia in Barcelona, Spain
5. Hagia Sophia mosque in Sultanahmet, Istanbul, Turkey
6. Hagia Sophia interior, Istanbul, Turkey
7. A stamp printed in the United States shows image of art by Giotto, series, circa 1995

1.

2.

3.

4.

5.

6.

7.

Images © Shutterstock, Inc.

Renaissance Period

1. Cathedral Santa Maria del Fiore in Florence, Italy

Pieter Brueghel

2. Peasants Dance
3. Village Holiday
4. Tower of Babel (Babylon), a famous painting by Pieter Brueghel the Elder created in 1563

Albrecht Durer

5. Praying Hands
6. Czechoslovakia shows a picture of artist Albrecht Durer. The Knight and Horse, circa 1969

Leonardo Da Vinci

7. Leonardo da Vinci Self-Portrait, 1512
8. Photo of the Vitruvian Man by Leonardo Da Vinci from 1492

1.

2.

3.

4.

5.
6.
7.
8.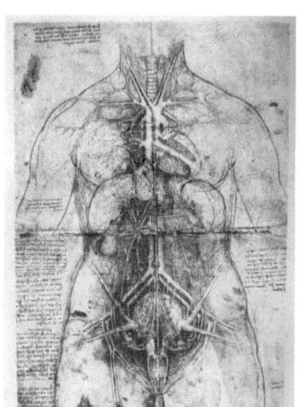

Images 1, 4, 6-8 © Shutterstock, Inc. Images 2-3, 5 courtesy of Corel.

Renaissance Period
Leonardo Da Vinci
9. Mona Lisa
10. Ginevra de Benci
11. Head of Leda
12. The Last Supper

Raphael Sanzio
13. The Conestabile Madonna
14. The Madonna of the Meadow
15. Madonna col Figlio e S Giovannino

Michelangelo
16. Sistine Hall

9.

10.

11.

12.

13.

14.

15.

16.

Images 9-11, 15 courtesy of Corel. Images 12-14, 16 © Shutterstock, Inc.

Appendix

Renaissance Period
Michelangelo
17. The Fall of Man
18. Sibilla Libica
19. Sibilla Erithrea
20. David
21. Pieta
22. The view on the Basilica of St. Peter, Vatican

Baroque Period
Sir Peter Paul Rubens
23. Helena Fourment and Her Children
24. Head of a Negro
25. Head of a Boy

17.

18.

19.

20.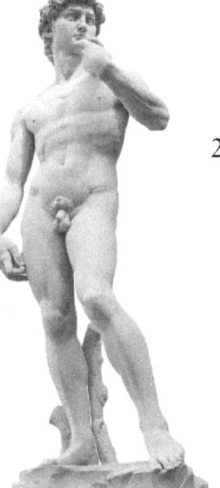

21.

22.

23.

24.

25.

Images 17-19, 23-25 courtesy of Corel. Images 20-22 © Shutterstock, Inc.

British Renaissance Period
Or Elizabethan Period (this was the term used in England and also called the English Renaissance)
William Shakespeare
1564-1616 Born in England

1. William Shakespeare, English poet and playwright. Engraving from *The Leisure Hour Magazine*, April 1864.

Mannerist Period (a short approximately 75 year period that extended the Renaissance and was between the Renaissance and the Baroque Period but the forms used by the Mannerist artists were elongated)

El Greco 1541-1616
1. View of Toledo
2. Mater Dolorosa
3. Gentleman with His Hand on His Breast

Shakespeare image © Shutterstock, Inc.   Images 1-3 courtesy of Corel.

Baroque Period

1. St. Paul Cathedral in London

Rembrandt

2. Stamp printed by Yemen, shows Self-Portrait by Rembrandt, circa 1972
3. Portrait of the Artists Father
4. Self Portrait as a Young Man
5. Old Man Praying
6. Aristotle Contemplating the Bust of Homer
7. Night Watch
8. A stamp printed in USSR shows an oil painting "The Return of the Prodigal Son" by Rembrandt, circa 1970.
9. Syndics of Draper's Guild

1.
2.
3.
4.
5.
6.
7.
8.
9.

Images 1-2, 7-9 © Shutterstock, Inc. Images 3-6 courtesy of Corel.

Baroque Period
Jan Vermeer
1632-1675 born in Delft, Netherlands

10. Madchen Mit Perle
11. A stamp printed in Yemen shows The Milkmaid by Johannes Vermeer, circa 1968
12. Girl with a Glass
13. The Letter

Neo-Classical Period
Jacques Louis David
Born in France 1748–1825

1. A stamp printed in Burundi shows paint "Portrait of Lenoir" by artist David, one stamp from series, circa 1974
2. Madame Seriziat 1795
3. Portrait of Madame Recamier

Images 2, 10 courtesy of Corel. Images 1, 3, 11-13 © Shutterstock, Inc.

Romantic Period
Francisco de Goya

1. Senora Sebasa Garcia
2. Donna Isaabel Cobos de Porcel
3. Don Manuel Osorio de Zuniga
4. Dona Isabel de Porcel
5. The shooting of the rebels on a night of May 3, 1808 also called "Excecution of the Citizens of Madrid" or the "Execution of the 3rd of May"
6. The Milkmaid of Bordeaux
7. "The Raft of the Medusa" by E. Gericault

1.
2.
3.
4.
5.
6.
7.

Images 1-3 courtesy of Corel. Images 4-6 © Shutterstock, Inc.

19TH CENTURY PERIOD
Claude Monet
1. Field of Poppies
2. Fisherman's Cottage on the Cliffs

Auguste Renoir
3. Child With Cat
4. Doncellas al Piano

Vincent Van Gogh
5. Fishing in Spring
6. Boats of Saintes-Maries
7. Bedroom at Arles

1.

2.

3.

4.

5.

6.

7.

Images courtesy of Corel.

19TH CENTURY PERIOD

Vincent Van Gogh
8. Night on the Coffee Terrace
9. Self-portrait of the artist Van Gogh

Paul Gauguin
10. Self Portrait
11. Ia Orana Maria
12. Crouching Tahitian Girl
13. Portrait of Madame Ginoux

Edgar Degas
14. Ballet Class

Mary Cassatt
15. Mother and Child
16. Child in a Straw Hat

8.
9.
10.
11.
12.
13.
14.
15.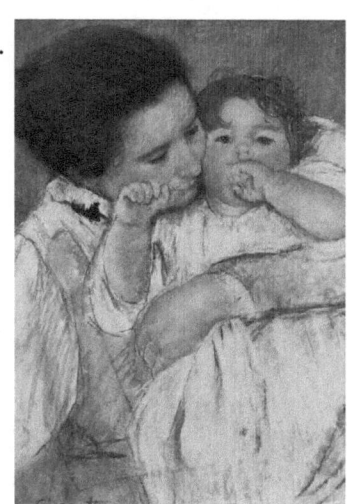
16.

Images 8-9, 13 © Shutterstock, Inc. Images 10-12, 14-16 courtesy of Corel.

19TH CENTURY PERIOD
Henri de Toulouse-Lautrec
17. At the Moulin Rouge
18. The Moulin Rouge 1890

Auguste Rodin
19. The Thinker

20TH CENTURY PERIOD
Kathe Kollwitz
1. More War, woman with raised arm
2. Katsushika Hokusai

Grant Wood
3. American Gothic in the Chicago Art Institute Chicago, Illinois

Images 17-18 courtesy of Corel. Images 19, 1-3 © Shutterstock, Inc.

20TH CENTURY PERIOD
Wassily Kandinsky
4. A stamp printed in France shows Painting by Wassily Kandinsky

Pablo Picasso
5. Les Demoiselles d'Avignon - The Young Ladies of Avignon

Andy Warhol
6. Marilyn Monroe

Diego Rivera
8. A Dream of a Sunday Afternoon in Alameda Park

Miscellaneous
7. Stamp printed in USA show popular 1960s American film director Alfred Hitchcock
9. A postage stamp printed in USA showing an image of Jackson Pollock painting
10. Fallingwater, Mill Run, Pennsylvania
11. Family Group by Henry Moore
12. A view of The "Gates" with the Midtown skyline in the background from Central Park, New York City. Christo and Jeanne Claude

Images © Shutterstock, Inc.

20TH CENTURY PERIOD
Ira and George Gershwin

Brothers Ira and George Gershwin worked almost exclusively together from the early 1920s until George's premature death in 1937. Their collaborations, including songs such as "I Got Rhythm" and "'S Wonderful," added immeasurably to American popular music. George wrote the music and Ira provided the lyrics for over a dozen musicals, including *Funny Face*, *Show Girl*, and *Strike Up the Band*. Their show *Of Thee I Sing* (1931) became the first musical to receive a Pulitzer Prize.

© Shutterstock.com

Benny Goodman

The child of immigrants, Benny Goodman (1909–1986) began studying clarinet when he was ten years old. He started playing professionally while a teenager and led his first band in 1934. Noted for his solo improvisations, Goodman became the first white bandleader to feature African-American jazz musicians in his band. In 1937, *Time* magazine dubbed him the "King of Swing," and the following year he led the first jazz band to play at Carnegie Hall. He received a Grammy Lifetime Achievement Award in 1986.

© Hulton Archive/Stringer/Getty Images

Jeff Parrott
American Painter

Psyexpressionism

Courtesy of Jeff Parrott.

REFERENCES

Bentley, Gerald Eades. *Shakespeare: A Biographical Sketch*, 3rd edition. New York: Yale University Press, 1964.

Bishop, *Adventures in the Human Spirit*, 2nd edition. Upper Saddle River: Prentice Hall, Inc, 1999.

Book of Knowledge, volumes 1–19, Boston: The Grolier Society, 1951.

Brooke Tucker. *Shakespeare of Stratford*. New Haven: Yale Publication Press, 1970.

Burgess, Anthony. *Shakespeare*. New Haven: Knopf Publishing, 1970.

Cirlot, Juan-Eduardo. *Picasso: Birth of a Genius*. New York/Washington: Praeger, 1972.

Cooper, Douglas. *Picasso Theatre*. New York: Harry N. Abrams, Incorporated, 1967.

Cunningham, Lawrence, and John Reich. *Culture and Values*. New York: CBS College Publishing, Holt, Rinehart and Winston, 1982.

Czwiklitzer, Christopher. *Picasso's Posters*. New York: Random House, Incorporated, 1971.

Daix, Pierre. *Picasso: The Blue and Rose Period*. NY: New York Graphic Society, 1967.

Dixon, Laurinda and William Fleming. *Arts and Ideas Study Guide*, 7th edition. New York: CBS College Publishing, Holt, Rinehart and Winston, 1986.

Eisman, Lawrence, Elizabeth Jones, and Raymond J. Malone. *Making Music Your Own 8*. Morristown: Silver Burdett Company, 1968.

Encyclopedia Americana. New York: Americana Corporation, Scholastic Library Publishing. 1961.

Encyclopedia of the World, 6th edition. Boston: Houghton Mifflin, 2001.

Fiero, Gloria K. *Landmarks in Humanities*. Boston: McGraw Hill Higher Education, 2005.

Fischner-Rathus, Lois. *Understanding Art*. Belmont, California: Wadsworth Publishing, 2006.

Fritz Zobeley. *Portrait of Beethoven: An Illustrated Biography*. New York: Herder and Herder, 1972.

Gilbert, McCarter. *Living with Art*. New York: McGraw-Hill Companies, 2002.

Goldsmith, Oliver. *Poems and Plays*. London: J. M. Dent & Sons, 1966.

Grant, Sandy C. *The Art of Seeing Teacher Guide*. Pleasantville, New York.

Hale, John. *Renaissance*: Time Life Education, Richmond, Virginia: Time Life Education, 1965.

Hobbs, Jack A. and Robert L. Duncan. *Arts, Ideas and Civilization*. Englewood Cliffs: Prentice-Hall, Inc., 1989.

Hoskin, G.L. *The Life and Times of Edward Alleyn*. London: LLC Jonathan Cape, 1952.

Huffington, Arianna. *Picasso: Creator and Destroyer*. New York: Simon & Schuster, 1988.

Jacobs, David. *Beethoven*. New York: American Heritage Publishing Co., 1970.

Janson, A. and H. W. Janson. *History of Art: The Western Tradition*. Englewood Cliffs, New Jersey: Pearson Education, 2005.

Kay, Dennis. *Shakespeare: His Life and Times*. New York: Twayne Publishers, 1994.

Kerman, Joseph. *Listen: Brief Edition*. New York: Worth Publishers, Inc., 1987.

Lamm, Robert C. and Neal M. Cross. *The Humanities in Western Culture*. 9th ed. Dubuque: Wm. C. Brown Communications, Inc., 1993.

Leighton, Patricia. *Re-ordering the Universe: Picasso and Anarchism*. Princeton, NJ: Princeton University Press, 1989.

Levi, Peter. *The Life and Times of William Shakespeare*. New York: Henry Holt & Co., 1989.

Machlis, Joseph. *The Enjoyment of Music*, New York W W Norton & Company, 1970.

McCandless, Lucie. *Goya: His Life and Works*. New York: Warren Schloat Production, 1969.

Meine, Franklin J. *The American People's Encyclopedia*. Chicago: The Spencer Press, 1956.

Miller, Hugh M. *History of Music*. 3rd ed. New York: Barnes & Noble, Inc., 1960.

Mittler, Gene. *Art in Focus*. Boston: McGraw-Hill/Glencoe, 1988.

Nadeau, Roland and William Tesson. *Listen: A Guide to the Pleasures of Music*. Boston: Allyn and Bacon, Inc., 1976.

Neilson, Frances. *Shakespeare and the Tempest*. New Hampshire, Richard R. Smith Publisher, Inc., 1956.

Parrott, Lois. *Instructor's Manual with Tests* for *Exploring the Humanities: Creativity and Culture in the West*. Upper Saddle River: Pearson Education, Inc., 2006.

Penrose, Roland. *The Sculpture of Picasso*. New York: Museum of Modern Art, 1967.

Phipps, Richard and Richard Wink. *Invitation to the Gallery: An Introduction to Art*. Dubuque: Wm. C. Brown Publishers, 1987.

Politoske, Daniel T. *Music*. 2nd ed. Englewood Cliffs: Prentice-Hall, Inc., 1979.

Rowe. R. L. *Shakespeare the Man*. New York: Harper & Row, 1973.

Rubin, William S. et al. *Les Demoiselles d'Avignon*. New York: Museum of Modern Art, 1994.

Sabertés, James. *Personal Reminiscences*. New York: Buchholz Gallery, 1951.

Sayre, Henry. *Discovering the Humanities*. Upper Saddle River: Prentice Hall, 2010.

Sayre, Henry. *Humanities, Culture, Continuity and Change*. Upper Saddle River: Prentice Hall-Pearson Education, 2010.

Schindler, Allan. *Listening to Music*. New York: Holt, Rinehart and Winston, 1980.

Sedgwick, John. *Art Appreciation Made Simple*. New York: Doubleday and Co. Inc., 1959.

Speaight, Robert. *Shakespeare: The Man and his Achievement*. Lanham, MD: Cooper Square Publishers Inc., 2000.

Sporre, Dennis. *Instructor's Manual to Perceiving the Arts*. Upper Saddle River: Prentice Hall, 2006.

Sporre. Dennis. *The Creative Impulse, 2nd ed*. Upper Saddle River: Prentice Hall, 1990.

Sporre, Dennis J. *Reality through the Arts*. 5th ed. Upper Saddle River: Prentice Hall, 2004.

Stein, Gertrude. *Picasso*. Boston: Beacon Press, 1959.

Stokstad, Marilyn. *21st Century Art History*. Upper Saddle River: Prentice Hall-Pearson Education, 2009.

Strawinsky, I. Craft, R. *Expositions and Developments*. London: Faber & Faber, 1962

Sur, William R., Robert E. Nye, and Charlotte DuBois. *This is Music 8*. Boston: Allyn and Bacon, Inc., 1965.

Ulrich and Pick. *A History of Music Style*, New York: Harcourt Brace & World, 1963.

Ulrich, Homer. *Chamber Music*. New York: Columbia University Press., 1967.

Ulrich, Homer. *Music: A Design for Listening*. New York: Harcourt Brace & World, 1962.

Ulrich, Homer. *Symphonic Music. IT 's Evolution Since the Renaissance*. New York: Columbia University Press, 1952.

Van de Bogart, Doris. *Introduction to the Humanities: Painting, Sculpture, Architecture, Music, and Literature*. New York: Barnes & Noble Books, 1968.

Webster's II Dictionary, revised edition. Boston: Houghton Mifflin Company, 1966.

Williams, Brian and Brenda Williams. *Encyclopedia of World History*. Bath, United Kingdom: Paragon Publishing, 2003.

Wilson, George and Buckley Laird. *A Dictionary of Ballet*. New York: Penguin Books, 1957.

Wold, Milo. *An Outline History of Music*. Dubuque: W. M. C. Brown Publishers, 1989.

Wold, Milo and Edmund Cykler. *An Introduction to Music and Art in the Western World*. 5th ed. Dubuque: Wm. C. Brown Company Publishers, 1976.

World Book Encyclopedia 2,3,4,5,9,10,11,17,18, 21. Chicago, Illinois: World Book Inc. a Scott Fetzer Co., 1972.